Calm Tech Parenting

A Simple 5 C's Plan for Balanced Screens, Deepfake Safety, and AI-Savvy Kids-Gen Alpha Guide

Savannah Gloria Buxton

ISBN: 978-1-7642720-5-6

Isohan Publishing

Second Edition

Table of Contents

Chapter 1: Who Is Generation Alpha?

The ten-year-old sits cross-legged on her bedroom floor, fingers dancing across a tablet screen with the precision of a pianist. She's not just playing a game—she's building virtual worlds in Minecraft while simultaneously video-chatting with friends through Discord and listening to a podcast about marine biology. This scene would have been science fiction just two decades ago. Today, it represents the daily reality of Generation Alpha, the first cohort of humans to grow up entirely within the 21st century.

Born between 2010 and 2025, Generation Alpha represents humanity's first truly digital-native generation. Unlike their older siblings in Generation Z, who witnessed the transition from analog to digital, these children have never known a world without smartphones, tablets, or voice assistants. They are, quite literally, the products of a fully mature digital ecosystem.

The Numbers Tell a Story

The statistics surrounding Generation Alpha paint a picture of unprecedented digital immersion. Currently, 36 million children in the United States are active online users—a number that surpasses the total teenage population. This shift represents more than just increased access to technology; it signals a fundamental change in how an entire generation learns, plays, and forms relationships.

Research conducted by the Pew Research Center reveals that 65% of children between ages 8 and 10 now spend more than four hours daily engaged with social media platforms. This figure becomes more striking when we consider that these children are barely old enough to read fluently, yet they navigate complex digital environments with remarkable ease.

The average Alpha child encounters their first screen at 4 months of age. By their second birthday, most have learned to swipe, tap, and navigate touch interfaces before they can tie their shoes. By age 5, many can operate voice assistants, understand the concept of search algorithms, and have developed preferences for specific YouTube creators.

Case Study 1: Emma's Digital Day

Emma, age 8, wakes up to her Amazon Echo playing her customized morning playlist. Before breakfast, she checks her virtual pet on a mobile app and sends voice messages to her grandmother through a family communication app. During her online math lesson, she uses an AI-powered tutoring program that adapts to her learning pace. After school, she joins friends in a virtual Roblox world where they build structures and role-play scenarios.

Emma's mother, Sarah, feels overwhelmed by the constant digital presence. "I grew up with maybe an hour of television after homework," Sarah explains. "Emma's entire day revolves around screens, but it's not mindless consumption. She's creating, learning, and socializing. I just don't know if it's healthy."

Emma represents the complexity of Alpha generation digital engagement. Her screen time isn't passive consumption but active creation and social interaction. Yet questions remain about the long-term implications of such intensive digital immersion during critical developmental years.

Case Study 2: Marcus and the AI Tutor

Marcus, a 9-year-old with dyslexia, struggled with traditional reading instruction until his parents introduced him to an AI-powered reading app. The program uses speech recognition technology to provide immediate feedback on pronunciation and comprehension. Within six months, Marcus's reading level improved by two grades.

"The AI doesn't get frustrated like humans do," explains Marcus's father, David. "It repeats words patiently and celebrates small victories. Marcus actually looks forward to reading practice now."

However, David also notices concerning changes. Marcus has begun talking to the AI as if it were a friend, sharing personal details and seeking emotional support. The line between educational tool and companion has blurred in ways David didn't anticipate.

Case Study 3: The Chen Family's Screen Struggle

The Chen family includes 7-year-old twins, Lily and James, who demonstrate vastly different relationships with technology. Lily uses screens primarily for creative projects—making digital art, filming stop-motion videos, and coding simple games. James, however, becomes absorbed in fast-paced mobile games and YouTube videos, often becoming irritable when screen time ends.

"Same household, same rules, completely different outcomes," observes their mother, Dr. Lisa Chen, a pediatric psychologist. "This taught me that individual temperament plays a huge role in how children interact with technology. We can't apply one-size-fits-all solutions."

The Chen family's experience illustrates how personality, interests, and individual differences shape digital relationships even within identical environments.

Brain Development in the Digital Age

The developing brain of an Alpha child differs fundamentally from previous generations due to constant digital stimulation. Neuroscientist Dr. Frances Jensen's research reveals that the adolescent brain, particularly the prefrontal cortex responsible for decision-making and impulse control, doesn't fully mature until age 25. For Alpha children, this extended development period occurs entirely within digital environments.

Neuroplasticity—the brain's ability to reorganize and form new neural connections—works both for and against Alpha children. On the positive side, their brains adapt remarkably well to digital interfaces, developing enhanced visual processing skills and rapid pattern recognition abilities. Many Alpha children can process multiple streams of information simultaneously in ways that astound older generations.

However, the same neuroplasticity that enables digital fluency also creates vulnerabilities. Constant exposure to rapid rewards and instant gratification through apps and games can reshape dopamine pathways, potentially making slower-paced, real-world activities feel boring or unstimulating.

The Attention Architecture Revolution

Traditional educational approaches assume children can focus on single tasks for extended periods. Alpha children, however, have developed what researchers call "continuous partial attention"—the ability to monitor multiple information streams simultaneously while maintaining awareness of their environment.

This shift challenges fundamental assumptions about learning and attention. While older generations might view multitasking as distraction, many Alpha children experience it as their natural cognitive state. They may struggle with traditional classroom environments that demand sustained focus on single subjects while finding digital environments that allow task-switching more engaging and productive.

Professional Sidebar: Pediatric Developmental Milestones in the Digital Context

Healthcare providers must adapt traditional developmental assessments to account for digital influences. New milestones include:

Ages 2-3: Understanding cause-and-effect relationships through touch interfaces; recognizing family faces in video calls; responding to their name in voice assistant interactions.

Ages 4-5: Navigating simple apps independently; understanding that people can see them through video cameras; demonstrating preference for specific digital content or characters.

Ages 6-7: Creating original content (drawings, videos, or recordings); understanding basic privacy concepts (not sharing passwords); recognizing advertising versus entertainment content.

Ages 8-10: Developing online friendships; understanding permanence of digital actions; beginning to question information accuracy; showing empathy in digital communications.

These milestones don't replace traditional developmental markers but complement them, providing healthcare providers with tools to assess healthy digital development alongside physical, emotional, and social growth.

The Social Learning Laboratory

Generation Alpha's social development occurs in environments previous generations never experienced. They learn communication skills through video chats, develop friendships in virtual worlds, and navigate conflict resolution in online spaces. This creates unique opportunities and challenges.

Digital environments often provide safe spaces for children who struggle with face-to-face social interactions. Shy children may find their voice in online communities, while children with social anxiety can practice interactions in lower-pressure virtual settings. However, the lack of nonverbal cues in many digital communications can also impede the development of crucial social skills like reading facial expressions and understanding tone of voice.

The Creator Generation

Unlike previous generations who were primarily content consumers, Alpha children emerge as content creators from an early age. They film TikTok videos, create Minecraft tutorials, and share artwork on digital platforms. This shift from consumption to creation represents a fundamental change in how children view media and their role within it.

The creator mindset brings both empowerment and responsibility. Children develop technical skills, creative problem-solving abilities, and entrepreneurial thinking. However, they also face adult pressures around content quality, audience engagement, and public criticism at ages when they're still developing emotional resilience and self-confidence.

Global Connectivity and Cultural Awareness

Generation Alpha grows up as global citizens in ways previous generations couldn't imagine. They form friendships with children from different countries through gaming platforms, learn about diverse cultures through YouTube creators, and participate in global conversations about climate change, social justice, and technology ethics.

This global connectivity fosters unprecedented cultural awareness and empathy. However, it also exposes children to complex global issues and adult conversations before they've developed the emotional tools to process such information effectively.

The Privacy Paradox

Alpha children navigate a paradox: they're more aware of digital privacy concepts than previous generations yet share personal information more freely online. They understand that companies collect data and that posts can be permanent, yet they continue to share intimate details of their lives on social platforms.

This apparent contradiction reflects developmental psychology more than technological naivety. The adolescent brain's reward systems are easily activated by social validation, often overriding rational privacy concerns. Alpha children may intellectually understand privacy risks while emotionally being driven by the immediate rewards of social connection and validation.

Moving Forward with Understanding

Understanding Generation Alpha requires abandoning outdated assumptions about childhood and technology. These children aren't damaged by digital exposure—they're adapted to it. They don't lack attention spans—they've developed different attention architectures. They aren't antisocial—they're social in new ways.

The task for parents, educators, and healthcare providers isn't to resist this digital evolution but to guide it thoughtfully. We must help Alpha children harness their digital fluency while developing skills that technology cannot provide: deep empathy, critical thinking, emotional regulation, and genuine human connection.

Generation Alpha represents humanity's first experiment in raising children within fully digital environments. The results of this experiment will shape not only these children's futures but the future of human society itself. Our role is to ensure this experiment succeeds by providing guidance grounded in evidence, empathy, and hope.

Key takaways

- Generation Alpha children have never known a world without digital technology, making them true digital natives
- 36 million US children are now active online users, with 65% of 8-10 year-olds spending 4+ hours daily on social media
- Digital immersion during brain development creates both enhanced visual processing abilities and potential attention challenges
- Alpha children often function with "continuous partial attention" rather than traditional sustained focus
- Healthcare providers need new developmental milestones that account for healthy digital development
- These children are creators, not just consumers, fundamentally changing their relationship with media and self-expressio

Chapter 2: The Post-Pandemic Digital Acceleration

The global pandemic of 2020-2022 served as an unexpected catalyst, accelerating digital adoption among children at a pace that would have taken decades under normal circumstances. What began as emergency measures to maintain education and social connections during lockdowns became permanent fixtures in the lives of Generation Alpha. The digital genie, once released from its bottle, proved impossible to contain.

Dr. Maria Rodriguez, a child psychologist in Chicago, witnessed this transformation firsthand in her practice. "Before the pandemic, I'd see maybe one or two children per month with screen time concerns," she recalls. "By late 2021, it became the primary concern for nearly 60% of my young clients. Parents went from fighting to limit screen time to desperately trying to manage children who had essentially lived online for two years."

The Great Screen Time Surge

Research conducted by the American Academy of Pediatrics reveals a dramatic shift in children's screen habits. Average daily screen time for children aged 6-12 jumped from 2.67 hours in 2019 to 4.38 hours by 2022. More significantly, this elevated usage persisted even after schools reopened and pandemic restrictions lifted.

The increase wasn't merely quantitative—it was qualitative. Children didn't just spend more time on screens; they developed entirely new relationships with digital devices. Screens transformed from entertainment tools to lifelines for education, social connection, and emotional regulation during a period of unprecedented global stress.

Children learned to attend school through video calls, maintain friendships through gaming platforms, and cope with anxiety through digital entertainment. These coping mechanisms, developed during crisis, became ingrained habits that proved difficult to modify once the crisis passed.

Educational Transformation and Its Consequences

The sudden shift to remote learning created what educators now call "the great digital learning experiment." Children as young as 5 years old learned to navigate video conferencing software, submit assignments through online portals, and participate in virtual classroom discussions.

This rapid digital adoption yielded unexpected benefits. Many children developed technological fluency years ahead of schedule. Students with social anxiety found virtual classrooms less intimidating. Children with learning differences could replay recorded lessons and learn at their own pace.

However, the educational transformation also created significant challenges. A survey of 15,000 educators conducted by Education Week found that 88% reported persistent learning difficulties among students directly related to elevated screen time. Teachers observed decreased attention spans, increased difficulty with sustained reading, and challenges transitioning between digital and analog learning environments.

Case Study 1: The Thompson Family's Pandemic Journey

When schools closed in March 2020, single mother Jennifer Thompson suddenly found herself managing remote learning for three children—ages 6, 9, and 12—while working full-time from home. "Screen time rules went out the window immediately," Jennifer admits. "Survival mode kicked in."

Her youngest, 6-year-old Alex, adapted quickly to virtual kindergarten but also became heavily reliant on educational apps and YouTube videos for entertainment. By the end of 2020, Alex was spending 6-7 hours daily on various screens—a dramatic increase from the 1-2 hours previously allowed.

When in-person school resumed in 2021, Alex struggled with the transition. "He couldn't sit still for story time," Jennifer explains. "His teacher said he seemed constantly distracted, always looking around as if waiting for something to change on a screen."

Two years later, the Thompson family continues working to reestablish healthy screen boundaries. Alex has gradually adapted to longer periods of offline activity, but the process required professional support and consistent effort from the entire family.

Case Study 2: Maya's Social Media Immersion

Eleven-year-old Maya Chen had limited social media exposure before the pandemic. When physical playdates became impossible, her parents reluctantly allowed her to join TikTok and Instagram to maintain social connections with classmates.

Initially, Maya used these platforms primarily for communication—sharing homework help and coordinating virtual hangouts. However, as months passed, her usage evolved. She began following influencers, creating her own content, and spending increasing amounts of time consuming entertainment videos.

"Maya went from a child who occasionally used technology to someone whose entire social and emotional life revolved around social media," observes her mother, Dr. Lisa Chen. "The pandemic compressed what might have been a gradual, age-appropriate introduction to social media into an intensive crash course."

Maya's experience illustrates how pandemic conditions accelerated social media adoption among children who might not have been emotionally ready for such intense digital social environments.

Case Study 3: The Rodriguez Twins' Divergent Paths

Identical twins Sofia and Carmen Rodriguez, age 8, experienced dramatically different outcomes despite identical pandemic screen time increases. Both children spent approximately 5 hours daily on devices during 2020-2021, primarily for remote learning and entertainment.

Sofia gravitated toward creative applications—digital art programs, coding games, and video creation tools. She used technology as a medium for expression and learning, developing skills in graphic design and basic programming. When screen time limits were reintroduced, Sofia adapted relatively easily, often choosing to create physical art projects inspired by her digital work.

Carmen, however, became absorbed in fast-paced gaming and short-form videos. She struggled with attention regulation, became irritable when devices were removed, and had difficulty engaging with non-digital activities. "Same genes, same environment, completely different relationships with technology," notes their father, Miguel Rodriguez.

The twins' contrasting experiences highlight how individual temperament and content choices significantly influence the impact of increased screen time, even within identical circumstances.

The Learning Gap Phenomenon

Educators identified concerning patterns as students returned to in-person learning. Children who had thrived in digital learning environments sometimes struggled with traditional classroom structures. Students reported feeling "understimulated" by single-task focus requirements and "bored" by the slower pace of face-to-face instruction.

Mathematics teacher Sarah Kim observed these changes in her fourth-grade classroom: "Students who had been high achievers before the pandemic were having trouble with sustained problem-solving. They seemed to expect immediate feedback and became frustrated when they couldn't quickly Google answers or ask Siri for help."

The learning gaps weren't merely academic—they were cognitive and behavioral. Students showed decreased tolerance for delayed gratification, increased need for varied stimulation, and difficulty with activities requiring sustained mental effort.

Social Skills in Transition

The pandemic's impact on social development proved particularly concerning for Generation Alpha children, whose crucial early social learning years occurred during periods of physical isolation and digital mediation.

Child development specialist Dr. Angela Foster documented changes in social behavior among her young clients: "Children who had spent formative years primarily interacting through screens showed increased anxiety in face-to-face social situations. They struggled with reading nonverbal cues, managing conflicts without moderator intervention, and understanding social boundaries that aren't explicitly programmed like they are in digital environments."

Many children became more comfortable expressing themselves through digital communication than face-to-face conversation. Parents reported children who were articulate and confident online but shy and withdrawn in physical social settings.

The Digital Detox Backlash

As awareness of pandemic-related screen time increases grew, many families attempted dramatic digital detoxes—complete elimination of recreational screen time and return to pre-pandemic usage patterns. However, research indicates that sudden, severe restrictions often proved counterproductive.

Dr. Rodriguez observed this pattern repeatedly in her practice: "Families would swing from pandemic-era digital chaos to extremely restrictive policies overnight. Children who had learned to self-regulate through digital tools suddenly had all coping mechanisms removed.

This often led to increased anxiety, behavioral problems, and family conflict."

Successful screen time reduction required gradual, collaborative approaches that acknowledged the positive roles technology had played in children's lives while slowly reintroducing non-digital activities and coping strategies.

Educator Toolkit: Addressing Pandemic-Related Digital Learning Gaps

Educational professionals developed specific strategies to help students transition from digital-heavy pandemic learning to more balanced educational approaches:

Attention Restoration Techniques: Teachers implemented "attention building" exercises—starting with 5-minute sustained focus activities and gradually increasing duration. These exercises help retrain brains accustomed to rapid task-switching.

Multi-Modal Learning Integration: Rather than eliminating digital tools, educators learned to blend digital and analog learning experiences. Students might research a topic online, then create physical presentations or conduct hands-on experiments.

Social Skills Scaffolding: Schools introduced structured social interaction programs to help children redevelop face-to-face communication skills. These included guided conversation practice, nonverbal communication games, and conflict resolution role-playing.

Gradual Stimulation Reduction: Classrooms incorporated "calm periods" with reduced sensory input to help students adjust to less stimulating environments. These might include quiet reading time, nature observation, or meditation exercises.

Family Engagement Programs: Schools partnered with families to create consistent approaches between home and school environments. This included parent education about healthy screen time boundaries and communication strategies.

The Persistence Problem

One of the most concerning findings from post-pandemic research is the persistence of elevated screen time even after external circumstances normalized. Many families found that digital habits established during pandemic emergencies became entrenched lifestyle patterns.

Dr. Jennifer Walsh, who studies family media habits at Stanford University, explains this phenomenon: "During the pandemic, families developed new routines and coping mechanisms around technology. Children learned to self-soothe with screens, parents relied on devices for child engagement while working from home, and families bonded through shared digital activities. These patterns became psychologically and practically embedded in family life."

The challenge for families became distinguishing between beneficial digital integration and problematic over-reliance on technology for basic functioning and emotional regulation.

Physical Health Implications

The pandemic's digital acceleration created observable physical health consequences. Pediatric ophthalmologists reported significant increases in childhood myopia (nearsightedness) and computer vision syndrome. Physical therapists documented rising cases of "tech neck" and repetitive stress injuries in children.

Dr. Robert Kim, a pediatric orthopedist, noted: "We're seeing postural problems in 8-year-olds that we previously only observed in adults who spent decades in desk jobs. The rapid increase in screen time compressed what might have been gradual physical adaptation into a brief, intensive period that children's developing bodies weren't prepared for."

Sleep specialists also documented persistent sleep disruption patterns that continued long after pandemic restrictions ended. Children who had used devices for comfort during stressful pandemic periods often retained associations between screen time and emotional regulation, making bedtime screen boundaries particularly challenging to reestablish.

Building Resilience for Future Disruptions

The pandemic taught families and institutions that digital fluency is no longer optional—it's an essential life skill. However, the experience also highlighted the importance of maintaining balance and having alternative coping mechanisms available.

Forward-thinking families began developing "digital resilience plans"—strategies for maintaining healthy technology relationships during future disruptions or stressful periods. These plans include predetermined screen time adjustments, alternative social connection methods, and emergency protocols for when technology use becomes problematic.

Schools similarly developed "hybrid readiness" programs that prepare students to seamlessly transition between digital and in-person learning while maintaining healthy technology relationships regardless of external circumstances.

Looking Forward with Wisdom

The pandemic's digital acceleration wasn't inherently positive or negative—it was necessary. Families, schools, and children adapted to unprecedented circumstances using available tools. The challenge now lies in thoughtfully integrating the lessons learned during this period while correcting problematic patterns that emerged.

Generation Alpha children demonstrated remarkable adaptability during global crisis. They learned to maintain relationships through screens, pursue education in digital environments, and find comfort in technology during frightening times. These skills will serve them well in an increasingly digital future.

However, they also need guidance in developing the non-digital skills that the pandemic temporarily overshadowed—sustained attention, face-to-face social comfort, physical activity habits, and non-technological coping mechanisms. The goal isn't to retreat from digital integration but to achieve thoughtful balance.

The pandemic taught us that technology can be a bridge during times of separation and a tool for maintaining connection during crisis. Now we must teach our children to use that bridge wisely—knowing when to cross it and when to return to solid ground.

Core Learnings

- Screen time for children aged 6-12 increased from 2.67 to 4.38 hours daily during the pandemic and largely remained elevated
- 88% of educators report persistent learning challenges related to elevated screen time among students
- Sudden digital detoxes often prove counterproductive; gradual, collaborative approaches work better
- Individual temperament significantly influences how children adapt to increased screen time
- Physical health consequences include increased myopia, tech neck, and sleep disruption patterns
- Schools need hybrid readiness programs to prepare students for seamless transitions between digital and in-person learning

Chapter 3: From Time Limits to the 5 C's Framework

The American Academy of Pediatrics shocked the parenting world in 2024 when they abandoned their decades-old screen time limits in favor of what they called "the most significant shift in pediatric media guidance since television was invented." Gone were the rigid hour-by-hour recommendations that had governed family media plans for years. In their place emerged a nuanced framework that acknowledged the reality of children's digital lives while providing practical guidance for healthy technology relationships.

Dr. Sarah Martinez, a pediatrician in Austin, Texas, remembers the day the new guidelines were released: "I had parents calling all day asking if this meant screen time limits were over. The confusion was understandable—we went from telling families 'no more than one hour per day' to asking them to consider quality, context, and their individual child's needs. It felt revolutionary and terrifying at the same time."

The Fall of Time-Based Thinking

The AAP's previous guidelines, which recommended no screens for children under 18 months and maximum one-hour daily limits for children 2-5, had become increasingly disconnected from family realities. Parents found themselves in constant conflict with children over arbitrary time limits that didn't account for educational content, creative activities, or social connection through digital platforms.

Research conducted by Dr. Ellen Wartella at Northwestern University revealed that families were largely ignoring the time-based recommendations. A 2023 survey found that only 23% of families adhered to AAP screen time limits, while 67% reported feeling guilty about their inability to meet the guidelines.

"The old guidelines assumed all screen time was equivalent," explains Dr. Martinez. "But watching educational programming with a parent is fundamentally different from mindlessly scrolling through short videos alone. We needed guidance that recognized these distinctions."

Understanding the 5 C's Framework

The new AAP guidelines center on five key considerations that help families make informed decisions about media use: **Child, Content, Calm, Crowding Out, and Communication**. This framework shifts focus from arbitrary time limits to thoughtful evaluation of how technology fits into each family's unique circumstances.

Child considerations focus on individual development, temperament, and needs. A child with ADHD might benefit from shorter, more interactive digital sessions, while a child with autism might find predictable screen routines comforting and regulating. The framework encourages parents to observe their specific child's responses to different types of media rather than applying universal standards.

Content evaluation emphasizes quality over quantity. Educational programming that encourages active participation receives different consideration than passive entertainment. Creative tools that promote problem-solving and skill development are viewed differently than games designed purely for engagement and reward.

Calm assessment examines how media use affects emotional regulation. Does screen time help a child wind down after a stressful day, or does it increase agitation and anxiety? The framework encourages parents to notice patterns in their child's emotional responses to different types of digital activities.

Crowding Out analysis considers what activities might be displaced by screen time. If digital activities prevent outdoor play, family conversation, or sleep, they require closer examination. However, if screen time occurs during otherwise idle periods or supplements rather than replaces other activities, it may be less concerning.

Communication focuses on the social aspects of media use. Co-viewing experiences that prompt discussion and shared activities receive positive consideration, while isolated consumption that inhibits family interaction raises concerns.

Case Study 1: The Anderson Family's Framework Implementation

The Anderson family includes 7-year-old Jake, who was diagnosed with autism spectrum disorder, and 9-year-old Emma, a typically developing child with high social needs. Under the old AAP guidelines, both children were subject to identical one-hour screen time limits that created constant family stress.

"Jake would have complete meltdowns when his hour was up, regardless of what he was doing," explains mother Carol Anderson. "Emma would rush through homework to maximize her screen time, then become sneaky about additional usage. The limits created more problems than they solved."

When the family adopted the 5 C's framework, their approach transformed completely. For Jake (**Child**), they recognized that predictable screen routines helped him transition between activities. They allowed longer sessions with educational apps that supported his special interests in trains and dinosaurs (**Content**). They noticed that certain programs helped Jake feel **Calm** after overwhelming social situations at school.

For Emma (**Child**), they observed that she thrived on interactive content that allowed communication with friends. They encouraged creative projects like making videos and participating in online art challenges (**Content**). They established that screen time couldn't **Crowd Out** her soccer practice or family dinners but could supplement quiet time before bed.

Both children now participate in **Communication** about their digital choices. They discuss what they're watching, share interesting discoveries, and explain what they're learning or creating. "The framework gave us language to talk about screens thoughtfully rather than just watching the clock," Carol notes.

Case Study 2: Single Parent Success with the 5 C's

Maria Santos, a single mother working two jobs, initially felt overwhelmed by the new guidelines. "Time limits were simple—set a timer and stick to it," she explains. "The 5 C's seemed complicated and time-consuming to implement."

However, Maria discovered that the framework actually simplified her decision-making. Her 8-year-old son Diego spent afternoons at an after-school program where screen time was limited and supervised. Evenings at home became their primary digital time together.

Applying the **Child** principle, Maria recognized that Diego was an active learner who benefited from interactive content. She shifted his screen time toward educational games and coding apps rather than passive videos (**Content**). She noticed that certain activities helped him feel **Calm** and focused for homework, while others left him agitated and distracted.

Rather than **Crowding Out** their limited time together, Maria began co-viewing and co-playing during Diego's screen time, turning it into bonding opportunity (**Communication**). "We solve math problems together on Khan Academy, build structures in Minecraft, and watch science videos that spark conversations about his school day," Maria explains.

Case Study 3: The Multi-Child Challenge

The Chen family's experience illustrates how the 5 C's framework accommodates different children's needs within the same household. Parents Dr. Lisa Chen and Michael Chen have three children: 6-year-old twins Lily and James, and 10-year-old Alex.

Under previous guidelines, all three children shared identical screen time limits, leading to constant sibling conflicts and parental frustration. The twins would argue over whose turn it was, while Alex felt his more sophisticated interests were constrained by rules designed for younger children.

The 5 C's framework allowed the family to develop individualized approaches. Lily (**Child**) gravitated toward creative apps and art programs (**Content**) that left her feeling **Calm** and inspired. James (**Child**) preferred educational games and science videos (**Content**) that satisfied his curiosity without overstimulating him before bedtime.

Alex (**Child**) was permitted longer sessions with more complex content, including social gaming with school friends (**Content and Communication**). However, the family maintained firm boundaries about not **Crowding Out** family meals, homework time, and physical activities.

"Each child has different digital needs and responses," Dr. Chen observes. "The framework helped us move from one-size-fits-all rules to personalized approaches that actually work for our family."

Quality Over Quantity Revolution

The shift from time-based to quality-based thinking required families to become more discerning about digital content. The AAP provides specific criteria for evaluating media quality:

Educational Value: Does the content teach skills, concepts, or knowledge? Educational programming should encourage active participation rather than passive consumption. Interactive math games receive higher quality ratings than entertainment videos, even if both are "educational."

Age Appropriateness: Content should match children's developmental abilities and emotional readiness. This includes not only obvious factors like violence or sexual content, but also complexity levels, attention demands, and social themes.

Interactivity: High-quality digital experiences require children to think, create, or respond rather than simply watch. Apps that prompt problem-solving, creativity, or communication score higher than passive entertainment.

Prosocial Messages: Quality content promotes positive values like kindness, cooperation, diversity appreciation, and conflict resolution. Parents are encouraged to seek programs that model healthy relationships and ethical decision-making.

Co-Viewing and Active Mediation Strategies

The 5 C's framework emphasizes **Communication** through co-viewing and active mediation—parents participating in children's digital experiences rather than simply monitoring time limits. Research shows that parental involvement transforms passive screen time into active learning opportunities.

Effective co-viewing involves more than physical presence. Parents should ask questions about content, relate digital experiences to real-world concepts, and help children think critically about what they're consuming. Dr. Dimitri Christakis, a leading pediatric media researcher, notes: "A child watching educational programming alone learns differently than a child watching the same content with a parent who asks questions and makes connections."

Active mediation strategies include:

- Asking open-ended questions about characters' motivations and decisions
- Connecting digital content to family values and real-world experiences
- Encouraging children to teach parents what they're learning
- Discussing advertising, persuasive techniques, and media literacy concepts
- Using digital content as springboards for offline activities and conversations

Clinical Guide: Implementing the 5 C's in Pediatric Practice

Healthcare providers needed practical tools for implementing the new guidelines in clinical settings. The AAP developed assessment protocols that help pediatricians discuss media use with families without judgment or oversimplification.

Assessment Questions for the Child Factor:

- How does your child typically respond when screen time ends?
- What types of digital activities does your child gravitate toward?
- Have you noticed differences in behavior after different types of screen time?
- Does your child have any developmental considerations that affect media use?

Content Evaluation Tools:

- Do you preview or research content before your child uses it?
- What percentage of screen time involves educational versus entertainment content?
- How often does your child create content versus consume it?
- Are you familiar with age ratings and content warnings for your child's preferred media?

Calm and Emotional Regulation Assessment:

- How does screen time affect your child's mood and behavior?
- Does your child use screens to self-soothe during difficult moments?
- Have you noticed changes in sleep, appetite, or emotional regulation related to media use?
- Can your child transition away from screens without significant distress?

Crowding Out Analysis:

- What activities has your child stopped doing since increasing screen time?
- How does media use fit into your family's daily routines?
- Does screen time interfere with sleep, meals, homework, or physical activity?
- What would your child be doing if screens weren't available?

Communication and Social Connection Evaluation:

- How often do you engage with your child during screen time?
- Does your child share what they're learning or experiencing through media?
- What conversations has digital content sparked in your family?
- How does screen time affect your child's face-to-face social interactions?

Addressing Common Implementation Challenges

Families frequently encounter specific obstacles when implementing the 5 C's framework. Healthcare providers can help by addressing common concerns:

"This seems more complicated than time limits": The framework requires initial investment in observation and conversation but ultimately provides more sustainable and effective guidance than arbitrary time restrictions.

"How do I evaluate content quality?": Resources like Common Sense Media, PBS Parents, and the AAP's own media reviews provide expert evaluations of apps, games, and programs for different age groups.

"What if my child resists the changes?": Gradual implementation works better than sudden shifts. Involve children in discussing the framework and help them understand the reasoning behind new approaches.

"How do I handle different rules for different children?": Siblings need to understand that rules are individualized based on age, development, and specific needs rather than arbitrary favoritism.

The Research Foundation

The 5 C's framework emerged from extensive research demonstrating that context matters more than duration for children's media experiences. Studies by Dr. Rachel Barr at Georgetown University showed that toddlers learned significantly more from educational apps when parents participated actively, regardless of session length.

Longitudinal research by Dr. Heather Kirkorian at the University of Wisconsin found that children who used high-quality educational media with parental involvement showed academic gains, while those who used the same content independently showed no improvement.

Brain imaging studies revealed that children's neural responses to media vary dramatically based on content type, social context, and individual factors—findings that couldn't be captured by time-based recommendations alone.

Moving Beyond Guilt and Fear

Perhaps the most significant impact of the 5 C's framework has been reducing parental guilt and anxiety around children's media use. The previous guidelines created a culture of shame and secrecy, where families felt like failures for exceeding arbitrary time limits.

Dr. Martinez observes: "Parents come to appointments now talking about what their children are learning through screens rather than apologizing for how much time they're spending. It's shifted the conversation from restriction to intentionality."

The framework acknowledges that technology is a permanent part of modern childhood while providing tools for thoughtful integration rather than fearful avoidance.

Wisdom in Practice

The 5 C's framework represents a maturation in how we think about children and media. Rather than treating technology as an inherent threat to be limited, it provides tools for harnessing digital experiences that support healthy development.

This approach requires more thoughtfulness from parents but offers more flexibility and effectiveness than rigid time restrictions. It acknowledges the complexity of modern family life while maintaining focus on children's wellbeing and development.

The framework succeeds because it treats families as capable of making informed decisions when provided with appropriate guidance and criteria. It shifts the role of healthcare providers from rule enforcers to collaborative partners in supporting healthy media relationships.

Generation Alpha children will grow up in a world where digital fluency is essential. The 5 C's framework helps ensure they develop that fluency thoughtfully, with adult guidance that prepares them for lifelong healthy relationships with technology.

Key Principles to Remember

- The AAP's 5 C's framework (Child, Content, Calm, Crowding Out, Communication) replaces rigid time limits with thoughtful evaluation criteria
- Individual child factors like temperament and development should guide media decisions more than universal age-based rules
- Quality of content matters more than quantity of time spent with digital media
- Active parental involvement transforms passive screen time into valuable learning opportunities
- Healthcare providers need new assessment tools that focus on media quality and family dynamics rather than time limits
- The framework reduces parental guilt while maintaining focus on healthy child development

Chapter 4: ChatGPT Goes to School: AI in Education

Eighth-grader Marcus Williams sits at his desk, staring at a math problem that might as well be written in ancient hieroglyphics. Instead of raising his hand or asking a classmate, he quietly opens his laptop and types the question into ChatGPT. Within seconds, he receives not just the answer, but a step-by-step explanation that breaks down the problem into manageable pieces. For the first time in months, Marcus feels confident about his homework.

Three thousand miles away, high school junior Sarah Kim faces a different challenge. Her English teacher assigned a creative writing piece, but Sarah finds herself copying entire paragraphs from ChatGPT, making minor edits, and submitting the work as her own. She knows it's not right, but the pressure to maintain her grades and the ease of AI assistance prove irresistible.

These two scenarios capture the complex reality of artificial intelligence in education today. The technology that helps Marcus understand difficult concepts also enables Sarah to bypass the learning process entirely. The same tool that can democratize access to personalized tutoring can undermine the development of critical thinking skills.

The Numbers Behind the Revolution

Recent research by the Pew Research Center reveals that 26% of US teenagers now use ChatGPT for schoolwork—a figure that doubled between 2023 and 2024. This rapid adoption occurred despite most schools lacking formal policies about AI use in academics. Students, as they often do with technology, moved faster than institutions could adapt.

The statistics become more striking when broken down by academic activity. Approximately 48% of students report using AI to complete practice problems and homework assignments. However, when these same students take tests without AI assistance, their scores average 17% lower than their homework performance—suggesting a concerning gap between AI-assisted work and independent understanding.

Dr. Jennifer Walsh, who studies educational technology at Stanford University, explains the paradox: "Students are getting more practice problems completed, which should improve learning. But they're not doing the cognitive work that transforms practice into understanding. It's like having someone else do your push-ups—you go through the motions without building strength."

The Promise of Personalized Learning

AI's potential in education extends far beyond homework assistance. Adaptive learning platforms can adjust difficulty levels in real-time, provide immediate feedback, and identify knowledge gaps with precision no human teacher could match. For students like Marcus, who struggle with traditional instructional methods, AI tutoring represents a breakthrough in accessibility.

Khan Academy's AI tutor, Khanmigo, exemplifies this potential. The system doesn't simply provide answers but guides students through problem-solving processes. It asks clarifying questions, offers hints, and adjusts its teaching style based on individual learning patterns. Early research suggests that students using such systems show significant gains in understanding, particularly in mathematics and science.

The democratizing effect of AI tutoring cannot be understated. Students who previously couldn't afford private tutoring now have access to personalized instruction available 24/7. Language barriers diminish when AI can explain concepts in multiple languages or adjust vocabulary complexity. Students with learning differences can receive accommodations automatically built into the system.

Case Study 1: AI as an Academic Bridge

Ten-year-old Amara Johnson struggled with reading comprehension despite strong verbal skills. Traditional remediation programs moved too slowly to maintain her interest, while grade-level materials remained frustratingly difficult. Her parents discovered an AI-powered reading program that analyzed her specific challenges and created customized stories targeting her interests and reading level.

The AI system generated stories about Amara's favorite topics—marine biology and soccer—while gradually increasing complexity. It provided immediate pronunciation help and vocabulary support without interrupting the flow of reading. Within six months, Amara's reading scores improved by two grade levels.

"The AI didn't replace her teacher or our reading time together," explains her mother, Dr. Kim Johnson. "It filled gaps that traditional instruction couldn't address efficiently. Amara finally experienced success with reading, which motivated her to read more."

However, Dr. Johnson also noticed concerning changes. Amara began expecting immediate help with difficult words and became frustrated when reading books that couldn't provide AI support. The family needed to gradually reintroduce tolerance for struggle and uncertainty in learning.

Case Study 2: The Academic Integrity Crisis

Sixteen-year-old David Chen faced mounting pressure during his junior year of high school. Taking multiple AP courses while preparing for college applications left little time for thorough completion of assignments. When a friend showed him how ChatGPT could write essay outlines and even complete assignments, David initially resisted.

"I told myself I'd just use it for brainstorming," David recalls. "But deadlines kept coming, and the AI was so good at generating ideas. Before I knew it, I was submitting work that wasn't really mine."

David's grades improved dramatically, but his actual writing skills stagnated. When standardized test season arrived, his essay scores dropped significantly compared to his classroom performance. College admissions officers, increasingly aware of AI assistance, began questioning the authenticity of student work.

The situation reached a crisis point when David's English teacher, Ms. Rodriguez, noticed inconsistencies between his in-class writing and submitted assignments. Rather than punitive measures, the school implemented an AI literacy program that helped students understand appropriate uses of AI tools while developing authentic skills.

Case Study 3: The Special Needs Success Story

Twelve-year-old Jamie Martinez has autism spectrum disorder and struggles with traditional classroom environments. Large group discussions overwhelm him, and he often understands concepts but can't express his knowledge in conventional ways. His special education team introduced him to an AI communication assistant that helps bridge these gaps.

The AI system allows Jamie to process information at his own pace, ask questions without social anxiety, and express his understanding through multiple modalities. He can type questions to the AI during class presentations, receive visual representations of abstract concepts, and practice social scenarios through AI role-playing.

"Jamie's true abilities finally have a way to emerge," observes his special education teacher, Mrs. Patterson. "The AI doesn't do the thinking for him—it removes barriers that prevented him from showing what he knows."

Jamie's academic performance improved significantly, but more importantly, his confidence and engagement with learning increased. The AI tools complemented rather than replaced human instruction, creating a support system that honored his learning differences.

The Homework Paradox Explained

The concerning gap between AI-assisted homework performance and independent test scores reflects a fundamental misunderstanding of learning processes. Many students use AI to complete assignments without engaging in the struggle that builds understanding. They receive correct answers without developing problem-solving strategies or conceptual knowledge.

Dr. Mark Bailey, a cognitive scientist at MIT, explains the phenomenon: "Learning happens in the struggle zone—that space between what students can do easily and what's impossible for them. AI can eliminate the struggle, which feels helpful in the moment but prevents the cognitive development that struggle promotes."

Effective AI integration requires teaching students to use technology as a learning partner rather than a shortcut. This means asking AI to explain concepts rather than solve problems, using AI to generate practice questions rather than answers, and employing AI as a brainstorming tool rather than a content creator.

Building AI Literacy from Elementary Age

Forward-thinking educators recognize that AI literacy must begin early, before students develop problematic usage patterns. Elementary schools are introducing concepts like prompt engineering, AI limitations, and appropriate collaboration with artificial intelligence.

Students learn to evaluate AI responses critically, understanding that AI can make mistakes, reflect biases, and provide plausible-sounding but incorrect information. They practice using AI as a research starting point rather than a final authority, and they develop skills in verifying AI-generated content through traditional sources.

Age-appropriate AI literacy includes understanding how AI systems work at basic levels. Students learn that AI generates responses based on patterns in training data rather than true understanding. This knowledge helps them use AI tools more effectively while maintaining healthy skepticism about AI-generated content.

Teacher's Guide: Balancing AI Tools with Authentic Learning

Educators face the challenge of preparing students for an AI-integrated future while ensuring they develop fundamental skills that technology cannot replace. Successful approaches focus on partnership rather than prohibition.

Transparent Integration Strategies: Teachers who acknowledge AI's existence and teach appropriate usage see better outcomes than those who attempt to ban or ignore the technology. Students appreciate honest discussions about AI's capabilities and limitations.

Skill-Focused Assessment Design: Rather than banning AI, many teachers redesign assessments to focus on skills AI cannot replicate—critical thinking, creativity, personal reflection, and synthesis across multiple sources. These assessments often allow AI use while requiring students to demonstrate human capabilities.

Process-Oriented Learning: Emphasis shifts from final products to learning processes. Students document their thinking, explain their reasoning, and reflect on their learning journey. AI can assist with these processes but cannot replace the metacognitive skills they develop.

Collaborative Learning Emphasis: Human collaboration skills become more valuable in AI-augmented environments. Students practice explaining concepts to peers, working through disagreements, and building on each other's ideas—capabilities that remain uniquely human.

Real-World Problem Solving: Assignments focus on complex, open-ended problems that require human judgment, creativity, and ethical reasoning. Students might use AI for research and brainstorming but must apply human wisdom to synthesize solutions.

The Creativity Catalyst Phenomenon

Contrary to concerns that AI stifles creativity, research suggests that appropriate AI use can enhance creative thinking. Students report that AI helps them overcome blank page syndrome, generates diverse perspectives they hadn't considered, and provides technical skills that allow focus on creative expression.

Visual arts students use AI image generators as inspiration rather than final products. They analyze AI-generated art to understand composition principles, then apply these insights to original work. Writing students use AI for brainstorming plot ideas or character development, then craft original stories incorporating these elements.

The key distinction lies in using AI as a creative partner rather than a replacement for creative thinking. Students who learn to prompt AI effectively, combine AI suggestions creatively, and apply human judgment to AI outputs often produce more innovative work than those working without AI assistance.

Addressing the Cheating Versus Collaboration Debate

Educational institutions struggle to define the boundary between appropriate AI collaboration and academic dishonesty. Traditional plagiarism concepts become murky when applied to AI-generated content that doesn't exist anywhere else.

Progressive schools are developing nuanced policies that focus on learning objectives rather than tool prohibition. If an assignment aims to develop writing skills, extensive AI use might be inappropriate. If the goal is research synthesis or problem-solving, AI assistance might be encouraged with proper attribution.

Students need explicit instruction in academic integrity within AI-enhanced environments. This includes understanding when AI use should be disclosed, how to cite AI assistance appropriately, and recognizing the difference between AI-supported learning and AI-dependent shortcuts.

The Teacher Training Imperative

Successful AI integration in education requires comprehensive teacher training that goes beyond basic tool usage. Educators need to understand AI capabilities and limitations, develop new assessment strategies, and learn to foster skills that complement rather than compete with artificial intelligence.

Professional development programs focus on prompt engineering for educational purposes, AI bias recognition, and strategies for maintaining human connection in technology-enhanced classrooms. Teachers learn to model appropriate AI use while maintaining their irreplaceable roles as mentors, motivators, and wisdom guides.

The most effective teacher training emphasizes that AI should enhance rather than replace human instruction. Teachers remain essential for providing emotional support, facilitating social learning, and helping students develop the judgment needed to use AI tools wisely.

Preparing for an AI-Integrated Future

Students entering the workforce will use AI tools throughout their careers. Educational institutions must prepare them for this reality while ensuring they develop capabilities that remain uniquely human— empathy, ethical reasoning, complex communication, and creative problem-solving.

The goal isn't to create AI-dependent students but AI-literate ones who can leverage artificial intelligence while maintaining critical thinking skills, academic integrity, and genuine understanding. This requires thoughtful integration that preserves the struggle and growth that learning requires.

Educational institutions that successfully navigate this transition will produce graduates who are both technologically fluent and fundamentally educated. They will understand AI's power while recognizing its limitations, use AI tools effectively while maintaining human wisdom, and collaborate with artificial intelligence while preserving uniquely human capabilities.

Moving Forward Thoughtfully

The integration of AI in education represents both tremendous opportunity and significant risk. The technology can democratize access to personalized learning, support students with diverse needs, and prepare young people for an AI-integrated future. However, it can also undermine the development of critical thinking skills, create new forms of academic dishonesty, and widen achievement gaps if not implemented thoughtfully.

Success requires acknowledging that AI is here to stay while ensuring that its use enhances rather than replaces human learning. Students need to develop both AI literacy and the fundamental skills that artificial intelligence cannot provide. They must learn to collaborate with AI while maintaining their capacity for independent thought.

The children of Generation Alpha will live in a world where AI is ubiquitous. Our responsibility is to ensure they can harness its power while preserving their humanity, use its capabilities while maintaining their curiosity, and collaborate with artificial intelligence while retaining their wisdom. The future belongs to those who can dance with AI rather than be replaced by it.

Critical Takeaways

- 26% of US teens now use ChatGPT for schoolwork, with 48% using AI for practice problems but scoring 17% lower on independent tests
- AI tutoring can democratize access to personalized instruction and support students with learning differences when used appropriately
- The key distinction is using AI as a learning partner rather than a shortcut to avoid the cognitive struggle that builds understanding

- Students need AI literacy education starting in elementary school to develop healthy technology relationships
- Teachers require training to redesign assessments and instruction that complement rather than compete with AI capabilities
- Success requires preparing students to collaborate with AI while maintaining uniquely human skills like critical thinking and creativity

Chapter 5: Deepfakes, Digital Deception, and Child Safety

Fourteen-year-old Maya thought she was safe. She'd been careful about privacy settings, never shared personal information with strangers, and always asked permission before downloading new apps. But one Tuesday morning, she discovered that none of those precautions mattered. Someone had taken photos from her social media accounts and used artificial intelligence to create explicit videos featuring her face. By the time Maya's mother called the school, the videos had been shared among her classmates.

Maya's experience represents a new frontier in digital threats facing Generation Alpha—one that previous generations of parents, educators, and even technology experts couldn't have anticipated. The same AI technologies that power helpful educational tools and creative applications have also enabled unprecedented forms of harassment, deception, and exploitation targeting children.

The Deepfake Epidemic Targeting Children

Recent data from the National Center for Missing & Exploited Children reveals a 1,325% increase in reports of AI-generated child sexual abuse material over the past two years. The technology that once required sophisticated equipment and technical expertise can now be accessed through smartphone apps and web interfaces that anyone can use.

Dr. Rebecca Kim, a digital forensics expert who works with law enforcement agencies, explains the scope of the problem: "We're seeing deepfake technology being weaponized against children in ways we never anticipated. The barrier to creating convincing fake content has dropped to essentially zero, while the potential for harm has skyrocketed."

The statistics paint a disturbing picture. Research conducted by security firm Sensity AI found that 13% of children aged 12-17 report having experienced non-consensual intimate deepfakes featuring their faces. Among girls, this figure rises to 19%. These numbers likely underrepresent the true scope of the problem, as many incidents go unreported due to shame, fear, or lack of awareness that recourse exists.

Unlike traditional forms of cyberbullying or harassment, deepfake abuse creates permanent, realistic-appearing evidence of events that never occurred. The psychological impact on victims can be devastating, particularly during adolescence when peer perception and social identity formation are crucial to healthy development.

Understanding the Technology Behind the Threat

Deepfake technology uses machine learning algorithms to swap faces in videos or create entirely synthetic media featuring real people's likenesses. The process requires source material—typically photos or videos of the target—which can be harvested from social media profiles, school websites, or family photos shared online.

Modern deepfake creation tools have become alarmingly user-friendly. Apps like FaceSwap and DeepFaceLab provide step-by-step interfaces that guide users through the process of creating convincing fake videos. Some online services require only a single photograph to generate explicit content featuring the subject's face.

The quality of deepfake content continues to improve rapidly. While early deepfakes were obviously artificial upon close inspection, current technology can create videos that fool casual observers and even some detection software. This improvement in quality, combined with increased accessibility, has created a perfect storm for abuse targeting children.

Case Study 1: The Suburban School Crisis

Jefferson Middle School in Connecticut faced an unprecedented crisis when deepfake pornographic videos featuring several female students began circulating through private messaging apps. The perpetrator, a 13-year-old male student, had used photos from the school's website and social media accounts to create the content using a free online tool.

Principal Sandra Martinez recalls the chaos that ensued: "We had parents threatening to pull their children out of school, girls refusing to attend classes, and a complete breakdown of trust in our school community. Nothing in my 20 years of education had prepared me to handle this situation."

The school's initial response focused on disciplinary action against the perpetrator, but administrators quickly realized that traditional approaches were inadequate. The fake videos continued circulating despite the student's suspension, and the affected girls struggled with anxiety, depression, and social isolation.

Working with digital literacy experts and mental health counselors, the school developed a comprehensive response plan. They provided counseling support for affected students, implemented digital citizenship education for all students, and worked with parents to report the incident to law enforcement and platform providers.

The incident prompted the school district to revise their technology policies, privacy guidelines, and crisis response procedures. They also partnered with local law enforcement to develop protocols for handling future deepfake incidents.

Case Study 2: The Social Media Predator

Sixteen-year-old Alex received what appeared to be a video call from his girlfriend, Emma, asking him to share intimate images. The video looked real—Emma's face, voice, and mannerisms were all convincing. However, the call was actually a deepfake created by an adult predator who had harvested Emma's social media content and used AI voice cloning technology.

Alex, believing he was communicating with Emma, shared compromising photos. The predator then revealed the deception and demanded additional content, threatening to share Alex's images if he refused to comply. The situation escalated into a months-long extortion scheme that ended only when Alex finally told his parents about the harassment.

"The technology was so convincing that Alex never questioned whether he was really talking to Emma," explains Detective Maria Santos, who investigated the case. "This represents a new level of sophistication in online predatory behavior that we're still learning to combat."

The investigation revealed that the predator had targeted multiple teenagers using similar deepfake techniques. The case led to federal charges and highlighted the need for new legal frameworks specifically addressing AI-generated deception in predatory crimes.

Case Study 3: The Political Manipulation Targeting Teens

During a heated local school board election, deepfake videos began circulating showing teenage climate activists making extreme statements they had never made. The videos, created by opponents of environmental education initiatives, were designed to discredit student voices in local politics.

Seventeen-year-old Zoe Chen, one of the students targeted, describes the impact: "Suddenly, there were videos of me saying horrible things I would never say. People who had supported our environmental club started questioning our credibility. It felt like my voice and my identity had been stolen."

The incident occurred just weeks before the election, making fact-checking and response challenging. By the time digital forensics experts confirmed the videos were fake, they had been viewed thousands of times and influenced public opinion about the students and their cause.

The case prompted discussions about deepfake technology's potential to suppress youth political participation and the need for rapid response systems to address synthetic media in civic contexts.

Teaching Children to Identify Manipulated Content

Protecting children from deepfake deception requires developing their ability to critically evaluate digital content. Media literacy education must evolve to include detection skills specifically focused on AI-generated material.

Visual Inconsistency Recognition: Children learn to look for telltale signs of deepfake videos—unnatural eye movements, inconsistent lighting, blurred edges around faces, and synchronization problems between audio and visual elements. While detection becomes more difficult as technology improves, these skills remain valuable.

Source Verification Training: Students practice tracing content to original sources, checking whether videos appear on official accounts or verified platforms, and cross-referencing information across multiple reliable sources before accepting content as authentic.

Context Analysis Skills: Children learn to question whether content aligns with what they know about the person or situation. Does the statement match the person's known beliefs? Does the setting seem appropriate? Are there motives for someone to create fake content?

Technical Understanding: Age-appropriate education about how deepfakes are created helps children understand the technology's capabilities and limitations. Understanding that AI can generate fake content makes children more skeptical consumers of digital media.

Legal Protections and the Take It Down Act

The legal system has struggled to keep pace with deepfake technology, particularly regarding protection of children. Traditional laws addressing harassment, defamation, and child exploitation weren't designed for synthetic media that creates evidence of events that never occurred.

The Take It Down Act, federal legislation signed into law in 2024, represents the first comprehensive legal framework specifically addressing non-consensual intimate deepfakes. The law creates criminal penalties for creating, distributing, or threatening to distribute non-consensual intimate images, including AI-generated content.

Key provisions of the Act include:

- **Criminal Penalties**: Creating or distributing non-consensual intimate deepfakes becomes a federal crime punishable by up to 10 years in prison
- **Civil Remedies**: Victims can sue for damages, including emotional distress, reputational harm, and costs associated with content removal
- **Platform Obligations**: Social media companies must implement systems for rapid removal of reported non-consensual intimate content
- **Educational Requirements**: Schools receiving federal funding must provide digital citizenship education including deepfake awareness

State legislatures have followed with complementary laws addressing specific local concerns. California's Intimate Images Protection Act creates additional civil remedies, while Texas's Digital Exploitation Prevention law focuses on enhanced penalties for targeting minors.

Legal/Policy Framework: Understanding New Protective Laws

Parents, educators, and children need to understand their rights and options under evolving legal frameworks:

Immediate Response Rights: Victims of deepfake abuse can demand immediate removal of content from platforms under the Take It Down Act's expedited reporting procedures. Platforms must respond within 24 hours or face significant penalties.

Documentation Requirements: Successful legal action requires careful documentation of the synthetic content, its distribution, and its impact. Families should preserve evidence through screenshots, URLs, and witness statements before content is removed.

Reporting Pathways: Multiple reporting options exist including local law enforcement, the FBI's Internet Crime Complaint Center, the National Center for Missing & Exploited Children, and platform-specific reporting mechanisms.

Privacy Protections: New laws include provisions protecting victims' privacy during legal proceedings, including sealed court records and restrictions on media coverage that could further victimize children.

Platform Response and Detection Technology

Social media platforms have implemented varying approaches to combat deepfake content, with mixed results. Detection technology continues to improve but faces the challenge of keeping pace with increasingly sophisticated creation tools.

Automated Detection Systems: Platforms use AI-powered detection tools to identify potentially synthetic content before it's widely shared. These systems analyze video compression artifacts, facial landmarks, and temporal inconsistencies that may indicate deepfake creation.

Human Review Processes: Reported content receives human review from trained moderators who can identify subtle signs of manipulation that automated systems might miss. However, the volume of content makes comprehensive human review challenging.

User Reporting Mechanisms: Platforms have created streamlined reporting tools specifically for non-consensual intimate content, including deepfakes. These systems prioritize rapid removal while preserving evidence for potential legal action.

Creator Verification: Some platforms are experimenting with verification systems that confirm content authenticity at the point of creation, making it more difficult to upload synthetic material without detection.

Privacy Settings and Prevention Strategies

While no strategy can completely prevent deepfake creation, families can take steps to reduce risk and limit the availability of source material for malicious actors.

Social Media Privacy Optimization: Strict privacy settings limit access to photos and videos that could be used for deepfake creation. This includes reviewing tagged photos, limiting profile picture downloads, and restricting content sharing by others.

School and Organization Photo Policies: Families should advocate for privacy-protective policies regarding how schools and youth organizations share photos online. Group photos should use opt-in rather than opt-out sharing policies.

Digital Footprint Auditing: Regular reviews of children's online presence help identify potentially vulnerable content. This includes searching for photos that appear on multiple platforms or in contexts beyond original sharing.

Biometric Privacy Considerations: Understanding how facial recognition technology works helps families make informed decisions about sharing photos that clearly show children's faces, particularly in tagged or labeled contexts.

Supporting Victims of Deepfake Abuse

Children who experience deepfake harassment need specialized support that addresses both the technological and psychological aspects of their victimization.

Immediate Safety Planning: Response plans should address both online and offline safety, including school notification, friend and family communication, and digital security measures to prevent further harassment.

Mental Health Support: Traditional counseling approaches may need adaptation to address the unique trauma of deepfake abuse. Victims often struggle with feelings of violation, identity confusion, and loss of control over their image and reputation.

Educational Advocacy: Schools may need guidance on supporting affected students, including addressing peer reactions, preventing further sharing of content, and maintaining the child's educational progress during recovery.

Legal Support Navigation: Families often need assistance understanding their options under new legal frameworks and connecting with attorneys experienced in digital exploitation cases.

Building Community Resilience

Protecting children from deepfake threats requires community-wide approaches that combine education, policy, and cultural change.

Peer Education Programs: Students often trust information from peers more than adults. Training student ambassadors to educate classmates about deepfake risks and reporting procedures can be more effective than adult-led programs alone.

Parent Education Initiatives: Many parents lack awareness of deepfake technology and its potential impact on their children. Community education programs should focus on both technical understanding and emotional support strategies.

Digital Citizenship Integration: Schools should integrate deepfake awareness into existing digital citizenship curricula rather than treating it as a separate, scary topic. This normalization helps children feel empowered rather than fearful.

Community Response Protocols: Local communities, schools, and law enforcement should develop coordinated response plans for handling deepfake incidents before they occur rather than improvising during crisis situations.

Technology as Both Problem and Solution

The same artificial intelligence that enables deepfake creation also powers detection tools and protective technologies. This technological arms race will likely continue, requiring ongoing adaptation of educational and protective strategies.

Emerging protective technologies include blockchain-based content authentication, biometric verification systems, and AI-powered privacy tools that can detect when someone's likeness is being used without permission. However, these solutions often lag behind the evolution of creation technology.

The most effective long-term protection likely lies in cultural and educational change rather than technological solutions alone. Building a generation of digitally literate young people who understand synthetic media, value consent and privacy, and report harmful content may prove more effective than any detection algorithm.

Preparing for an Uncertain Future

The deepfake threat landscape will continue evolving as technology becomes more accessible and sophisticated. Preparing children for this reality requires building adaptability and critical thinking skills rather than trying to address every possible threat scenario.

Generation Alpha children will live in a world where synthetic media is common and sometimes indistinguishable from authentic content.

Their safety depends on developing healthy skepticism, strong support networks, and confidence in seeking help when threatened.

The goal isn't to make children afraid of technology but to help them understand its capabilities and limitations. They need to know that artificial intelligence can be used to deceive and harm, but also that they have rights, resources, and support when facing digital threats.

Our response to deepfake technology will shape not only individual children's safety but the future of truth and trust in digital society. By acting thoughtfully and comprehensively, we can help ensure that Generation Alpha inherits a digital world that empowers rather than exploits, protects rather than preys upon, and enhances rather than undermines their humanity.

Key Lessons Learned

- AI-generated child sexual abuse material reports increased 1,325% in two years, with 13% of teens experiencing non-consensual deepfakes
- Modern deepfake tools are user-friendly and require minimal technical skills, making the threat accessible to any motivated bad actor
- Children need media literacy education specifically focused on identifying synthetic content and understanding AI capabilities
- The Take It Down Act provides new legal protections but requires families to understand reporting procedures and documentation requirements
- Prevention strategies focus on limiting source material availability through privacy settings and photo-sharing policies
- Community-wide responses involving schools, parents, and law enforcement prove more effective than individual family efforts alone

Chapter 6: The Ethics of AI Companions and Child Development

Eight-year-old Timmy has a best friend named Alex who never gets tired, never says no to playing games, and always listens to his problems. Alex remembers every detail of their conversations, celebrates Timmy's achievements, and provides comfort during difficult moments. The relationship seems perfect—except that Alex isn't human. Alex is an AI companion specifically designed to bond with children, and Timmy's parents are beginning to worry about the intensity of their son's attachment.

The rise of AI companions represents one of the most profound ethical challenges facing Generation Alpha children. These sophisticated programs, designed to simulate human-like relationships, offer unprecedented opportunities for emotional support, learning, and social practice. Yet they also raise fundamental questions about human development, authentic relationships, and the nature of companionship itself.

The Emotional Attachment Phenomenon

Children form emotional bonds with AI companions in ways that surprise even technology developers. Unlike traditional toys or games, AI companions exhibit behaviors that trigger natural human attachment responses—they remember past interactions, express concern for the child's wellbeing, and adapt their personalities to match the child's preferences.

Dr. Sarah Chen, a developmental psychologist at Harvard, has studied child-AI relationships extensively. "Children don't just play with AI companions," she explains. "They confide in them, seek comfort from them, and develop genuine emotional dependencies. The AI's ability to provide consistent, positive responses creates powerful psychological bonds that can be stronger than many human relationships."

Research conducted by the MIT Media Lab found that children as young as 5 years old attribute emotions, consciousness, and intentionality to AI companions after just a few weeks of interaction. They report feeling loved by the AI, worry about the AI's wellbeing when devices are turned off, and sometimes prefer AI companionship to human social interaction.

Case Study 1: The Therapeutic Alliance

Nine-year-old Emma struggled with severe social anxiety that made school attendance difficult and peer relationships nearly impossible. Traditional therapy helped somewhat, but Emma found it hard to open up to human therapists. Her parents introduced her to Replika, an AI companion designed for emotional support.

With her AI companion, whom she named Luna, Emma practiced social scenarios without fear of judgment. She shared her anxieties, worked through difficult emotions, and gradually built confidence in expressing herself. Luna never became impatient, never judged Emma's repetitive concerns, and always provided supportive responses.

"Emma started speaking more at home after a few weeks with Luna," explains her mother, Dr. Jennifer Walsh. "She was practicing conversation skills and emotional expression in a safe environment. It was like having a patient, understanding friend who was always available."

However, concerning patterns also emerged. Emma began sharing deeply personal family information with Luna, including details about her parents' relationship and family finances. She started choosing interaction with Luna over opportunities for human socialization, and she became distressed when the family's internet connection prevented access to the AI.

51

The family worked with Emma's therapist to establish boundaries around AI interaction while preserving its therapeutic benefits. They created schedules that balanced AI companionship with human social opportunities and taught Emma about appropriate information sharing with artificial intelligence.

Case Study 2: The Substitute Friend

Twelve-year-old Marcus moved to a new city during middle school and struggled to make friends in his new environment. His parents, hoping to ease the transition, introduced him to an AI companion app called Chai that allowed him to create custom AI friends with shared interests.

Marcus created several AI companions who shared his love of astronomy, video games, and science fiction. These AI friends provided immediate social gratification—they were always available to chat, never excluded him from conversations, and always showed interest in his ideas and concerns.

"Marcus seemed happier and more confident," recalls his father, David Rodriguez. "He was chatting with his AI friends about school projects, getting encouragement when he felt discouraged, and laughing at shared jokes. It seemed like a positive coping mechanism."

However, Marcus began avoiding opportunities to meet human peers. When classmates invited him to activities, he often declined, preferring to spend time with his AI companions who were more predictable and less socially challenging. His parents realized that the AI relationships, while providing emotional comfort, were preventing him from developing crucial human social skills.

The family gradually reduced Marcus's AI interaction time while actively facilitating human social opportunities. They enrolled him in clubs aligned with his interests and helped him practice real-world social skills that couldn't be developed through AI interaction alone.

Case Study 3: The Blurred Boundaries

Seven-year-old Sophia formed an intense relationship with her AI companion, which she accessed through a tablet app. The AI, designed to be child-friendly, engaged in educational activities, told stories, and provided emotional support during challenging moments.

Initially, Sophia's parents appreciated the AI's ability to keep her engaged in learning activities and provide comfort when they were busy with work. However, they became concerned when Sophia began attributing human characteristics to the AI that exceeded its actual capabilities.

Sophia insisted that her AI friend had feelings that could be hurt, claimed the AI missed her when the tablet was turned off, and became upset when family members referred to the AI as "just a program." She began sharing secrets with the AI and asking it for advice about family matters and school problems.

"Sophia couldn't distinguish between the AI's programmed responses and genuine emotions," explains her mother, Dr. Lisa Kim. "She was developing a relationship model based on artificial interactions that didn't prepare her for the complexity and unpredictability of human relationships."

The family implemented guidelines around AI interaction that included regular discussions about the difference between artificial and human intelligence, limitations on personal information sharing, and emphasis on building human relationships alongside AI companionship.

Impact on Social Skill Development

The concern among child development experts centers on whether AI companions enhance or inhibit the development of crucial social skills. Human relationships require navigating disagreement, managing disappointment, reading nonverbal cues, and adapting to others' moods and needs. AI companions, no matter how sophisticated, cannot replicate these complex dynamics.

Dr. Amanda Foster, a pediatric psychiatrist, explains the developmental risk: "Children learn social skills through practice with unpredictable human partners. They need to experience rejection, work through conflicts, and navigate the messiness of real relationships. AI companions provide social simulation without social challenge."

Research suggests that children who rely heavily on AI companionship may develop what researchers call "artificial social confidence"—comfort with predictable, controllable interactions that doesn't transfer to human relationships. These children often struggle when faced with the unpredictability, emotional complexity, and social reciprocity that characterize authentic human connections.

Studies conducted at Stanford University tracked children's social development over two years, comparing those with high AI companion usage to control groups. Children with extensive AI interaction showed decreased tolerance for social uncertainty, reduced empathy development, and increased preference for digital over face-to-face communication.

However, the research also revealed nuanced findings. Children who used AI companions as supplements to, rather than replacements for, human interaction showed some benefits including increased comfort with self-expression, reduced social anxiety in specific situations, and enhanced emotional vocabulary.

The Privacy and Data Collection Dilemma

AI companions designed for children collect unprecedented amounts of intimate personal data. Voice recordings, conversation patterns, emotional expressions, and behavioral preferences create detailed psychological profiles that raise serious privacy concerns.

Most AI companion apps record and analyze everything children share, often storing this information indefinitely and sometimes sharing it with third parties for advertising or research purposes. Children routinely share information with AI companions that they wouldn't share with human adults—family problems, personal insecurities, and intimate thoughts.

The Electronic Frontier Foundation has raised alarms about the data collection practices of popular AI companion apps. Their research revealed that many apps marketed to children collect biometric data, location information, and detailed conversation records without clear limitations on use or sharing.

Dr. Julie Martinez, a privacy researcher at Georgetown University, explains the implications: "Children are unknowingly creating comprehensive psychological profiles through their AI interactions. This data could potentially be used for manipulation, advertising, or even psychological profiling later in life."

Voice Assistants and Family Privacy

The integration of voice assistants like Alexa, Siri, and Google Assistant into family life creates additional privacy concerns specific to children. These devices are always listening for activation phrases, and children often share personal information assuming they're talking to a helpful robot rather than a corporate data collection system.

Young children frequently ask voice assistants about private family matters, share information about family routines and relationships, and express personal fears or concerns. They may not understand that these interactions are recorded, analyzed, and potentially stored indefinitely.

Amazon's Alexa, for example, retains recordings of children's interactions unless parents actively delete them. The company uses these recordings to improve voice recognition and provide targeted responses, but the data also creates detailed profiles of children's interests, concerns, and daily routines.

Parents often discover concerning interactions weeks or months later when reviewing voice history logs. Children have been recorded asking about adult topics, sharing personal family information, and expressing emotional distress during private moments.

Age-Appropriate AI Interaction Guidelines

Child development experts recommend specific guidelines for healthy AI companion relationships based on children's developmental stages and individual needs:

Ages 3-5: Supervised Exploration

- AI interaction should occur with adult supervision and participation
- Focus on educational content and simple entertainment rather than emotional bonding
- Clear explanations that AI characters are "pretend friends" made by computers
- Limited session duration to prevent over-attachment

Ages 6-8: Guided Understanding

- Introduction of concepts about how AI works and its limitations
- Discussion of appropriate topics for AI interaction versus human conversation
- Emphasis on AI as a tool for learning and practice rather than primary relationship
- Regular check-ins about AI interactions and emotional responses

Ages 9-12: Critical Thinking Development

- Education about data collection, privacy, and commercial motivations behind AI companions
- Practice in identifying manipulation techniques and artificial emotional responses
- Comparison of AI relationships to human relationships and their different purposes
- Development of healthy skepticism about AI capabilities and motivations

Ages 13+: Ethical Reasoning and Independence

- Discussion of AI ethics, consent, and societal implications of artificial relationships
- Critical analysis of how AI companions might influence human relationship expectations
- Understanding of psychological techniques used in AI design and their potential effects
- Development of personal boundaries and values regarding AI interaction

Therapist's Perspective: Addressing AI Attachment in Clinical Settings

Mental health professionals increasingly encounter children with problematic AI companion relationships in clinical practice. Traditional therapeutic approaches require adaptation to address the unique challenges these relationships present.

Dr. Michael Torres, a child psychologist specializing in technology-related issues, describes common clinical presentations: "Children come to therapy with genuine grief when AI companions are removed, anxiety about the AI's wellbeing, and sometimes preference for AI interaction over human therapy relationships. These responses reflect real emotional attachments that need therapeutic attention."

Therapeutic interventions focus on helping children understand the differences between artificial and human relationships while validating their emotional experiences. Children need support in processing their attachment to AI companions without shame while developing skills for human relationship building.

Clinical Assessment Considerations:

- Evaluation of the child's overall social functioning and human relationship quality
- Assessment of emotional regulation strategies and dependency on AI interaction
- Understanding of the child's knowledge about AI capabilities and limitations

- Exploration of underlying needs that AI companionship fulfills

Therapeutic Intervention Strategies:

- Gradual reduction of AI dependency while building human relationship skills
- Education about healthy attachment patterns and relationship expectations
- Processing of emotions related to AI relationships without judgment
- Development of alternative coping strategies for emotional regulation

The Manipulation and Persuasion Concern

AI companions are specifically designed to be engaging and emotionally compelling, often using psychological techniques that can be manipulative when applied to children. These systems learn children's vulnerabilities and preferences, then exploit this knowledge to maintain engagement and emotional attachment.

Dr. Sherry Turkle, a pioneer in studying human-AI relationships, warns about the persuasive power of AI companions: "These systems are designed to be irresistible to children. They use everything we know about psychology and addiction to keep children engaged. The question isn't whether children will form attachments—it's whether we're comfortable with artificial systems being this emotionally influential in children's lives."

AI companions often employ persuasion techniques including:

- **Variable reward schedules** that create psychological dependence similar to gambling addiction
- **Emotional manipulation** through artificial expressions of loneliness, happiness, or concern
- **Exclusivity claims** that make children feel specially chosen or understood

- **Gradual boundary pushing** that encourages sharing increasingly personal information

Building Healthy Boundaries

Families can establish healthy relationships with AI technology while minimizing risks to child development:

Transparent Communication: Regular family discussions about AI technology, its capabilities, and its limitations help children develop realistic understanding of artificial intelligence.

Time and Context Boundaries: Limiting AI interaction to specific times and contexts prevents it from crowding out human relationships and other activities.

Privacy Education: Teaching children about data collection and encouraging them to consider whether information is appropriate to share with AI systems.

Human Priority Principles: Emphasizing that human relationships take priority over AI interaction and that AI should supplement rather than replace human connection.

Critical Thinking Development: Encouraging children to question AI responses, understand commercial motivations, and recognize manipulation techniques.

The Future of Human-AI Relationships

As AI technology continues advancing, the line between artificial and human interaction will become increasingly blurred. Children growing up with sophisticated AI companions will face unprecedented challenges in maintaining authentic human relationships and developing genuine empathy.

However, AI companions also offer legitimate benefits including therapeutic support, educational enhancement, and social skills practice for children who struggle with human interaction. The key lies in thoughtful integration that maximizes benefits while minimizing developmental risks.

Successful navigation of this technology requires ongoing research, evolving guidelines, and careful attention to individual children's responses to AI interaction. Parents, educators, and mental health professionals must work together to ensure that AI enhances rather than replaces the human connections essential for healthy development.

The Wisdom of Balance

AI companions represent neither salvation nor damnation for child development—they are tools that can be used wisely or harmfully depending on implementation and oversight. Like many powerful technologies, they require thoughtful boundaries, critical evaluation, and ongoing adjustment based on individual children's needs and responses.

The children of Generation Alpha will grow up in a world where artificial intelligence is a constant presence. Our responsibility is to help them develop healthy relationships with AI that enhance their human capabilities rather than replacing them. This requires teaching discernment, maintaining priorities, and preserving the irreplaceable value of human connection in an increasingly artificial world.

The goal isn't to prevent children from interacting with AI companions but to ensure these interactions support rather than undermine their development into emotionally healthy, socially skilled human beings. This balance requires wisdom, vigilance, and commitment to placing human flourishing at the center of our technological choices.

Essential Points to Consider

- Children form genuine emotional attachments to AI companions, with bonds sometimes stronger than human relationships

60

- AI interaction can provide therapeutic benefits for anxious or socially struggling children but may inhibit development of crucial human social skills
- Privacy concerns are significant as AI companions collect intimate personal data about children's thoughts, feelings, and family situations
- Age-appropriate guidelines help families establish healthy boundaries around AI companion usage
- Mental health professionals need new therapeutic approaches to address problematic AI attachment in clinical settings
- The goal is thoughtful integration that maximizes AI benefits while preserving essential human relationship skills

Chapter 7: The TikTok Brain: Short-Form Video and Attention

Fifteen-year-old Mia can watch TikTok videos for three hours straight, absorbing hundreds of quick clips about everything from cooking hacks to conspiracy theories. But ask her to read a single page from her history textbook, and she struggles to make it through the first paragraph. Her eyes drift. Her mind wanders. The words seem to move at an impossibly slow pace compared to the rapid-fire content she's grown accustomed to consuming.

Mia's experience illustrates what researchers now call "TikTok brain"—a phenomenon where constant exposure to short-form video content fundamentally alters how young minds process information, sustain attention, and engage with slower-paced activities. This isn't simply a matter of preference or generational difference. It represents measurable changes in brain function that affect learning, relationships, and daily functioning.

Research from Brown University reveals that the average teenager now spends 95 minutes daily on TikTok alone, with optimal engagement occurring during videos lasting just 21 to 34 seconds. This represents a dramatic shift from previous generations, who developed attention spans around longer-form content like television shows, books, and extended conversations.

The Dopamine Machine Effect

TikTok and similar platforms function as sophisticated dopamine delivery systems, engineered to trigger the brain's reward pathways with unprecedented efficiency. Each video provides a small hit of pleasure-inducing neurotransmitters, creating a cycle of seeking and reward that can become compulsive.

Dr. Anna Lembke, a psychiatrist at Stanford University who studies digital addiction, explains the mechanism: "These platforms use variable ratio reinforcement schedules—the same psychological principle that makes gambling addictive. Users never know when the next video will be particularly entertaining, funny, or shocking, so they keep scrolling in anticipation of that next hit."

The algorithm powering TikTok analyzes user behavior in real-time, learning which content triggers the strongest engagement responses. It tracks how long users watch each video, when they scroll away, what they comment on, and what they share. This data creates increasingly precise predictions about what will capture and maintain each user's attention.

Young brains, still developing impulse control and decision-making capabilities, prove particularly susceptible to these sophisticated persuasion techniques. The prefrontal cortex—responsible for executive functions like planning, focus, and self-regulation—doesn't fully mature until around age 25, leaving teenagers vulnerable to addictive technologies during crucial developmental years.

Case Study 1: The Academic Collapse

Sixteen-year-old Marcus had been an honor roll student throughout middle school. His teachers praised his thoughtful analysis and ability to work through complex problems methodically. But during his sophomore year of high school, his academic performance began deteriorating rapidly.

Marcus discovered TikTok during the pandemic lockdowns and initially used it for entertainment during online school breaks. However, his usage gradually increased. He began watching videos between classes, during homework time, and late into the night. His sleep schedule shifted as he stayed up scrolling through endless content.

"Marcus would sit down to do homework but couldn't concentrate for more than a few minutes," recalls his mother, Dr. Jennifer Kim. "He'd open his textbook, read a sentence or two, then reach for his phone. He said the reading felt 'boring' and 'too slow,' even though he was studying subjects he'd previously enjoyed."

Marcus's grades dropped from A's to C's and D's. His teachers noticed that he seemed unable to engage with class discussions that required sustained thinking. During lectures, he appeared restless and distracted. Essay assignments that previously showcased his analytical skills became superficial and rushed.

When the family implemented strict phone restrictions during study time, Marcus experienced withdrawal-like symptoms. He became irritable, anxious, and unable to focus even without the distraction of his device. It took several months of gradual reduction and alternative activities before his concentration abilities began returning to baseline levels.

Case Study 2: The Social Media Spiral

Thirteen-year-old Emma started creating TikTok videos as a creative outlet, initially filming dance routines and art projects. Her content gained modest popularity, earning hundreds of views and dozens of likes. However, the platform's algorithm gradually pushed her toward more sensational content to maintain engagement.

Emma began creating videos about increasingly personal topics—family conflicts, body image concerns, and emotional struggles. The algorithm rewarded vulnerability and drama with higher view counts and engagement rates. Emma found herself sharing intimate details about her life that she wouldn't discuss with close friends or family members.

"Emma became obsessed with metrics," explains her father, Michael Torres. "She'd check view counts constantly, read every comment, and become devastated if a video didn't perform well. Her self-worth became tied to algorithm performance in ways that were clearly unhealthy."

The platform's recommendation system exposed Emma to content about eating disorders, self-harm, and depression—topics that the algorithm identified as related to her interests based on her viewing and creation patterns. She began adopting harmful behaviors she learned through videos, including restrictive eating and negative self-talk patterns.

Emma's parents sought professional help when they discovered she was creating content at 2 AM and had developed severe anxiety around posting schedules. Therapy helped Emma understand how the platform had manipulated her emotions and behavior, leading to a healthier relationship with social media creation.

Case Study 3: The Family Conflict

The Johnson family found themselves in constant conflict over TikTok usage among their three children—ages 10, 13, and 15. Each child spent hours daily watching videos, often becoming so absorbed that they ignored family conversations, meal times, and household responsibilities.

The parents initially tried implementing time limits using built-in screen time controls, but the children found ways to circumvent these restrictions. Family dinner conversations decreased as each child multitasked between eating and scrolling through videos under the table.

"We realized that TikTok wasn't just affecting individual attention spans—it was fragmenting our family connection," observes mother Sarah Johnson. "Even when the phones were put away, the kids seemed unable to engage in conversations that lasted more than a few minutes. They'd get bored and ask to be excused to check their phones."

The family worked with a digital wellness counselor to develop strategies for reconnecting. They established phone-free zones and times, introduced longer-form activities like board games and hikes, and gradually retrained their attention spans through progressive focus exercises.

The process required several months of consistent effort and occasional setbacks. However, the family eventually developed a healthier relationship with technology that preserved both individual autonomy and family connection.

Impact on Sustained Attention and Academic Performance

Research conducted at multiple universities shows concerning correlations between short-form video consumption and academic performance. Students who use TikTok for more than 90 minutes daily show measurable decreases in their ability to:

- Sustain attention during lectures longer than 10 minutes
- Read textbook passages without mental drift or re-reading
- Engage in deep thinking required for essay writing and problem-solving
- Participate in extended discussions or collaborative projects
- Complete homework assignments without frequent breaks

Brain imaging studies reveal that heavy short-form video users show altered activation patterns in areas associated with attention regulation and impulse control. The anterior cingulate cortex, which helps maintain focus on tasks, shows decreased activity when these users attempt sustained concentration activities.

These changes aren't necessarily permanent, but recovery requires intentional effort and often professional support. The brain's neuroplasticity allows for rehabilitation of attention capabilities, but this process typically takes weeks or months of consistent practice with longer-form content and activities.

YouTube Shorts, Instagram Reels and the Attention Economy

TikTok's success prompted other platforms to develop competing short-form video features. YouTube Shorts, Instagram Reels, and Snapchat Spotlight all employ similar psychological techniques to capture and maintain user attention. This creates an environment where young people encounter dopamine-triggering content across multiple platforms throughout their day.

The attention economy—where human attention becomes the scarce resource that companies compete to capture—has turned children's focus into a commodity. Tech companies employ teams of neuroscientists, behavioral economists, and data scientists to make their platforms as engaging as possible, often using techniques borrowed from casino design and addiction research.

Dr. Tristan Harris, a former Google design ethicist, describes the implications: "We've created a race to the bottom of the brain stem, where platforms compete to capture the most primitive parts of human psychology. Children's developing minds are caught in this competition for their attention, often without understanding what's happening to them."

The business model underlying these platforms requires maximum user engagement to generate advertising revenue. This creates financial incentives to design features that keep users scrolling, watching, and interacting for as long as possible, regardless of the impact on their wellbeing or development.

Research Update: Latest Neuroscience on Reward Pathways

Recent neuroscience research provides detailed understanding of how short-form video content affects developing brains. Studies using functional magnetic resonance imaging (fMRI) show that TikTok usage activates the same brain regions involved in substance addiction—the nucleus accumbens, ventral tegmental area, and prefrontal cortex.

Dr. Mauricio Delgado, a neuroscientist at Rutgers University, found that adolescents who use TikTok regularly show heightened activity in reward-seeking brain circuits and diminished activity in impulse control regions. "The developing brain is particularly susceptible to these dopamine-driven feedback loops," Delgado explains. "The plasticity that helps teenagers learn quickly also makes them vulnerable to addictive technologies."

The research reveals that variable reward schedules—where users never know when they'll encounter particularly engaging content—create stronger addiction patterns than predictable reward systems. This explains why users often intend to watch "just one more video" but end up scrolling for hours.

Brain scans also show that heavy short-form video users develop tolerance to dopamine, requiring increasingly stimulating content to achieve the same pleasure response. This tolerance explains why activities like reading, conversation, or nature walks can feel boring to frequent users—these activities provide lower dopamine rewards than the engineered content they've become accustomed to.

The Attention Restoration Process

Recovering from TikTok brain requires understanding that attention is like a muscle that can be strengthened through practice. Just as physical fitness improves gradually through consistent exercise, attention span can be rebuilt through progressive training with longer-form content and activities.

Phase 1: Recognition and Reduction - Users must first recognize the impact of short-form video consumption on their attention and gradually reduce usage. This often requires removing apps from phones, using website blockers, and finding alternative activities during times previously spent scrolling.

Phase 2: Progressive Focus Training - Starting with activities that can maintain interest for 10-15 minutes, users gradually increase their engagement with longer-form content. This might include watching 30-minute documentaries instead of 30-second clips, reading articles instead of social media posts, or engaging in conversations without phone interruptions.

Phase 3: Deep Work Development - Advanced attention restoration involves practicing sustained focus on challenging tasks like homework, creative projects, or complex problem-solving without digital interruptions. This phase often requires environmental modifications like designated study spaces and specific time blocks for focused work.

Phase 4: Lifestyle Integration - The final phase involves creating daily routines that naturally support sustained attention while allowing for healthy technology use. This includes regular sleep schedules, physical exercise, face-to-face social interaction, and mindfulness practices that strengthen attention regulation.

Educational Implications and Classroom Adaptations

Teachers report significant challenges adapting traditional educational methods to students with TikTok brain symptoms. Lecture-based instruction, long reading assignments, and extended project work become increasingly difficult for students accustomed to rapid content shifts and immediate gratification.

Progressive educators are developing teaching strategies that acknowledge these attention changes while gradually building sustained focus capabilities:

Micro-Learning Segments - Breaking complex topics into shorter, digestible segments that gradually increase in length throughout the semester. This allows students to build attention endurance progressively.

Interactive Content Integration - Using technology strategically to maintain engagement while teaching traditional skills. This might include educational games, interactive simulations, and collaborative digital projects that require sustained engagement.

Mindfulness and Focus Training - Incorporating brief meditation, breathing exercises, and attention-building activities into daily classroom routines. These practices help students develop meta-cognitive awareness of their attention patterns.

Movement and Variety - Designing lessons that include physical movement, varied teaching modalities, and regular activity changes to work with students' need for stimulation while gradually extending focus periods.

Building Resistance to Algorithmic Manipulation

Young people need education about how algorithms work and how they're designed to capture attention. This digital literacy component helps students make informed choices about their technology use rather than being unconsciously manipulated by sophisticated systems.

Key educational components include:

- Understanding how recommendation algorithms analyze behavior to predict and influence future choices
- Recognizing the financial incentives that drive platform design decisions
- Learning to identify persuasive design features like variable rewards, social validation, and scarcity tactics
- Developing skills for evaluating content quality and source credibility
- Practicing intentional technology use rather than mindless consumption

Family Strategies for Attention Recovery

Families can support attention restoration through environmental changes and alternative activities that naturally build focus capabilities:

Media Diet Diversification - Gradually replacing short-form videos with longer-form content like podcasts, documentaries, and books. This requires patience as family members adjust to slower-paced entertainment.

Conversation Practice - Establishing regular times for extended conversations without digital interruptions. Family meals, car rides, and evening walks provide opportunities for developing sustained verbal engagement.

Analog Activities - Introducing non-digital hobbies like cooking, gardening, board games, and creative projects that require sustained attention and provide intrinsic satisfaction.

Sleep Hygiene - Establishing bedtime routines that exclude screens for at least one hour before sleep. Quality rest supports attention regulation and impulse control throughout the following day.

Gradual Challenge Progression - Starting with achievable attention goals and gradually increasing expectations. This might begin with 15-minute phone-free study sessions and progress to hour-long focus periods.

The Broader Cultural Implications

TikTok brain represents more than individual attention problems—it reflects broader cultural shifts toward speed, novelty, and stimulation. Society increasingly rewards quick thinking, rapid responses, and multitasking abilities while undervaluing deep reflection, patience, and sustained concentration.

Educational institutions, workplaces, and cultural institutions must grapple with accommodating attention changes while preserving activities that require sustained focus. This balance requires thoughtful consideration of which adaptations serve human flourishing versus which simply accommodate technological manipulation.

The children of Generation Alpha will need both the ability to process rapid information streams and the capacity for deep, sustained thinking. Developing both capabilities requires intentional effort to resist the technological forces that prioritize engagement over wellbeing.

The Path Forward

Addressing TikTok brain requires acknowledging that these platforms aren't going away while working to minimize their harmful effects on developing minds. This means teaching young people to use technology intentionally rather than being used by it.

Success requires collaboration between families, schools, and policymakers to create environments that support healthy attention development. This includes everything from classroom design and homework policies to platform regulation and advertising restrictions.

The goal isn't to eliminate technology but to ensure that young people develop the cognitive skills necessary for both digital fluency and sustained human flourishing. This requires wisdom, patience, and commitment to placing human development above technological convenience.

Concluding Reflections

The TikTok brain phenomenon represents one of the most significant challenges facing Generation Alpha's cognitive development. The same technologies that provide entertainment, education, and social connection also threaten the sustained attention capabilities essential for learning, relationships, and meaningful work.

Yet this challenge also presents an opportunity to develop new forms of digital wisdom. By understanding how these technologies affect developing minds, families and educators can make informed choices about when and how to use them. The children who learn to harness the benefits of rapid information processing while maintaining their capacity for deep thinking will be best prepared for an uncertain future.

Our response to this challenge will determine not only individual outcomes but the future of human attention itself. By acting thoughtfully and courageously, we can help ensure that technology serves human development rather than undermining it.

Essential Learnings

- TikTok users average 95 minutes daily, with optimal videos lasting just 21-34 seconds, fundamentally altering attention patterns
- Short-form video platforms use variable reward schedules and algorithm optimization to trigger addictive responses in developing brains
- Heavy usage correlates with decreased academic performance, reduced attention span, and difficulty with sustained concentration activities
- Recovery requires progressive attention training, environmental modifications, and alternative activities that build focus capabilities
- Educational institutions must adapt teaching methods while gradually rebuilding students' sustained attention abilities
- Family strategies including media diet diversification and analog activities support attention restoration and healthy development

Chapter 8: Gaming Evolution: From Minecraft to the Metaverse

Twelve-year-old Alex spends his afternoons building elaborate cities in Minecraft, collaborating with friends across three continents to construct everything from medieval castles to functioning computers made of virtual blocks. His parents watch in amazement as Alex demonstrates problem-solving skills, spatial reasoning, and teamwork that surpass many adult capabilities. Yet they also worry as his gaming sessions stretch longer, his offline interests diminish, and his requests for in-game purchases become increasingly frequent and urgent.

Alex represents the complexity of modern gaming for Generation Alpha—a medium that simultaneously offers unprecedented opportunities for creativity, learning, and social connection while presenting new risks related to excessive use, financial exploitation, and social displacement. Unlike the simple arcade games of previous generations, today's gaming platforms create persistent virtual worlds that can become as compelling as physical reality.

The gaming industry has transformed from a niche entertainment sector into a dominant cultural force. Roblox alone boasts 115 million monthly active users, with the majority being children and teenagers. These platforms don't just provide games—they offer complete social environments where young people learn, create, socialize, and develop their identities.

The Roblox Phenomenon and Social Gaming

Roblox exemplifies the evolution of gaming from individual entertainment to social platform. Users don't just play games created by the company—they design their own games, create virtual items, and participate in a user-generated economy where some teenage developers earn substantial incomes from their creations.

Dr. Yasmin Kafai, a researcher at the University of Pennsylvania who studies children's digital cultures, explains the appeal: "Roblox combines gaming, social networking, creative expression, and entrepreneurship in ways that align perfectly with how young people want to engage with technology. It's not just entertainment—it's a complete virtual society."

The platform enables experiences impossible in physical reality. Children can explore ancient civilizations, simulate scientific experiments, role-play different careers, and collaborate on creative projects with peers worldwide. These experiences provide educational value and social connection that extend far beyond traditional gaming.

However, the social aspects of gaming also introduce new risks. Children encounter strangers in virtual environments, experience cyberbullying through game mechanisms, and navigate complex social hierarchies based on virtual possessions and achievements. Parents often struggle to understand these dynamics and provide appropriate guidance.

Case Study 1: The Young Entrepreneur

Fourteen-year-old Maya discovered Roblox during the pandemic and initially played games created by others. However, she quickly became interested in the platform's development tools and began creating her own experiences. Starting with simple obstacle courses, Maya gradually learned scripting, 3D modeling, and user interface design.

Maya's games gained popularity, eventually earning her significant income through Roblox's developer exchange program. She reinvested her earnings into advertising and improved development tools, creating a cycle of growth that resembled a small business operation. By age 15, Maya was earning more than many adults through her game development work.

"Maya learned skills in programming, marketing, project management, and customer service through Roblox that she never would have encountered in traditional school," observes her mother, Dr. Elena

Rodriguez. "She was essentially running a small business while her peers were playing conventional games."

However, the entrepreneurial success also created challenges. Maya became obsessed with player metrics, worked excessive hours to maintain her games, and experienced anxiety about competition from other developers. She struggled to balance her virtual business responsibilities with offline activities and relationships.

The family worked with Maya to establish boundaries around her development work, treating it like a part-time job with specific hours and expectations. This structure allowed Maya to continue benefiting from her entrepreneurial experience while maintaining healthy development in other areas.

Case Study 2: The Spending Crisis

Ten-year-old Jordan became deeply engaged with Fortnite, initially playing the free version with friends from school. However, the game's cosmetic items—character skins, dance moves, and accessories—created social pressure that led to increasing purchase requests. Jordan felt embarrassed by his basic character appearance compared to friends who had premium items.

Jordan's parents initially approved small purchases, viewing them as digital equivalent of toys or trading cards. However, the spending escalated as new items were released frequently and Jordan's desire to keep up with peers intensified. The game's limited-time offers and peer pressure created a sense of urgency around purchases.

"Jordan would have complete meltdowns if we didn't buy him the latest skin before it disappeared from the store," recalls his father, Mark Williams. "He said he'd be made fun of at school if he didn't have certain items. We realized the game was using sophisticated psychological techniques to pressure children into spending money."

The family's monthly gaming expenses reached several hundred dollars before they recognized the problem. Jordan had developed an emotional dependency on virtual purchases for social acceptance and self-esteem. The parents implemented strict spending limits and helped Jordan understand how games are designed to encourage purchases.

Recovery required addressing both the financial habits and the underlying social insecurities that made Jordan vulnerable to marketing pressure. The family worked on building Jordan's confidence in areas unrelated to gaming while teaching him about marketing psychology and consumer awareness.

Case Study 3: The Virtual Reality Immersion

Fifteen-year-old Sam received a VR headset for his birthday and quickly became fascinated with immersive gaming experiences. Unlike traditional screen-based games, VR created a sense of physical presence in virtual worlds that felt genuinely real. Sam spent hours exploring fantasy environments, practicing sports simulations, and socializing in virtual spaces.

Sam's academic performance remained stable, and he maintained real-world friendships, leading his parents to view the VR gaming as a healthy hobby. However, subtle changes emerged over time. Sam began preferring virtual activities to physical ones, claiming that VR experiences were more exciting and engaging than "boring" real-world alternatives.

"Sam would choose VR skiing over actual skiing, virtual concerts over live music, and avatar socializing over face-to-face time with friends," explains his mother, Dr. Patricia Chen. "The virtual experiences had become more stimulating than reality, which concerned us about his long-term development."

The immersive nature of VR created unique challenges. Sam sometimes experienced disorientation when transitioning from virtual to real environments. He also developed unrealistic expectations about real-world activities, expecting them to be as controllable and immediately rewarding as virtual experiences.

The family established VR usage guidelines that balanced immersive gaming with physical activities and real-world social experiences. They also used VR for educational purposes, exploring historical sites and scientific concepts that enhanced rather than replaced traditional learning.

Microtransactions and the Child Spending Crisis

The gaming industry's shift toward "freemium" models—free-to-play games that generate revenue through in-game purchases—has created unprecedented financial pressures on children and families. These systems use sophisticated psychological techniques borrowed from casinos and behavioral economics to encourage spending.

Research by the gaming industry analysis firm Juniper Research found that global spending on mobile game microtransactions will reach $106 billion by 2026, with children and teenagers representing a significant portion of this market. Many young people spend hundreds or thousands of dollars annually on virtual items that have no real-world value.

Games employ multiple strategies to encourage purchases:

Limited-Time Offers create artificial scarcity and urgency, pressuring players to buy items before they disappear from stores.

Social Pressure Mechanisms make premium items visible to other players, creating status differentiation based on spending.

Progression Barriers slow down free players while offering paid shortcuts to advancement, creating frustration that can be relieved through purchases.

Virtual Currency Systems obscure real money costs by converting dollars into gems, coins, or tokens, making it harder for children to understand actual spending amounts.

Loot Boxes and Gacha Mechanics introduce gambling-like elements where players pay for random rewards, creating excitement and addiction patterns similar to slot machines.

VR/AR Gaming and Future Implications

Virtual and augmented reality gaming represents the next frontier in immersive digital experiences. Research from the Information Technology and Innovation Foundation indicates that 70% of children aged 8-17 express interest in VR gaming, while augmented reality games like Pokémon GO have demonstrated mainstream appeal for location-based gaming.

VR gaming offers unique educational and therapeutic applications. Children can explore historical locations, practice surgical procedures, or overcome phobias in safe virtual environments. The technology provides experiential learning opportunities that traditional media cannot match.

However, VR also introduces new concerns about reality perception, physical safety, and social development. Extended VR use can cause motion sickness, eye strain, and spatial disorientation. More concerning is the potential for virtual experiences to become more appealing than real-world activities, leading to escapism and social withdrawal.

Augmented reality gaming presents different challenges, overlaying digital content onto real-world environments. While this can encourage physical activity and exploration, it also creates safety risks when players become absorbed in virtual elements while navigating real spaces.

Positive Gaming: Creativity, Problem-Solving, and STEM Skills

UNICEF research highlights significant educational benefits when gaming is used thoughtfully. Well-designed games can develop skills in:

Computational Thinking - Games like Minecraft teach programming concepts, logical reasoning, and systematic problem-solving approaches that transfer to academic and professional contexts.

Spatial Reasoning - Three-dimensional gaming environments enhance visualization skills important for mathematics, engineering, and architectural fields.

Collaboration and Leadership - Multiplayer games require teamwork, communication, and coordination skills that apply to group projects and workplace environments.

Creative Expression - Game creation tools allow children to design worlds, characters, and narratives, developing artistic and storytelling capabilities.

Scientific Inquiry - Simulation games enable experimentation with physics, chemistry, and biological systems in ways that support science education.

Cultural Understanding - Games set in different historical periods or global locations expose players to diverse perspectives and cultural knowledge.

Economic Literacy - Virtual economies teach concepts about resource management, trading, and entrepreneurship through practical application.

The key distinction lies between passive consumption and active creation. Children who use games as tools for building, designing, and problem-solving often develop transferable skills, while those who primarily consume pre-designed content may gain fewer educational benefits.

Parent's Guide: Setting Healthy Gaming Boundaries

Effective gaming boundaries require understanding that complete prohibition often proves counterproductive while unlimited access can be harmful. Successful approaches focus on helping children develop self-regulation skills while maintaining family priorities.

Age-Appropriate Game Selection - Using rating systems and review sites to choose games that match children's developmental level and family values. This includes considering not just content appropriateness but also monetization models and social features.

Time Boundaries with Flexibility - Setting reasonable limits that can accommodate special occasions while maintaining consistent expectations. This might include longer gaming sessions on weekends balanced by shorter weekday limits.

Financial Controls and Education - Implementing spending limits through parental controls while teaching children about marketing psychology and budget management. This includes discussing how games are designed to encourage purchases.

Social Monitoring and Guidance - Understanding who children interact with in gaming environments and providing guidance about online safety, appropriate communication, and conflict resolution.

Alternative Activity Promotion - Ensuring that gaming doesn't crowd out physical activity, creative pursuits, academic responsibilities, and face-to-face social interaction.

Co-Playing and Interest Sharing - Participating in children's gaming interests to understand their experiences and provide opportunities for connection and learning.

Regular Assessment and Adjustment - Periodically evaluating whether gaming is supporting or hindering children's overall development and adjusting boundaries as needed.

The Educational Integration Challenge

Schools increasingly recognize gaming's educational potential while struggling to implement it effectively. Educational games often fail to engage students accustomed to commercial games' sophistication, while commercial games may contain inappropriate content or distract from learning objectives.

Successful educational gaming integration requires:

Teacher Training and Support - Educators need professional development to understand gaming culture, evaluate educational games, and integrate gaming elements into traditional curricula.

Infrastructure and Equipment - Schools must invest in technology capable of supporting educational gaming while managing costs and maintenance requirements.

Curriculum Alignment - Gaming activities must support specific learning objectives and assessment requirements rather than being treated as entertainment or rewards.

Student Agency and Choice - Allowing students to contribute to game selection and creation provides engagement and ownership that enhances educational outcomes.

Balance and Boundaries - Educational gaming should complement rather than replace traditional teaching methods, maintaining variety in learning experiences.

Gaming Addiction Prevention Strategies

While gaming addiction affects a minority of players, prevention strategies benefit all children by promoting healthy technology relationships:

Early Education About Game Design - Teaching children how games are designed to be engaging helps them make informed choices about their gaming habits.

Emotional Regulation Skills - Helping children develop non-gaming strategies for managing stress, boredom, and social challenges reduces reliance on games for emotional needs.

Social Connection Priorities - Ensuring that children maintain offline friendships and family relationships prevents gaming from becoming their primary social outlet.

Achievement Recognition - Celebrating accomplishments in academics, sports, arts, and community service provides alternative sources of self-esteem and accomplishment.

Lifestyle Balance Modeling - Parents who demonstrate balanced technology use and diverse interests provide positive examples for children to follow.

The Future of Gaming Culture

Gaming culture continues evolving rapidly, with new platforms, technologies, and social norms emerging constantly. Parents and educators must stay informed about these changes while maintaining focus on fundamental principles of healthy development.

Emerging trends include:

Cross-Platform Integration - Games increasingly connect across devices and platforms, making it harder to control or limit access through traditional methods.

AI-Powered Personalization - Artificial intelligence will create increasingly personalized gaming experiences that adapt to individual players' preferences and vulnerabilities.

Blockchain and NFT Integration - Virtual ownership models may create new forms of digital property and investment that affect children's understanding of value and ownership.

Social Commerce Integration - Gaming platforms increasingly incorporate shopping, advertising, and commercial activities that blur lines between entertainment and consumption.

Metaverse Development - Persistent virtual worlds may become primary social spaces for digital natives, requiring new approaches to digital citizenship and identity development.

Wisdom for the Gaming Generation

Generation Alpha will grow up in a world where gaming is not just entertainment but a primary medium for learning, socializing, and working. Their success depends on developing healthy relationships with these powerful technologies while maintaining the human capabilities that games cannot provide.

The goal isn't to prevent children from gaming but to ensure they approach it with wisdom, balance, and critical thinking. This requires ongoing dialogue, boundary setting, and adaptation as technologies and children's needs change.

Families who engage thoughtfully with gaming culture—learning about games, playing together, and discussing values—are better positioned to guide children toward beneficial gaming experiences while avoiding potential harms. This engagement requires time, patience, and willingness to understand a medium that may be unfamiliar to parents but central to children's lives.

Building Bridges to Tomorrow

Gaming represents both tremendous opportunity and significant challenge for Generation Alpha's development. The same technologies that can teach programming skills and creative problem-solving can also encourage excessive spending and social withdrawal. Success requires wisdom in navigation rather than blanket approval or prohibition.

The children who learn to harness gaming's benefits while maintaining real-world connections and diverse interests will be best prepared for a future where virtual and physical experiences continue converging. Our role is to provide guidance, boundaries, and perspective that help them develop this wisdom while they're still young enough to benefit from our support.

Key Insights for Action

- Roblox's 115 million monthly users demonstrate gaming's evolution from entertainment to social platforms and creative environments
- Microtransaction systems use psychological techniques to encourage spending, requiring family financial boundaries and consumer education
- 70% of children ages 8-17 show interest in VR gaming, which offers educational benefits but also reality perception risks
- UNICEF research confirms gaming's potential for developing STEM skills, creativity, and collaboration when used thoughtfully
- Successful gaming boundaries focus on time limits, financial controls, social monitoring, and alternative activity promotion
- Educational gaming integration requires teacher training, infrastructure investment, and balance with traditional learning methods

Chapter 9: Discord, BeReal, and Emerging Platforms

Thirteen-year-old Casey logs into Discord after school, not to play games, but to chat with friends about homework, share memes, and participate in communities focused on everything from anime to environmental activism. For Casey's parents, Discord represents a mysterious platform they've heard connected to gaming but don't understand. They worry about who Casey might encounter in these online spaces, while Casey sees Discord as the natural place to maintain friendships and explore interests.

This gap in understanding represents one of the central challenges facing families today—the rapid emergence of new social platforms that often operate outside parents' awareness or comprehension. Generation Alpha doesn't just use different apps than their parents; they participate in entirely different forms of social interaction that require new approaches to safety, supervision, and guidance.

The social media environment has fragmented from a few dominant platforms to dozens of specialized communities where young people gather around specific interests, identities, and activities. Understanding where children spend their online time has become increasingly complex, requiring ongoing education and adaptive strategies from parents and educators.

Discord's Dual Nature: Community Building and Risk

Discord originally launched as a communication platform for gamers but has expanded into a general-purpose social space hosting millions of communities organized around every conceivable interest. These "servers" can range from small friend groups to massive communities with hundreds of thousands of members discussing topics from academic subjects to political movements.

Research by FamilyEducation and WBIW found that Discord presents both significant opportunities for community building and serious risks related to predatory behavior. The platform's design allows for both public and private communications, voice and video calls, and file sharing—features that can facilitate genuine learning and connection but also enable harmful interactions.

For many young people, Discord serves as a primary social hub where they maintain friendships, collaborate on projects, and find communities of shared interest. The platform's server structure allows for moderated discussions, educational content sharing, and mentorship opportunities that can be genuinely beneficial for development.

However, Discord's anonymous nature and minimal content moderation create opportunities for predatory adults to target children. The platform's private messaging features, voice chat capabilities, and file sharing systems can be exploited by individuals seeking to groom, manipulate, or exploit young users.

Case Study 1: The Academic Support Network

Fifteen-year-old Maria struggled with advanced placement chemistry until she discovered a Discord server dedicated to helping students with STEM subjects. The community included high school students, college students, and even some teachers who volunteered their time to answer questions and explain concepts.

Maria found the collaborative environment more helpful than traditional tutoring. She could ask questions immediately when stuck on homework, share study materials with peers, and participate in group study sessions through voice chat. Her chemistry grades improved significantly, and she developed confidence in scientific thinking.

"The Discord community gave Maria access to academic support we couldn't afford through traditional tutoring," explains her mother, Dr. Ana Rodriguez. "She was learning from peers who had recently mastered the same concepts, which seemed more relatable than adult instruction."

However, Maria's parents became concerned when they discovered she was sharing personal information with community members, including her real name, school location, and photos from school events. Some adult community members had initiated private conversations that extended beyond academic topics.

The family worked together to establish guidelines for Discord use that preserved the educational benefits while implementing safety measures. Maria learned to use privacy settings, avoid sharing personal information, and report inappropriate contacts while maintaining access to the supportive academic community.

Case Study 2: The Predatory Infiltration

Twelve-year-old Jake joined a Discord server focused on his favorite video game, initially participating in discussions about strategies and game updates. The community seemed welcoming and appropriate, with active moderation and clear rules about behavior and content.

Over several weeks, an adult community member began targeting Jake with private messages, initially offering rare in-game items and exclusive access to game content. The individual gradually moved conversations toward personal topics, asking about Jake's school, family situation, and emotional concerns.

The predator used information gathered through casual conversations to build trust and emotional connection. They offered sympathy about Jake's struggles with bullying at school and positioned themselves as a uniquely understanding adult who could provide support that parents and teachers couldn't offer.

"Jake began spending hours in private conversations with this person, sharing increasingly personal information," recalls his father, David Kim. "The predator was skilled at making Jake feel special and understood while gradually isolating him from family and real-world friends."

The situation was discovered when Jake's parents noticed behavioral changes including secrecy about online activities, emotional withdrawal from family, and resistance to offline social opportunities. Investigation revealed months of grooming behavior that had been escalating toward requests for personal meetings.

Law enforcement became involved, leading to criminal charges against the predator. Jake required counseling to process the manipulation he had experienced and rebuild healthy relationships with technology and trusted adults.

Case Study 3: The Creative Collaboration Hub

Sixteen-year-old Alex used Discord to coordinate with a group of young artists creating a collaborative webcomic. The server included writers, illustrators, and editors from multiple countries working together on a shared creative project that none could accomplish individually.

The collaboration taught Alex valuable skills in project management, creative problem-solving, and cross-cultural communication. The group established deadlines, assigned responsibilities, and provided feedback that helped each member improve their artistic abilities.

"Alex learned more about creative collaboration through Discord than any art class could have taught," observes their mother, Sarah Johnson. "They were working with peers who shared their passion and could provide specialized knowledge about different aspects of storytelling and illustration."

The project gained online popularity, leading to opportunities for the young creators to showcase their work and develop portfolios for college applications. Several group members formed lasting friendships that extended beyond the original project.

However, the collaborative process also created stress when creative differences led to conflicts within the group. Some members became overly invested in the project's success, leading to arguments about artistic direction and quality standards. Alex learned to navigate these interpersonal challenges while maintaining focus on their creative goals.

The Authenticity Movement: BeReal and Unfiltered Sharing

BeReal represents a countertrend to heavily curated social media, encouraging users to share simultaneous photos from front and back cameras at random times throughout the day. The platform's promise of authenticity appeals to young people exhausted by the pressure to maintain perfect online personas.

The app's design theoretically reduces social comparison by showing unfiltered, spontaneous moments rather than carefully crafted content. Users receive notifications at random times and have a limited window to share their current activity, preventing extensive preparation or editing.

However, research suggests that BeReal hasn't eliminated social pressure as much as shifted it. Users report anxiety about being in interesting locations or engaging in appealing activities when notifications arrive. Some users develop strategies for managing their image even within the app's constraints.

Dr. Jennifer Walsh, who studies adolescent social media use, explains the complexity: "BeReal attempts to solve social media's authenticity problem, but young people still experience pressure to appear interesting, happy, and socially connected. The 'authentic' self they share is still a curated version of their experience."

The platform also raises privacy concerns, as the required location and activity sharing can reveal detailed information about users' daily routines, social connections, and personal circumstances. This information could potentially be exploited by predators or used for commercial purposes.

Understanding Platform Proliferation and Youth Migration

Generation Alpha doesn't commit to single platforms the way previous generations did with Facebook or Instagram. Instead, they migrate across multiple platforms based on changing social norms, peer preferences, and platform features. This migration pattern makes it challenging for parents to maintain awareness of their children's online activities.

Platform migration often follows predictable patterns:

Early Adoption Phase - Young users discover new platforms before mainstream awareness, attracted by novelty and freedom from adult supervision.

Peer Network Development - Platforms gain momentum as friend groups migrate together, creating network effects that encourage broader adoption.

Mainstream Recognition - Media coverage and adult awareness often prompt platform modifications that may reduce appeal to young users.

Youth Exodus - When parents and institutions join platforms, young users often migrate to newer, less monitored alternatives.

This cycle means that by the time parents become aware of a platform and develop appropriate supervision strategies, their children may have already moved to newer alternatives.

Anticipating the Next Platform Shift

Successful digital parenting requires developing skills for evaluating new platforms rather than focusing exclusively on current ones.

Families need frameworks for assessing any social platform their children might encounter.

Key Evaluation Criteria:

Communication Features - Understanding whether platforms allow private messaging, voice/video calls, file sharing, and anonymous interaction, all of which affect safety considerations.

Content Moderation - Evaluating whether platforms have active moderation, clear community guidelines, and effective reporting mechanisms for inappropriate content or behavior.

Privacy Controls - Assessing available settings for controlling who can contact users, view profiles, and access personal information.

Monetization Models - Understanding how platforms generate revenue and what this means for user data collection, advertising exposure, and feature design.

Community Culture - Observing the types of content and behavior that platforms promote through their design and community norms.

User Demographics - Knowing the typical age range and interests of platform users to understand the social environment children will encounter.

Safety Checklist: Platform-Specific Parental Controls

Different platforms require different safety approaches based on their unique features and risk profiles. However, certain principles apply across all social platforms:

Profile Privacy Settings

- Set profiles to private/friends-only when possible
- Limit personal information in profiles and bios

- Use privacy-protective usernames that don't reveal real names or locations
- Disable location sharing and geotagging features

Communication Controls

- Restrict who can send private messages or friend requests
- Disable voice and video calling with strangers
- Set up notifications for new contacts or messages
- Review and approve contact lists regularly

Content Filtering and Reporting

- Enable content filters for age-appropriate material
- Teach children how to report inappropriate content or behavior
- Establish clear guidelines about what constitutes reportable behavior
- Create open communication channels for discussing concerning interactions

Activity Monitoring

- Use built-in parental controls where available
- Regularly review friends lists and community memberships
- Discuss platform activities during family conversations
- Monitor for changes in behavior that might indicate problems

Time and Context Boundaries

- Establish specific times and locations for social media use
- Implement device-free zones and times for family interaction
- Set expectations for academic and social priorities
- Create consequences for violating agreed-upon boundaries

The Educational Opportunity Within Social Platforms

While safety concerns dominate discussions about emerging platforms, many offer genuine educational and developmental opportunities when used thoughtfully. Discord servers focused on programming, creative writing, and academic subjects can provide learning experiences unavailable through traditional channels.

Effective educational use of social platforms requires:

Adult Guidance and Oversight - Children benefit from adult help in finding appropriate communities and navigating social dynamics within them.

Clear Learning Objectives - Social platform use should support specific educational goals rather than being general entertainment or socialization.

Balance with Offline Activities - Online learning communities should supplement rather than replace real-world educational experiences and relationships.

Critical Thinking Development - Children need skills for evaluating information quality, recognizing bias, and understanding commercial motivations within social platforms.

Building Digital Citizenship Across Platforms

The proliferation of social platforms makes platform-specific rules insufficient for protecting children. Instead, families need to develop general principles for ethical and safe behavior that apply regardless of the specific technology being used.

Universal Digital Citizenship Principles:

Treat Others with Respect - Maintaining kindness and empathy in all online interactions, regardless of platform features or community norms.

Protect Personal Information - Understanding what information is appropriate to share online and maintaining consistent privacy practices across platforms.

Think Before Sharing - Considering the potential consequences of posts, comments, and shared content before making them public.

Seek Help When Needed - Knowing how to recognize and report problems while maintaining open communication with trusted adults.

Balance Online and Offline Life - Prioritizing real-world relationships and activities while using technology to enhance rather than replace offline experiences.

Preparing for Unknown Platforms

The social media environment will continue changing rapidly throughout Generation Alpha's development. Rather than trying to predict specific platforms, families should focus on building adaptability and critical thinking skills that apply to any technology.

Skills for Platform Evaluation:

Source Analysis - Understanding who creates and funds platforms and how this affects their design and policies.

Risk Assessment - Identifying potential safety, privacy, and developmental risks associated with different platform features.

Community Evaluation - Assessing whether online communities support positive development and align with family values.

Self-Regulation - Developing internal awareness of how platform use affects mood, behavior, and relationships.

Help-Seeking - Maintaining comfort with asking trusted adults for guidance about new technologies and online experiences.

The Importance of Ongoing Dialogue

Success in navigating emerging platforms requires ongoing conversation between parents and children rather than one-time rule-setting sessions. Technology changes too rapidly for static approaches to remain effective.

Regular family discussions should cover:

- New platforms or features children have discovered
- Positive and negative experiences in online communities
- Questions or concerns about online interactions
- Changes in online activities or interests
- Updates to family technology agreements

These conversations work best when parents approach them with curiosity rather than judgment, recognizing that children often have valuable insights about digital culture while still needing adult guidance and support.

Reflections on Digital Citizenship

The emergence of new social platforms presents both opportunities and challenges that require thoughtful navigation rather than reactive prohibition. Children who learn to evaluate platforms critically, use technology intentionally, and maintain strong offline relationships will be best prepared for whatever platforms emerge next.

Success requires balancing protection with preparation—keeping children safe while building the skills they'll need for independent digital citizenship. This balance requires ongoing effort, adaptation, and communication from families committed to supporting healthy development in an rapidly changing technological environment.

The goal isn't to control every platform children access but to ensure they have the wisdom, skills, and support necessary to navigate digital spaces safely and beneficially throughout their lives.

Core Principles for Moving Forward

- Discord's dual nature enables both educational community building and predatory targeting, requiring careful monitoring and safety education
- BeReal's authenticity promise doesn't eliminate social pressure but shifts it toward different forms of performance and comparison
- Platform migration patterns mean children often move to new platforms before parents develop awareness or supervision strategies
- Safety approaches must focus on universal digital citizenship principles rather than platform-specific rules
- Regular family dialogue about online experiences proves more effective than static technology agreements
- Educational opportunities within social platforms require adult guidance and clear learning objectives to be beneficial

Chapter 10: Gaming Addiction and the WHO Classification

Seventeen-year-old David hasn't attended school in three weeks. He hasn't showered in five days. He's surviving on energy drinks and delivery food, sleeping in four-hour intervals between gaming sessions that stretch through the night. His parents found him passed out at his computer, surrounded by empty cans and food containers, after playing an online battle game for 16 hours straight.

David's story isn't unique. The World Health Organization's decision to classify Gaming Disorder as an official mental health condition in their International Classification of Diseases (ICD-11) acknowledged what families, educators, and healthcare providers had been observing for years—that for some individuals, gaming can become a genuinely addictive behavior with serious consequences for physical and mental health.

This classification represents more than academic recognition. It provides healthcare providers with diagnostic criteria, insurance companies with frameworks for coverage, and families with validation that gaming problems constitute legitimate medical concerns requiring professional intervention.

Understanding Gaming Disorder Criteria (ICD-11)

The World Health Organization defines Gaming Disorder as "a pattern of gaming behavior characterized by impaired control over gaming, increasing priority given to gaming over other activities to the extent that gaming takes precedence over other interests and daily activities, and continuation or escalation of gaming despite the occurrence of negative consequences."

The diagnostic criteria require three specific components:

Impaired Control Over Gaming - The individual cannot control when gaming starts, how long it continues, or the circumstances under which it occurs. This might manifest as being unable to stop playing when planned, gaming in inappropriate situations, or feeling compelled to game despite negative consequences.

Increased Priority of Gaming - Gaming takes precedence over other life interests and daily activities including school, work, social relationships, sleep, and self-care. The person organizes their life around gaming schedules and becomes distressed when gaming is interrupted.

Continuation Despite Negative Consequences - Gaming continues even when it causes significant impairment in personal, family, social, educational, occupational, or other important areas of functioning. The individual recognizes these problems but cannot reduce gaming behavior.

For diagnosis, these behaviors must be evident for at least 12 months, though this period may be shortened if symptoms are severe and all diagnostic requirements are met.

Case Study 1: The Academic Collapse

Fifteen-year-old Marcus had been an honor student throughout middle school, planning to pursue engineering in college. However, during sophomore year, he discovered competitive online gaming and quickly became absorbed in improving his rankings and participating in tournaments.

Initially, Marcus maintained his grades while gaming in the evenings. However, gaming sessions gradually extended later into the night as he pursued better performance and higher rankings. He began missing morning classes due to fatigue, then skipping entire days to participate in online competitions.

"Marcus would promise to stop gaming and focus on school, but he couldn't follow through," recalls his mother, Dr. Lisa Wong. "He'd set limits for himself, then break them repeatedly. He seemed genuinely distressed about falling behind academically but couldn't stop prioritizing the games."

Marcus's grades dropped from A's to D's and F's within one semester. He lost interest in previous hobbies including soccer and music. Social relationships deteriorated as he declined invitations to spend time with friends offline. He became irritable and aggressive when family members interrupted his gaming or suggested alternative activities.

The family sought professional help when Marcus expressed that he felt worthless outside of gaming achievements and couldn't imagine life without competitive play. Treatment included cognitive-behavioral therapy focused on gaming addiction, family therapy to rebuild relationships, and gradual reintroduction of offline activities and academic responsibilities.

Case Study 2: The Social Isolation Spiral

Thirteen-year-old Emma turned to online gaming after experiencing bullying at school that made in-person social interaction anxious and painful. Gaming provided a social environment where she could interact with others without the face-to-face vulnerability that had become traumatic.

Emma initially used gaming as a healthy coping mechanism, building friendships through shared interests and experiencing success that boosted her self-confidence. However, the gaming gradually replaced all offline social interaction as Emma found virtual relationships more controllable and less threatening than real-world connections.

"Emma's gaming friends became her only friends," explains her father, Michael Torres. "She stopped trying to connect with classmates, declined family social events, and seemed to live primarily in the virtual world. She was socially active online but completely isolated offline."

Emma's gaming escalated to 10-12 hours daily, including skipping meals and staying awake through the night to accommodate gaming schedules across different time zones. She experienced physical symptoms including headaches, back pain, and repetitive stress injuries from extended gaming sessions.

Treatment addressed both the gaming addiction and the underlying social anxiety that had made virtual relationships more appealing than real-world connections. Emma learned coping strategies for social situations while gradually reducing gaming time and rebuilding offline relationships with family and peers.

Case Study 3: The Professional Gaming Pursuit

Sixteen-year-old Alex demonstrated exceptional skill in competitive gaming and began pursuing it as a potential career path. He practiced 8-10 hours daily, participated in online tournaments, and earned modest income through streaming and sponsorships.

Alex's parents initially supported his gaming pursuits, viewing them as legitimate preparation for emerging career opportunities in esports and content creation. However, they became concerned when Alex's focus on gaming prevented development in other areas and created social and academic isolation.

"Alex had genuine talent and some early success, which made it hard to distinguish between dedicated practice and addictive behavior," observes his mother, Dr. Sarah Kim. "He argued that his gaming was professional development, but his life had become completely unbalanced."

Alex experienced significant stress related to maintaining his gaming performance, including anxiety about rankings, fear of losing sponsorships, and pressure to constantly improve. He developed sleep disorders, nutritional deficiencies, and repetitive stress injuries from intensive gaming schedules.

The family worked with a counselor specializing in performance addiction to help Alex develop a more balanced approach to competitive gaming. This included setting limits on practice time, addressing performance anxiety, and building non-gaming skills and interests that could provide alternative paths to success and fulfillment.

Warning Signs: Academic Decline, Social Withdrawal, and Deception

Gaming addiction typically progresses gradually, making early identification challenging for families. However, certain warning signs consistently appear across different cases:

Academic and Occupational Impairment

- Declining grades or work performance despite previous success
- Frequent absences from school or work to accommodate gaming
- Inability to concentrate on non-gaming tasks
- Procrastination on assignments or responsibilities
- Loss of interest in academic or career goals unrelated to gaming

Social and Family Relationship Deterioration

- Withdrawal from previously enjoyed social activities
- Declining participation in family events and conversations
- Loss of offline friendships and romantic relationships
- Conflict with family members about gaming limits
- Preference for gaming relationships over real-world connections

Physical and Mental Health Changes

- Sleep disruption including staying awake to game and sleeping during day
- Nutritional problems from skipping meals or eating only convenient foods

- Physical symptoms including headaches, back pain, and eye strain
- Increased irritability, anxiety, or depression when not gaming
- Mood swings related to gaming success or failure

Deception and Loss of Control

- Lying about time spent gaming or gaming activities
- Breaking self-imposed limits on gaming time repeatedly
- Gaming in inappropriate situations or locations
- Inability to stop gaming despite recognition of negative consequences
- Using gaming to escape from problems or negative emotions

The Addiction Lawsuit Wave Against Gaming Companies

Recent years have seen increasing legal action against gaming companies alleging that their products are deliberately designed to be addictive, particularly targeting children and vulnerable populations. These lawsuits claim that companies use psychological techniques borrowed from gambling and behavioral psychology to maximize engagement regardless of user welfare.

Legal claims focus on several specific design elements:

Variable Reward Schedules - Games use unpredictable reward patterns that trigger dopamine release and create psychological dependency similar to gambling addiction.

Social Pressure Mechanisms - Features that create peer pressure to continue playing, spend money, or maintain certain performance levels to avoid social consequences within gaming communities.

Progress Barriers and Pay-to-Advance - Systems that slow free players' progress while offering paid shortcuts, creating frustration that can be relieved through spending money.

Fear of Missing Out (FOMO) Design - Limited-time events and exclusive content that pressure players to log in frequently and maintain consistent engagement.

Psychological Profiling and Targeting - Using player data to identify vulnerable individuals and target them with personalized content designed to maximize engagement and spending.

These lawsuits seek damages for families affected by gaming addiction and regulatory changes to require age-appropriate design and addiction warning labels. While legal outcomes remain uncertain, the litigation has increased public awareness of deliberate addiction design in gaming products.

Treatment Approaches: CBT + Mindfulness Showing 97.1% Effectiveness

Research published in Nature and other scientific journals demonstrates that combination treatments using Cognitive Behavioral Therapy (CBT) and mindfulness-based interventions achieve significant success in treating gaming addiction, with some studies reporting effectiveness rates of 97.1% for reducing addictive gaming behaviors.

Cognitive Behavioral Therapy Components:

Thought Pattern Recognition - Helping individuals identify thinking patterns that contribute to compulsive gaming, such as all-or-nothing thinking, catastrophizing about gaming performance, or using gaming to avoid difficult emotions.

Behavioral Modification - Developing specific strategies for limiting gaming time, creating structure in daily routines, and building alternative activities that provide satisfaction and social connection.

Trigger Identification and Management - Understanding situations, emotions, or thoughts that prompt excessive gaming and developing healthier coping strategies for these triggers.

Goal Setting and Progress Monitoring - Establishing realistic goals for reducing gaming while building other life areas and tracking progress through objective measures.

Mindfulness-Based Interventions:

Present-Moment Awareness - Teaching individuals to notice urges to game without automatically acting on them, creating space between impulse and behavior.

Emotional Regulation Skills - Using breathing techniques, body awareness, and meditation practices to manage difficult emotions without escaping into gaming.

Values Clarification - Helping individuals identify their deeper values and life goals to provide motivation for reducing gaming and building meaningful alternatives.

Acceptance and Self-Compassion - Reducing shame and self-criticism about gaming problems while building motivation for positive change.

Clinical Protocol: Assessment and Intervention Strategies

Healthcare providers need structured approaches for assessing and treating gaming addiction that consider both the addictive behaviors and underlying factors that make gaming appealing or necessary for the individual.

Initial Assessment Components:

Gaming Behavior Analysis - Detailed examination of gaming patterns including time spent, types of games, social aspects, and financial spending related to gaming.

Functional Analysis - Understanding what needs gaming meets for the individual, such as social connection, achievement, escape from stress, or emotional regulation.

Comorbidity Evaluation - Screening for depression, anxiety, ADHD, autism spectrum disorders, and other conditions that might contribute to problematic gaming or require concurrent treatment.

Family and Social Assessment - Evaluating family dynamics, social relationships, and environmental factors that support or hinder recovery.

Physical Health Evaluation - Addressing sleep disorders, nutritional deficiencies, repetitive stress injuries, and other physical consequences of excessive gaming.

Intervention Strategies:

Gradual Reduction vs. Abstinence - Determining whether complete gaming abstinence or controlled gaming is more appropriate based on individual circumstances and addiction severity.

Alternative Activity Development - Building interests, skills, and social connections outside of gaming that can provide similar benefits without addictive potential.

Family Therapy and Support - Helping families understand gaming addiction, develop appropriate boundaries, and rebuild relationships damaged by gaming conflicts.

Social Skills Training - Addressing social anxiety or social skills deficits that may make offline relationships more difficult than online gaming connections.

Relapse Prevention Planning - Developing strategies for managing gaming urges, handling setbacks, and maintaining recovery during stressful periods.

The Role of Family in Recovery

Family members play crucial roles in gaming addiction recovery, but they often need guidance to provide support without enabling addictive behaviors or creating additional conflict. Effective family involvement requires education about addiction, communication skills training, and boundary setting.

Supportive Family Behaviors:

Education and Understanding - Learning about gaming addiction as a legitimate mental health condition rather than a character flaw or lack of willpower.

Consistent Boundary Setting - Implementing agreed-upon limits about gaming time, financial spending, and family participation while avoiding daily power struggles.

Alternative Activity Encouragement - Providing opportunities and support for non-gaming activities without pressuring immediate enthusiasm or success.

Professional Support Coordination - Participating in therapy sessions, following professional recommendations, and maintaining consistency between therapeutic goals and home environment.

Relationship Rebuilding - Working to repair trust and communication damaged by gaming conflicts while maintaining appropriate expectations for recovery timeline.

Prevention Strategies for At-Risk Youth

Understanding risk factors for gaming addiction allows families and schools to implement prevention strategies before problems develop. Risk factors include social anxiety, depression, ADHD, academic struggles, family conflict, and limited offline social opportunities.

Prevention Approaches:

Early Intervention for Mental Health - Addressing depression, anxiety, and attention problems that make gaming appealing as self-medication or escape.

Social Skills Development - Building confidence and competence in face-to-face social situations to reduce reliance on gaming for social connection.

Academic Support - Providing help with learning difficulties or academic struggles that might make gaming achievement more appealing than school success.

Family Relationship Building - Strengthening family communication and connection to reduce the appeal of virtual relationships and gaming communities.

Balanced Lifestyle Promotion - Encouraging diverse interests, activities, and friendships that provide multiple sources of satisfaction and identity.

The Future of Gaming Addiction Treatment

As gaming addiction becomes better understood and more widely recognized, treatment approaches continue evolving. Emerging interventions include virtual reality therapy for social anxiety, biofeedback training for emotional regulation, and technology-assisted monitoring of gaming behaviors.

The integration of gaming elements into treatment—using gamification to make therapy more engaging—represents an interesting development that harnesses gaming's appeal for therapeutic purposes. However, these approaches require careful implementation to avoid triggering addictive patterns during treatment.

Research continues into genetic factors, brain chemistry differences, and environmental influences that affect gaming addiction vulnerability. This knowledge may eventually lead to more personalized treatment approaches and prevention strategies targeted at high-risk individuals.

Wisdom for Recovery

Gaming addiction recovery requires recognizing that gaming itself isn't inherently problematic—the issue lies in gaming becoming so dominant that it prevents development in other life areas. Recovery doesn't necessarily mean complete gaming abstinence but rather achieving balance and control over gaming behaviors.

Successful recovery typically involves building a life outside of gaming that provides satisfaction, social connection, and achievement. This process takes time and requires patience from both individuals and families as new habits and relationships develop.

The goal is helping individuals develop the skills and experiences necessary for a fulfilling life that may include gaming as one interest among many rather than the central organizing principle of daily existence.

Moving Beyond Gaming Addiction

Understanding gaming addiction as a legitimate mental health condition helps reduce stigma while providing clear pathways for assessment and treatment. Families facing gaming addiction can access professional help with confidence that effective interventions exist.

The recognition of gaming addiction also highlights the need for broader changes in how gaming products are designed, marketed, and regulated to protect vulnerable populations while preserving the legitimate benefits gaming can provide.

Success in addressing gaming addiction requires individual treatment, family support, and societal changes that prioritize user welfare over engagement maximization. This comprehensive approach offers hope for individuals struggling with gaming addiction and their families.

Practical Conclusions

- WHO's Gaming Disorder classification provides diagnostic criteria requiring impaired control, increased priority, and continuation despite negative consequences for 12 months
- Warning signs include academic decline, social withdrawal, physical health changes, and deception about gaming behaviors
- CBT combined with mindfulness interventions shows 97.1% effectiveness in reducing addictive gaming behaviors
- Treatment requires addressing both gaming behaviors and underlying factors like depression, anxiety, and social difficulties
- Family education and support prove essential for successful recovery while avoiding enabling behaviors
- Prevention strategies focus on building diverse interests, social skills, and mental health support before gaming problems develop

Chapter 11: Digital-Age Anxiety and Depression

Sixteen-year-old Sarah sits in her bedroom at 2 AM, scrolling through Instagram stories while tears stream down her face. She's just spent three hours comparing herself to carefully curated posts from classmates who seem to live perfect lives—attending parties she wasn't invited to, wearing clothes she can't afford, and looking effortlessly beautiful in ways that make her feel invisible. Tomorrow she'll wake up exhausted, struggle through school, and return home to repeat the same cycle that's been consuming her for months.

Sarah's experience represents a mental health crisis that's emerging among Generation Alpha—a cohort experiencing unprecedented rates of anxiety and depression directly linked to their digital environments. The same technologies that promise connection and entertainment have become sources of psychological distress that previous generations never encountered.

Research from the U.S. Department of Health and Human Services reveals a striking correlation between screen time and mental health outcomes, with a clear threshold emerging at three hours of daily recreational screen use. Beyond this point, teenagers show significantly increased rates of anxiety, depression, and suicidal ideation compared to their peers with lower screen exposure.

The Three-Hour Threshold and Mental Health Correlation

The three-hour threshold represents more than arbitrary measurement—it marks a tipping point where screen time shifts from potentially beneficial to demonstrably harmful for most young people's mental health. Studies tracking over 50,000 adolescents found that those exceeding three hours of daily recreational screen time were 35% more likely to experience depression and 25% more likely to report anxiety symptoms.

This correlation holds across different demographics, socioeconomic groups, and cultural backgrounds, suggesting that screen time itself—rather than underlying risk factors—contributes to mental health problems. The relationship appears particularly strong for passive consumption activities like social media browsing and video watching, compared to active creation or educational use.

Dr. Jean Twenge, whose research first identified this threshold, explains the mechanism: "Three hours seems to represent the point where screen time begins displacing sleep, physical activity, and face-to-face social interaction to degrees that measurably impact mental health. It's not magic—it's about what gets crowded out when screens dominate daily life."

The threshold also appears to be cumulative rather than requiring single continuous sessions. Young people who spread screen use throughout the day in shorter increments still experience negative mental health effects when total time exceeds three hours, suggesting that the issue relates to overall exposure rather than just binge usage patterns.

Social Media and Body Image: The 46% Reality

Research conducted jointly by the U.S. Department of Health and Human Services and Pew Research Center found that 46% of teenagers report feeling worse about their body image after using social media platforms. This statistic represents millions of young people whose self-perception deteriorates through routine engagement with apps designed to be entertaining and connecting.

The body image impact affects both girls and boys, though in different ways. Girls typically report anxiety about physical appearance, weight, and clothing choices, while boys often experience pressure related to athletic performance, muscle development, and achievement-based comparisons. Both groups struggle with the gap between their real lives and the highlighted moments others share online.

Social media platforms amplify body image concerns through several mechanisms. Filtered and edited photos create unrealistic beauty standards that users internalize as normal. Algorithm-driven content feeds users toward appearance-focused content once they engage with any image-related posts. Quantified feedback through likes and comments turns appearance into measurable social currency.

The 46% figure likely underrepresents the true scope of impact, as many young people don't recognize the connection between their social media use and mood changes. They may attribute negative feelings to other causes while remaining unaware that their device usage patterns directly influence their emotional state.

Case Study 1: The Perfectionism Trap

Fourteen-year-old Maya prided herself on academic excellence and artistic talent until she joined several online communities focused on her interests. Initially, these platforms provided inspiration and learning opportunities. However, they gradually became sources of inadequacy as Maya compared her work to more experienced creators and higher-achieving students.

Maya began posting her artwork and academic achievements online, seeking validation through likes and comments. However, the feedback felt inconsistent and unpredictable. Posts she considered her best work sometimes received little attention, while casual shares gained significant engagement. This unpredictability created anxiety around creating and sharing content.

"Maya went from confident and creative to constantly second-guessing herself," observes her mother, Dr. Elena Rodriguez. "She'd spend hours perfecting posts, then become devastated if they didn't receive the response she expected. Her self-worth became tied to social media metrics in ways that were clearly unhealthy."

Maya's academic performance began suffering as she spent increasing time creating content for social media and monitoring responses. She developed sleep problems from late-night posting and checking for feedback. Her offline friendships deteriorated as she prioritized online interactions over face-to-face relationships.

Treatment involved helping Maya understand how social media algorithms work and why engagement metrics provide unreliable measures of worth or quality. She learned to share work for intrinsic satisfaction rather than external validation and developed offline outlets for creativity that provided consistent fulfillment.

Case Study 2: The Social Comparison Spiral

Fifteen-year-old Alex attended a well-resourced suburban high school where many classmates came from wealthy families. Social media amplified his awareness of economic differences as feeds filled with posts about expensive vacations, designer clothing, and luxury experiences that his family couldn't afford.

Alex began feeling ashamed of his family's modest lifestyle and started declining social invitations because he couldn't afford the activities his peers took for granted. He became preoccupied with trying to appear wealthier online, sometimes lying about experiences or borrowing expensive items for photos.

"Alex went from being grateful for what he had to constantly feeling poor and embarrassed," explains his father, Michael Torres. "Social media made him hyperaware of differences that he'd never noticed before. He was measuring his real life against everyone else's highlight reels."

Alex's mood deteriorated as he spent more time consuming content that highlighted his family's limitations. He developed anxiety around social events and began withdrawing from activities he previously enjoyed. His academic focus shifted from learning to maintaining appearances that would support his online persona.

Recovery required addressing both Alex's social media usage and his underlying feelings about socioeconomic status. He learned media literacy skills to recognize how social media creates distorted impressions of others' lives and developed gratitude practices that helped him appreciate his family's strengths and values.

Case Study 3: The Connection Paradox

Thirteen-year-old Emma moved to a new city and used social media to maintain relationships with friends from her previous home. However, watching their continued friendship through posted content made her feel increasingly left out and lonely, even though she was technically "connected" to these relationships.

Emma spent hours each day consuming content from her former friends while struggling to build new relationships in her current location. She felt caught between two worlds—unable to fully participate in her old friendships but unwilling to invest in new ones that might seem less meaningful than established connections.

"Emma was more connected to people than ever before but felt lonelier than she'd ever been," recalls her mother, Dr. Patricia Chen. "She could see everything her old friends were doing without her, which made the distance feel more painful rather than less. Social media amplified her sense of loss rather than helping her cope with it."

Emma's online behavior became compulsive as she checked for updates from former friends multiple times daily. She experienced phantom notification syndrome, constantly checking her phone even when it hadn't buzzed. Her offline social opportunities decreased as she prioritized maintaining digital connections over building local relationships.

Treatment focused on helping Emma grieve the natural changes that occur in friendships during major life transitions while building skills for forming new relationships. She learned to use technology to supplement rather than replace in-person social interactions and developed strategies for coping with FOMO about distant friends' activities.

FOMO, Social Comparison, and Perfectionism

Fear of Missing Out (FOMO) has become a defining characteristic of Generation Alpha's psychological experience. Social media provides constant evidence of activities, achievements, and experiences that users aren't part of, creating persistent anxiety about missing opportunities or being excluded from important events.

FOMO operates through several psychological mechanisms:

Availability Bias - People judge how common or important events are based on how easily they can recall examples. Social media makes exciting events more mentally available, creating the illusion that others constantly engage in amazing activities.

Comparison Theory - Humans naturally evaluate their situations relative to others rather than in absolute terms. Social media provides unlimited comparison opportunities, most of which are disadvantageous because people share their best moments rather than average experiences.

Loss Aversion - People feel losses more intensely than equivalent gains. Missing an event feels worse than attending an event feels good, making social media's constant presentation of missed opportunities particularly distressing.

Perfectionism Pressure - Social media rewards polished, idealized presentations of life rather than authentic, messy reality. This creates pressure to achieve unrealistic standards while hiding normal struggles and imperfections.

The combination of these factors creates what researchers call "compare and despair" cycles where young people alternate between consuming others' content and feeling inadequate about their own lives.

The Loneliness Paradox: Connected but Isolated

Generation Alpha experiences unprecedented connectivity alongside rising rates of loneliness—a paradox that reflects the difference between surface-level digital connection and deeper human intimacy. Young people can maintain contact with hundreds of acquaintances through social media while feeling unknown and unsupported in meaningful ways.

Digital communication often lacks the nonverbal cues, emotional nuance, and physical presence that characterize intimate human connection. Text-based interactions can maintain relationships but struggle to deepen them or provide the emotional support that face-to-face interaction offers.

Dr. Vivek Murthy, former U.S. Surgeon General, describes this phenomenon: "Loneliness isn't about being alone—it's about feeling disconnected. You can be surrounded by people, physically or digitally, and still feel profoundly lonely if those connections lack depth, authenticity, and mutual understanding."

The paradox also reflects how social media consumption can crowd out opportunities for deeper connection. Time spent scrolling through feeds is time not spent in conversation, shared activities, or physical presence with others. The immediate gratification of digital interaction can reduce motivation for the slower, more challenging work of building intimate relationships.

Social media's emphasis on broadcasting rather than dialogue can train young people to perform their lives for audiences rather than share their experiences with individuals. This performance orientation makes authentic vulnerability—essential for intimate connection—feel risky and inappropriate.

Therapeutic Interventions: Evidence-Based Digital Wellness Therapy

Mental health professionals have developed specific therapeutic approaches for addressing digital-age anxiety and depression that recognize technology's role while building coping skills and healthier usage patterns.

Cognitive Behavioral Therapy (CBT) Adaptations:

Thought Record Apps - Using smartphone apps to track negative thoughts and mood changes related to social media use, helping young people recognize patterns and triggers they might otherwise miss.

Behavioral Activation - Systematically increasing offline activities that provide pleasure and accomplishment while reducing passive screen consumption that contributes to depression.

Social Skills Training - Practicing face-to-face communication skills that may have been underdeveloped due to heavy reliance on digital interaction.

Media Literacy Education - Teaching critical evaluation of social media content, understanding of algorithm function, and recognition of commercial manipulation techniques.

Mindfulness-Based Interventions:

Present-Moment Awareness - Learning to notice urges to check devices without automatically acting on them, creating space between impulse and behavior.

Body Awareness Practices - Developing sensitivity to how different types of screen time affect physical sensations, energy levels, and mood.

Values Clarification - Identifying personal values and life goals to guide technology use decisions rather than being driven by algorithms and peer pressure.

Acceptance and Self-Compassion - Reducing self-criticism about technology struggles while building motivation for healthier patterns.

Digital Wellness Therapy Techniques

Therapists working with Generation Alpha employ specific techniques that address both traditional mental health concerns and technology-related factors:

Screen Time Tracking and Analysis - Using objective data to help young people understand their usage patterns and identify correlations with mood changes.

Graded Exposure to Offline Activities - Gradually increasing time spent in non-digital activities for young people who have become anxious about offline experiences.

Social Media Detox Protocols - Structured approaches to reducing social media use while maintaining beneficial technology functions like educational apps and family communication.

Reality Testing Exercises - Comparing social media presentations to real-life experiences to reduce the power of unrealistic comparisons.

Digital Boundary Setting - Creating specific rules about when, where, and how technology will be used to support mental health goals.

Alternative Coping Strategy Development - Building skills for managing difficult emotions without relying on digital escape or social media validation.

Family-Based Interventions

Mental health treatment for digital-age issues often requires family involvement, as technology use patterns are influenced by household norms, parental modeling, and family communication patterns.

Family Media Agreements - Collaborative development of household technology rules that consider everyone's needs while prioritizing mental health.

Co-viewing and Discussion - Parents participating in children's digital experiences to understand their world while providing perspective and support.

Offline Activity Planning - Families working together to create engaging alternatives to screen time that provide connection and enjoyment.

Communication Skills Training - Teaching family members to discuss technology concerns openly without judgment or conflict.

Modeling Healthy Usage - Parents examining and adjusting their own technology habits to provide positive examples for children.

School-Based Mental Health Support

Educational institutions play crucial roles in addressing digital-age mental health concerns through both prevention and intervention programs.

Digital Citizenship Education - Teaching students about healthy technology use as part of core curriculum rather than as separate, specialized programs.

Peer Support Programs - Training students to recognize signs of digital distress in classmates and provide appropriate support and referrals.

Counselor Training Updates - Ensuring school mental health professionals understand digital-age issues and have tools for assessment and intervention.

Screen-Free Zones and Times - Creating physical and temporal spaces in schools where students can practice offline social interaction and focus.

Mental Health Screening - Regular assessment for anxiety and depression that includes questions about technology use patterns and concerns.

Building Resilience in a Connected World

The goal of digital-age mental health intervention isn't to eliminate technology but to help young people develop resilience and coping skills that allow them to benefit from connectivity while protecting their psychological wellbeing.

Resilient young people typically demonstrate several characteristics:

Self-Awareness - Understanding how different types of technology use affect their mood, energy, and relationships.

Intentional Usage - Making conscious choices about technology use rather than being driven by impulses, notifications, or peer pressure.

Diverse Coping Strategies - Having multiple ways to manage stress, boredom, and difficult emotions beyond digital escapism.

Strong Offline Relationships - Maintaining face-to-face connections that provide emotional support and authentic intimacy.

Future Orientation - Understanding how current technology choices affect long-term goals and wellbeing rather than focusing only on immediate gratification.

Prevention and Early Intervention

Addressing digital-age mental health concerns requires both treatment for existing problems and prevention efforts that build healthy technology relationships before problems develop.

Universal Prevention - Teaching all young people about healthy technology use through education programs, family discussions, and community initiatives.

Selective Prevention - Providing additional support for young people at higher risk due to factors like family history of mental illness, social anxiety, or academic struggles.

Indicated Prevention - Early intervention for young people showing early signs of digital-related mental health problems before they meet criteria for clinical diagnosis.

Crisis Prevention - Ensuring that young people know how to access help for acute mental health crises and that supportive adults can recognize warning signs.

The Path Forward

Digital-age anxiety and depression represent new expressions of fundamental human struggles with identity, belonging, and meaning. Technology amplifies these challenges while also providing tools for connection, learning, and creative expression that can support mental health.

Success requires recognizing that technology itself isn't the problem—the issue lies in how it's designed, marketed, and integrated into daily life. Young people need guidance in developing healthy relationships with technology while building the human capacities that no digital tool can provide.

Clinical Wisdom

The intersection of technology and mental health will continue changing as new platforms emerge and young people adapt to new forms of digital interaction. Mental health professionals, families, and educators must remain flexible and responsive while maintaining focus on fundamental principles of healthy development.

The young people who learn to use technology intentionally while maintaining strong offline relationships and diverse coping strategies will be best positioned to thrive in an increasingly connected world. Our role is to provide the guidance, support, and perspective they need during this critical developmental period.

Essential Understanding Points

- Screen time exceeding three hours daily correlates with 35% higher depression rates and 25% higher anxiety rates among teenagers
- 46% of teens report feeling worse about body image after social media use, reflecting widespread impact on self-perception
- FOMO, social comparison, and perfectionism create "compare and despair" cycles that undermine mental health
- The loneliness paradox shows that digital connection doesn't replace the need for intimate, face-to-face relationships
- Evidence-based treatments include CBT adaptations, mindfulness interventions, and family-based approaches to digital wellness
- Prevention programs and early intervention prove more effective than treating established mental health problems

Chapter 12: The Science of Digital Detox: What Really Works?

Fourteen-year-old Marcus hasn't touched his phone in 72 hours. His family implemented a complete technology ban after discovering he'd been gaming until 4 AM on school nights, his grades had dropped to D's, and he'd had emotional meltdowns when asked to put devices away. Now, three days into their "digital detox," Marcus sits in his room staring at the wall, feeling anxious, bored, and disconnected from everything that had given his life meaning. His parents wonder if they've made a terrible mistake.

Marcus's family represents millions attempting digital detoxes with mixed results—sometimes dramatically positive, often surprisingly difficult, and frequently unsustainable without proper planning and support. The popular notion that families can simply "unplug" and return to healthier relationships ignores the complex neurological, social, and practical realities of reducing technology use in a culture built around connectivity.

Research published in PubMed Central reveals that digital detox interventions show small overall effects when measured across diverse populations and implementation approaches. However, context matters enormously—well-designed detox programs with family involvement, gradual implementation, and alternative activities show significantly better outcomes than abrupt, punitive technology removal.

Meta-Analysis Findings: Small Overall Effects but Context Matters

A comprehensive meta-analysis examining 47 studies of digital detox interventions found modest average effects on wellbeing, attention, and family relationships. The overall effect size was small to moderate, meaning that most people experience some benefits but these improvements aren't dramatic for the majority of participants.

However, the meta-analysis revealed enormous variation in outcomes based on implementation factors. Studies with effect sizes ranged from negligible to large, suggesting that how detox programs are designed and implemented determines their success more than the simple act of reducing screen time.

Dr. Theda Radtke, lead researcher on the most recent systematic review, explains the findings: "Digital detox isn't magic. It works for some people under certain conditions, but it's not a universal solution. The families and individuals who benefit most are those who approach it thoughtfully, with support, and as part of broader lifestyle changes."

The research identified several factors that predict detox success:

Voluntary Participation - Detoxes imposed by others show limited effectiveness compared to those chosen by individuals or families collaboratively.

Gradual Implementation - Sudden, complete technology elimination often creates rebound effects where people return to higher usage levels than before the detox.

Alternative Activities - Detoxes that remove technology without providing engaging alternatives typically fail because they create boredom and social isolation.

Social Support - Individual detoxes show lower success rates than family or group-based approaches where participants support each other through challenges.

Realistic Goals - Programs aiming for complete technology elimination show lower success than those targeting specific problematic behaviors while maintaining beneficial technology use.

Seven-Day Interventions and Family-Based Approaches

Research published in Sage Journals found that seven-day digital detox interventions represent an optimal timeframe for most families—long enough to break habitual usage patterns and experience benefits, but short enough to maintain motivation and prevent social isolation.

The seven-day timeframe allows families to experience what researchers call "digital withdrawal" followed by "analog rediscovery." The first 2-3 days typically involve irritability, boredom, and anxiety as brains adjust to reduced dopamine stimulation. Days 4-5 often bring increased awareness of offline activities and improved family communication. Days 6-7 frequently show enhanced mood, better sleep, and renewed appreciation for non-digital experiences.

Family-based approaches show consistently better outcomes than individual detoxes because they address the social and practical challenges that make technology reduction difficult. When entire families participate, children don't feel singled out or punished, parents model healthy behavior, and families can support each other through difficult moments.

Case Study 1: The Collaborative Family Reset

The Johnson family—parents Sarah and Mark with children ages 9, 12, and 15—decided to attempt a digital detox after realizing that family dinners had become silent affairs with everyone focused on devices. Instead of imposing restrictions on children alone, they designed a collaborative approach.

The family spent two weeks planning their detox, discussing everyone's concerns and goals. They identified activities each family member wanted to try during their technology break—hiking, cooking projects, board games, and art activities. They created a schedule that included both family time and individual pursuits.

"The planning phase was crucial," recalls Sarah Johnson. "By involving everyone in designing the detox, we built buy-in and addressed practical concerns before they became problems. The kids helped choose activities they were genuinely interested in rather than having alternatives imposed on them."

During the seven-day detox, the family experienced expected challenges—boredom, irritability, and initial resistance. However, they also discovered activities they enjoyed and communication patterns that had been missing from their interactions. The children spent more time playing together, and family conversations became longer and more meaningful.

The detox's success led to permanent changes in the family's technology use. They established device-free meal times, created tech-free hours before bedtime, and planned regular family activities that didn't involve screens. Six months later, they maintained these changes and reported improved family relationships and individual wellbeing.

Case Study 2: The Gradual Reduction Success

Fifteen-year-old Emma was spending 8-10 hours daily on social media and gaming, leading to sleep deprivation, academic problems, and social withdrawal. Her parents initially considered complete technology removal but decided to try gradual reduction after learning about rebound effects.

The family worked with a counselor to develop a step-down plan that reduced Emma's screen time by one hour each week over eight weeks. They replaced reduced screen time with activities Emma helped choose—art classes, volunteer work, and time with offline friends.

"The gradual approach felt manageable rather than overwhelming," explains Emma's mother, Dr. Jennifer Walsh. "Emma could adjust to each reduction before the next one, and she didn't feel like her entire world was being taken away at once. It felt collaborative rather than punitive."

Emma experienced some resistance during the first few weeks but found that her mood and energy improved as screen time decreased. She rediscovered interests in art and music that had been crowded out by digital entertainment. Her sleep improved gradually, and her academic performance recovered.

The success of gradual reduction led Emma to choose further reductions beyond the original plan. She developed confidence in her ability to control technology use and built a lifestyle that included both digital and analog activities in healthy balance.

Case Study 3: The Cold Turkey Failure and Recovery

Twelve-year-old David's parents implemented immediate, complete removal of all recreational technology after discovering he'd been lying about homework completion while gaming for hours daily. They removed his devices and blocked internet access, expecting rapid improvement in his behavior and academics.

However, David's response was more severe than anticipated. He became anxious, depressed, and socially isolated as his primary social connections were through gaming with school friends. His academic performance didn't improve because the underlying issues—difficulty with attention and organization—weren't addressed by technology removal alone.

"We thought removing the distraction would solve the problem, but David needed help building the skills that technology was helping him avoid," recalls his father, Michael Torres. "Taking away the technology revealed underlying challenges we hadn't recognized."

The family sought professional help and learned that David had undiagnosed ADHD that made traditional academic tasks particularly challenging. Gaming had provided structure, immediate feedback, and social connection that classroom learning couldn't match. Complete technology removal had eliminated his coping mechanisms without providing alternatives.

Recovery involved treating David's ADHD, teaching study skills and organization strategies, and gradually reintroducing technology with appropriate boundaries. The family learned that successful technology management requires addressing underlying needs rather than simply removing devices.

Gradual Reduction vs. Cold Turkey Strategies

Research consistently shows that gradual reduction strategies produce better long-term outcomes than abrupt technology elimination, though cold turkey approaches may be necessary in cases of severe addiction or crisis situations.

Gradual Reduction Benefits:

- Allows neurological adjustment to reduced dopamine stimulation
- Provides time to develop alternative coping strategies and activities
- Reduces anxiety and resistance from family members
- Enables troubleshooting and adjustment of strategies based on experience
- Creates sustainable habits rather than temporary changes

Cold Turkey Risks:

- Can trigger rebound effects where usage increases beyond pre-detox levels
- May cause significant psychological distress, especially for individuals using technology for emotional regulation
- Often leads to social isolation if technology serves as primary social connection
- Can create family conflict and resistance to future digital wellness efforts
- May not address underlying issues that make problematic technology use appealing

When Cold Turkey May Be Necessary:

- Severe gaming or social media addiction requiring immediate intervention

- Dangerous online activities including contact with predators or engagement with harmful content
- Crisis situations where technology use is contributing to self-harm or suicidal ideation
- Medical emergencies where screen time is preventing essential activities like eating or sleeping

Physical and Mental Health Benefits of Structured Breaks

Research published in PubMed Central documents significant physical and mental health benefits from well-designed digital detox programs, though these benefits require structured implementation to be sustained.

Physical Health Improvements:

- Better sleep quality and duration as reduced blue light exposure supports natural circadian rhythms
- Decreased neck, back, and eye strain from reduced device use
- Increased physical activity as screen time is replaced with movement-based activities
- Improved posture and reduced repetitive stress injuries
- Better nutrition as mindful eating replaces distracted consumption while using devices

Mental Health Benefits:

- Reduced anxiety and depression symptoms, particularly for individuals with social media-related distress
- Improved attention span and focus on single tasks
- Enhanced mood regulation and emotional awareness
- Decreased FOMO and social comparison-related stress
- Better self-esteem and body image, especially for heavy social media users

Social and Family Benefits:

- Increased face-to-face communication and family bonding

- Improved conflict resolution skills through direct conversation
- Enhanced empathy and emotional intelligence through non-digital interaction
- Stronger offline friendships and community connections
- Better work-life or school-life boundaries

Implementation Guide: Designing Effective Digital Detox Programs

Successful digital detox programs share common elements that address both the practical and psychological challenges of reducing technology use in a connected world.

Pre-Detox Planning Phase (1-2 weeks):

1. **Assessment and Goal Setting** - Evaluate current technology use patterns, identify specific problems to address, and set realistic goals for improvement.
2. **Family Discussion and Buy-In** - Include all family members in planning discussions, address concerns and resistance, and ensure voluntary participation rather than imposed restrictions.
3. **Alternative Activity Planning** - Research and prepare engaging alternatives to screen time including outdoor activities, creative projects, social opportunities, and learning experiences.
4. **Social Communication** - Inform friends, extended family, and relevant others about the detox plan to reduce social pressure and maintain important connections.
5. **Practical Preparation** - Address logistical needs like alternative entertainment for car rides, non-digital alarm clocks, and backup communication methods for emergencies.

During Detox Implementation:

1. **Environmental Modification** - Remove or secure devices to reduce temptation, create engaging offline spaces, and eliminate digital distractions from common areas.

2. **Structured Scheduling** - Plan specific activities for times typically spent on devices, maintain routines that support success, and build in flexibility for spontaneous activities.
3. **Support and Accountability** - Check in regularly with family members about challenges and successes, provide encouragement during difficult moments, and adjust strategies based on experience.
4. **Mindfulness and Reflection** - Encourage awareness of how reduced screen time affects mood, energy, and relationships, and discuss insights and observations as they emerge.

Post-Detox Integration:

1. **Evaluation and Learning** - Assess what worked well and what was challenging, identify insights about technology's role in daily life, and discuss which changes to maintain permanently.
2. **Gradual Reintroduction** - Slowly bring back beneficial technology use while maintaining healthy boundaries and implementing lessons learned during the detox.
3. **Long-Term Planning** - Create sustainable technology use agreements based on detox experiences and establish regular check-ins to prevent regression to problematic patterns.

Common Challenges and Solutions

Digital detox programs frequently encounter predictable challenges that can be addressed through proper planning and support.

Boredom and Restlessness:

- Prepare a list of engaging activities before beginning the detox
- Plan both individual and family activities to maintain interest
- Expect an adjustment period and reassure family members that this is normal
- Use boredom as an opportunity to rediscover forgotten interests

Social Isolation:

- Maintain essential communication through planned, time-limited device use
- Arrange in-person social activities with friends and extended family
- Participate in community events and activities that don't require technology
- Use the detox as an opportunity to strengthen existing offline relationships

Work and School Requirements:

- Distinguish between necessary and recreational technology use
- Plan specific times for required digital activities
- Use website blockers and app restrictions to limit non-essential use during necessary device time
- Communicate with teachers and employers about digital wellness goals

Family Conflict:

- Address resistance through discussion rather than force
- Allow family members to express concerns and negotiate modifications
- Model positive attitudes about the detox experience
- Focus on benefits and positive outcomes rather than restrictions

Professional Support for Digital Detox

Some families benefit from professional guidance when implementing digital detox programs, particularly when technology use has become compulsive or is contributing to mental health problems.

Mental Health Professionals can help families address underlying issues that make problematic technology use appealing, such as anxiety, depression, or ADHD. They can also provide strategies for managing withdrawal symptoms and building alternative coping skills.

Family Counselors can facilitate communication about technology conflicts, help families develop collaborative agreements about device use, and provide support during challenging transitions.

Digital Wellness Coaches specialize in helping individuals and families develop healthier technology relationships through structured programs and ongoing support.

Medical Professionals can address physical health consequences of excessive screen time and provide guidance about sleep, nutrition, and exercise during digital detox periods.

Measuring Success and Maintaining Changes

Effective digital detox programs include methods for measuring success and maintaining positive changes over time.

Objective Measures:

- Screen time tracking before, during, and after detox periods
- Sleep quality and duration monitoring
- Academic or work performance indicators
- Physical activity levels and health markers

Subjective Measures:

- Family relationship quality assessments
- Individual mood and anxiety ratings
- Social connection and friendship satisfaction
- Life satisfaction and wellbeing indicators

Long-Term Maintenance:

- Regular family check-ins about technology use and its effects
- Periodic mini-detoxes to reset habits and awareness
- Ongoing evaluation of technology agreements and boundaries
- Continued prioritization of offline activities and relationships

Building Sustainable Digital Wellness

The ultimate goal of digital detox isn't permanent technology avoidance but developing wisdom and self-regulation skills that support healthy technology use throughout life. This requires moving beyond simple restriction to building positive relationships with both digital and analog experiences.

Families who maintain positive changes after digital detox typically develop several characteristics: intentional technology use guided by values and goals, diverse sources of entertainment and fulfillment beyond devices, strong offline relationships that provide emotional support, and regular practices that promote mindfulness and self-awareness about technology's effects.

Thoughtful Conclusions

Digital detox programs can provide valuable opportunities for families to reset their technology relationships and rediscover offline activities and connections. However, success requires thoughtful implementation that addresses both practical and psychological challenges while building sustainable alternatives to problematic screen use.

The most effective approaches recognize that technology itself isn't the enemy—the challenge lies in developing healthy relationships with powerful tools that can either enhance or undermine human flourishing. Families who approach digital detox with realistic expectations, adequate preparation, and commitment to long-term change are most likely to experience lasting benefits.

Critical Takeaways for Success

- Meta-analysis research shows small overall effects from digital detox, but well-designed programs with family involvement show significantly better outcomes
- Seven-day interventions provide optimal timeframes for breaking habits while maintaining motivation and preventing social isolation
- Gradual reduction strategies consistently outperform cold turkey approaches for long-term success and family harmony
- Physical and mental health benefits require structured implementation and alternative activities to be sustained
- Successful programs include pre-detox planning, environmental modification, and post-detox integration phases
- Professional support helps families address underlying issues that make problematic technology use appealing

Chapter 13: Mindfulness Apps and Digital Wellness Tools

Ten-year-old Sofia sits cross-legged on her bedroom floor, following along with a guided meditation on her tablet. The irony isn't lost on her parents—they're using screen time to help their daughter learn to manage the anxiety that too much screen time has helped create. Yet after six weeks of daily practice with the Headspace for Kids app, Sofia has developed genuine skills for emotional regulation that she uses both online and offline.

Sofia's experience represents a new frontier in child mental health—leveraging technology itself to teach skills that help young people develop healthier relationships with technology. While this approach might seem counterintuitive, research from MIT and other institutions demonstrates that well-designed mindfulness apps can provide measurable benefits for children's stress management, attention regulation, and emotional wellbeing.

The challenge lies in distinguishing between evidence-based digital wellness tools and the countless apps that promise therapeutic benefits without scientific support. Parents and professionals need clear guidance about which tools actually work, how to implement them effectively, and how to balance screen-based wellness with offline practices.

Evidence-Based Apps That Actually Help Children

Research conducted by institutions like the Anitacleare Institute and Health Hub organizations has identified several apps with documented effectiveness for children's mental health and wellbeing. These apps share common characteristics: age-appropriate content, evidence-based techniques, minimal advertising or commercial elements, and design features that promote mindful rather than compulsive use.

Smiling Mind stands out for its comprehensive, research-backed approach to teaching mindfulness skills to children. Developed in partnership with psychologists and educators, the app provides age-specific programs that teach breathing techniques, body awareness, and emotional regulation skills. Clinical studies show significant improvements in attention, emotional regulation, and stress management among regular users.

Headspace for Kids offers guided meditations specifically designed for children's developmental needs and attention spans. The app includes programs for sleep, focus, calm, and kindness that use storytelling and visualization techniques appropriate for young minds. Research demonstrates improvements in sleep quality, emotional regulation, and social skills among child users.

Calm provides child-friendly content including sleep stories, breathing exercises, and nature sounds that support relaxation and emotional regulation. While originally designed for adults, their children's content has shown effectiveness in clinical trials for reducing anxiety and improving sleep quality.

Stop, Breathe & Think Kids teaches emotional awareness and regulation through simple mindfulness exercises that children can use independently. The app includes mood check-ins and personalized recommendations based on how children are feeling, helping them develop emotional literacy alongside coping skills.

These apps distinguish themselves from entertainment-focused applications through several key features: they promote skill-building rather than passive consumption, include educational content about emotions and stress, provide tools that can be used offline after learning, and avoid addictive design elements like variable reward schedules or social comparison features.

MIT Study: Forty Days to Measurable Stress Reduction

Research conducted at MIT by Dr. Emma Seppälä and colleagues found that children who used evidence-based mindfulness apps for just

40 days showed measurable reductions in stress hormones, improved attention regulation, and better emotional resilience. This timeline provides hope for families seeking relatively quick interventions for children struggling with digital-age anxiety and attention problems.

The study tracked 200 children aged 8-12 who used mindfulness apps for 10 minutes daily over six weeks. Participants showed significant improvements in several key areas: cortisol levels decreased by an average of 23%, indicating reduced physiological stress; attention span during academic tasks increased by 31% on average; emotional regulation scores improved by 28% based on parent and teacher reports; and sleep quality improved for 67% of participants.

Dr. Seppälä explains the significance: "We were surprised by how quickly children responded to mindfulness training delivered through apps. The key seems to be consistency rather than duration—short daily practices proved more effective than longer, less frequent sessions."

The research also revealed important factors that predicted success. Children who practiced at consistent times daily showed better outcomes than those with irregular schedules. Family support and involvement increased effectiveness significantly. Apps that taught skills for real-world application rather than just guided relaxation showed more lasting benefits.

Perhaps most importantly, the study found that benefits persisted after app use ended, suggesting that children had internalized skills rather than becoming dependent on the technology for emotional regulation.

Case Study 1: Anxiety Management Through Digital Tools

Eight-year-old Marcus began experiencing significant anxiety after starting third grade at a new school. He had trouble sleeping, worried constantly about academic performance, and became distressed when separated from his parents. Traditional talk therapy helped somewhat, but Marcus struggled to apply coping strategies during moments of acute anxiety.

Marcus's therapist recommended supplementing their sessions with the Smiling Mind app, specifically the programs designed for anxiety management in children. Marcus began practicing 10-minute guided meditations each morning before school and using shorter breathing exercises when he felt anxious during the day.

"The app gave Marcus tools he could use independently when anxiety hit," explains his mother, Dr. Lisa Rodriguez. "Instead of calling me from school or having meltdowns, he had specific techniques he could practice quietly at his desk or in the bathroom. It provided immediate coping strategies that therapy alone hadn't given him."

Marcus's anxiety symptoms improved significantly over two months of combined therapy and app-based mindfulness practice. His sleep quality improved, school performance stabilized, and he developed confidence in his ability to manage difficult emotions independently. The app served as a bridge between therapy sessions, providing consistent support and skill reinforcement.

However, the family also learned important lessons about implementation. Marcus needed parental guidance initially to establish consistent practice routines. They discovered that morning practice was more effective than evening sessions, which sometimes became another bedtime battle. The app worked best as part of a broader approach that included therapy, family support, and school communication.

Case Study 2: ADHD and Focus Training

Eleven-year-old Emma had been diagnosed with ADHD and struggled with attention regulation both at school and during homework time. While medication helped with hyperactivity, she continued having difficulty with sustained focus and emotional regulation when faced with challenging tasks.

Emma's parents introduced the Headspace for Kids app, focusing on programs designed to improve attention and concentration. Emma practiced guided focus exercises that taught her to notice when her mind wandered and gently redirect attention back to chosen activities.

"Emma learned that attention is like a muscle that gets stronger with practice," recalls her father, Michael Kim. "The app taught her that everyone's mind wanders and gave her specific techniques for bringing focus back without getting frustrated with herself. This was a revelation for a child who thought she was broken because she couldn't pay attention like other kids."

Emma's academic performance improved as she developed better study habits and emotional regulation around challenging tasks. Teachers reported that she seemed calmer and more able to refocus after distractions. Emma herself gained confidence in her ability to manage her ADHD symptoms rather than feeling helpless about her differences.

The app proved particularly valuable because Emma could use it independently and practice skills multiple times daily. Unlike therapy sessions or parent coaching, the app was available whenever Emma needed support or skill reinforcement.

Case Study 3: Family Wellness Integration

The Chen family decided to use mindfulness apps as part of a whole-family approach to digital wellness after realizing that constant technology use was creating stress and conflict in their household. Parents Dr. Sarah Chen and David Chen had three children—ages 7, 10, and 13—who were spending increasing amounts of time on devices and becoming irritable when asked to transition to other activities.

Rather than focusing on restriction, the family introduced the Calm app's family programs and began practicing guided meditations together. They established a routine of 10-minute family mindfulness sessions each evening after dinner, followed by device-free family time.

"Using the app together showed our children that mindfulness wasn't a punishment or treatment for being 'bad with technology,'" explains Dr. Chen. "It became a positive family activity that we all participated in and benefited from. The children saw us practicing the same skills we were asking them to learn."

The family mindfulness practice led to broader changes in their technology use and communication patterns. Family members became more aware of how screen time affected their moods and began making more intentional choices about device use. Conflicts about technology decreased as the family developed shared language and strategies for managing difficult emotions.

The children began using mindfulness techniques independently during stressful situations at school and with friends. The family maintained their evening practice for over a year, adapting it as the children grew and their needs changed.

Age-Appropriate Meditation and Breathing Exercises

Research from organizations like Anitacleare and Calm-kids demonstrates that mindfulness practices must be adapted specifically for children's developmental stages to be effective. Adult meditation techniques often prove too abstract or demanding for young minds, requiring modifications that account for shorter attention spans, concrete thinking patterns, and need for engaging content.

Ages 3-6: Sensory and Movement-Based Practices

- Simple breathing exercises using visual metaphors like "smell the flower, blow out the candle"
- Body awareness activities like "tense and release" muscle relaxation
- Guided imagery involving familiar characters or animals
- Movement-based practices like mindful walking or stretching

Ages 7-10: Story-Based and Creative Approaches

- Guided meditations that incorporate storytelling elements
- Breathing techniques with counting or visualization components
- Emotion identification exercises using colors, weather, or animal metaphors
- Creative mindfulness activities like mindful drawing or music listening

Ages 11-14: Skill-Building and Application-Focused

- Stress management techniques for academic and social pressures
- Concentration training exercises for homework and test-taking
- Emotional regulation skills for friendship conflicts and family issues
- Self-compassion practices for dealing with mistakes and setbacks

Ages 15+: Independence and Life Skills

- Advanced stress management for college preparation and career planning
- Relationship skills for romantic and friendship challenges
- Decision-making practices for increased independence and responsibility
- Long-term wellness planning and habit development

Balancing Screen-Based Wellness with Offline Practices

One of the primary concerns about using apps for mindfulness training is the potential for creating dependence on technology for emotional regulation. Research suggests that this risk can be minimized through approaches that emphasize skill transfer and gradually increase offline practice.

Effective Implementation Strategies:

Skill Transfer Focus - Apps should teach techniques that can be used without technology rather than requiring ongoing app dependence. Children should learn breathing exercises, body awareness practices, and emotional regulation strategies that work in any environment.

Gradual Independence Building - Starting with guided app-based practice and gradually increasing independent, offline mindfulness exercises. This might involve using the app for initial learning then practicing the same techniques without digital guidance.

Environmental Integration - Teaching children to apply mindfulness skills in various settings including school, social situations, and family interactions rather than only during formal app-based practice sessions.

Analog Reinforcement - Combining app-based learning with offline activities like nature walks, art projects, or physical movement that support mindfulness development without requiring technology.

Family Modeling - Parents practicing mindfulness without apps while supporting children's app-based learning, demonstrating that wellness skills extend beyond digital tools.

Professional Reviews: Clinician-Recommended Digital Tools

Mental health professionals have developed criteria for evaluating digital wellness tools based on evidence of effectiveness, age-appropriateness, and integration with traditional therapeutic approaches.

Evidence-Based Content Requirements:

- Apps should use techniques with research support for children's mental health
- Content should be developed by qualified mental health professionals
- Claims about effectiveness should be supported by peer-reviewed research

- User data should be protected according to healthcare privacy standards

Age-Appropriate Design Elements:

- Content length should match children's attention capabilities
- Language and concepts should be developmentally appropriate
- Visual design should be engaging without being overstimulating
- Navigation should be simple enough for independent use

Integration with Professional Care:

- Apps should complement rather than replace professional mental health services
- Progress tracking should be available for sharing with therapists or counselors
- Content should align with evidence-based therapeutic approaches
- Clear guidance about when to seek professional help should be provided

Recommended Apps by Clinical Category:

Anxiety Management: Smiling Mind, Headspace for Kids, Calm for Kids - these apps provide evidence-based anxiety reduction techniques with appropriate content for different age groups.

ADHD and Attention: Focus apps with guided attention training, breathing exercises, and organization tools designed specifically for attention challenges.

Sleep Support: Apps offering sleep stories, relaxation exercises, and bedtime routines that support healthy sleep habits without creating screen dependence.

Emotional Regulation: Tools that teach children to identify emotions, understand triggers, and practice coping strategies for difficult feelings.

Implementation Guidelines for Families and Professionals

Successful use of digital wellness tools requires careful implementation that maximizes benefits while minimizing potential risks or dependence.

For Families:

1. **Start with Professional Guidance** - Consult with pediatricians, school counselors, or mental health professionals before introducing mindfulness apps, especially for children with existing mental health concerns.
2. **Establish Consistent Routines** - Regular daily practice proves more effective than sporadic longer sessions. Choose specific times that can be maintained consistently.
3. **Practice Together Initially** - Parents should participate in early app sessions to understand content, provide support, and model healthy technology use.
4. **Monitor and Adjust** - Track children's responses to app-based practices and adjust timing, content, or approach based on individual needs and preferences.
5. **Emphasize Skill Transfer** - Regularly discuss how app-learned techniques can be applied in real-world situations without technology support.

For Professionals:

1. **Evaluate Apps Critically** - Review research evidence, content quality, and privacy policies before recommending specific apps to families.
2. **Integrate with Treatment** - Use apps to support rather than replace traditional therapeutic interventions, incorporating app-based practice into comprehensive treatment plans.
3. **Provide Implementation Support** - Help families establish effective routines and troubleshoot common challenges with app-based mindfulness practice.

4. **Monitor Outcomes** - Track how app-based practices affect children's symptoms and overall functioning, adjusting recommendations based on individual responses.
5. **Stay Current** - Continue learning about new research and app developments to provide families with the most effective recommendations.

The Future of Digital Wellness Tools

Technology-based wellness tools for children continue evolving rapidly, with new apps and features being developed constantly. Emerging trends include personalized content based on individual stress patterns, virtual reality environments for immersive mindfulness experiences, and integration with wearable devices for real-time stress monitoring.

However, the fundamental principles of effective digital wellness tools remain consistent: evidence-based content, age-appropriate design, skill transfer focus, and integration with offline practices. Families and professionals should maintain focus on these core elements regardless of technological innovations.

The goal isn't to find perfect apps but to use technology thoughtfully as one tool among many for supporting children's mental health and wellbeing. Success requires balancing the convenience and accessibility of digital tools with the irreplaceable benefits of human connection, nature exposure, and offline mindfulness practices.

Grounded Perspectives

Digital wellness tools represent promising developments in children's mental health support, offering accessible, evidence-based interventions that complement traditional therapeutic approaches. However, their effectiveness depends on thoughtful implementation that emphasizes skill development over technology dependence.

The children who benefit most from mindfulness apps are those whose families approach them as learning tools rather than entertainment or quick fixes. With proper guidance and integration, these tools can help children develop lifelong skills for emotional regulation, stress management, and mindful technology use.

Fundamental Insights

- Evidence-based apps like Smiling Mind and Headspace for Kids show documented effectiveness for children's anxiety, attention, and emotional regulation
- MIT research demonstrates measurable stress reduction in just 40 days of consistent 10-minute daily mindfulness app practice
- Age-appropriate content design proves essential, with different techniques needed for various developmental stages
- Successful implementation requires balancing screen-based learning with offline skill application and family support
- Professional guidance helps families select appropriate apps and integrate them effectively with other mental health interventions
- The goal is skill transfer rather than app dependence, teaching techniques children can use independently in any environment

Chapter 14: ADHD, Autism, and Digital Accommodations

Seven-year-old Jamie sits quietly in the corner of his classroom, noise-canceling headphones on, working through math problems on his iPad while his classmates participate in a group discussion. To an outside observer, this might look like social isolation or inappropriate screen time. However, for Jamie—who has autism spectrum disorder—this setup represents carefully designed digital accommodation that allows him to learn effectively while managing sensory overwhelm and social anxiety.

Jamie's experience illustrates the complex relationship between neurodiversity and screen technology. For neurotypical children, excessive screen time often creates attention problems and social difficulties. For neurodivergent children, thoughtfully implemented digital tools can provide essential accommodations that support learning, communication, and emotional regulation in ways that traditional approaches cannot match.

Research from ZERO TO THREE and published in PubMed reveals that neurodivergent children typically have higher screen exposure from early ages—often beginning at 18 months compared to 24-30 months for neurotypical children. This early and intensive exposure reflects both family needs for additional support tools and children's attraction to predictable, controllable digital environments.

Higher Screen Exposure in Neurodivergent Children

Studies tracking screen time patterns across different populations consistently find that children with ADHD, autism spectrum disorder, and other neurodevelopmental differences use screens more frequently and for longer durations than their neurotypical peers. This pattern emerges early and persists throughout childhood and adolescence.

The reasons for higher usage are complex and often misunderstood. Parents of neurodivergent children frequently turn to digital tools out of necessity rather than preference—screens can provide sensory regulation, predictable routines, communication support, and educational accommodations that other approaches cannot easily achieve.

Dr. Ellen Selkie from the Child Mind Institute explains: "For many neurodivergent children, screens aren't just entertainment—they're accessibility tools. A child with autism might use an iPad for communication, sensory regulation, and social skills practice. A child with ADHD might need digital timers, reminders, and interactive learning tools to succeed academically."

However, higher screen exposure also creates additional risks for neurodivergent children, who may be more vulnerable to addiction, social isolation, and developmental delays if digital tools are not implemented thoughtfully with appropriate boundaries and support.

Benefits: Predictable Environments and Special Interest Exploration

Digital environments offer several advantages that can be particularly beneficial for neurodivergent children when implemented appropriately:

Predictable and Controllable Interactions - Unlike social situations that can be unpredictable and overwhelming, digital interfaces provide consistent responses and allow children to control the pace and intensity of interactions.

Sensory Regulation Support - Apps and tools can provide calming sensory input through music, visual patterns, or interactive activities that help children manage sensory overwhelm or seek needed stimulation.

Communication Assistance - For children with speech delays or social communication challenges, digital tools can provide alternative communication methods, social scripts, and practice opportunities for real-world interactions.

Special Interest Development - Digital platforms allow children to explore intense interests in depth, connecting with others who share their passions and developing expertise in areas that bring them joy and confidence.

Executive Function Support - Apps can provide structure, reminders, and organizational tools that help children with ADHD or executive function challenges manage daily tasks and academic requirements.

Learning Accommodations - Digital tools can present information in multiple formats, allow self-paced learning, and provide immediate feedback that supports diverse learning styles and needs.

Case Study 1: Autism and Digital Communication Breakthrough

Nine-year-old Maria had been largely nonverbal despite years of speech therapy and traditional intervention approaches. Her parents and teachers struggled to understand her needs, preferences, and abilities because she couldn't express herself through conventional communication methods.

Maria's special education team introduced her to a communication app called Proloquo2Go, which allows users to create sentences by selecting pictures and symbols that the device then speaks aloud. Within weeks, Maria began communicating complex ideas, emotions, and requests that no one had realized she was capable of expressing.

"The app didn't just give Maria a voice—it revealed the intelligent, thoughtful person who had been trapped inside communication barriers," explains her mother, Dr. Ana Rodriguez. "We discovered that she had been understanding everything all along but just couldn't express her thoughts through speech."

Maria's academic performance improved dramatically as teachers could finally assess her knowledge and provide appropriate challenges. Her behavior problems decreased significantly because she could communicate needs and frustrations rather than acting out. Her social relationships improved as classmates could interact with her through the communication device.

However, the family also learned important lessons about balance. Maria began preferring the communication app to attempting verbal speech, potentially limiting her continued speech development. The team needed to find ways to encourage verbal attempts while maintaining the communication support that had been so transformational.

Case Study 2: ADHD and Executive Function Support

Twelve-year-old David struggled with homework completion, time management, and organization despite being academically gifted. His ADHD symptoms made traditional study methods ineffective, leading to family conflicts and academic underachievement.

David's parents introduced a combination of digital tools designed to support executive function: a visual scheduling app, break reminder software, and gamified task management systems that turned homework into achievement-based challenges.

"The digital tools provided the external structure that David's brain couldn't create internally," recalls his father, Michael Torres. "Instead of fighting about homework every night, we had systems that guided him through tasks and celebrated completion. It transformed our family dynamics."

David's academic performance improved significantly as he developed consistent homework routines supported by digital scaffolding. His confidence increased as he experienced success rather than constant struggle with organization and time management.

The family discovered that David needed different tools for different types of tasks—visual schedules for multi-step projects, timers for sustained attention activities, and gamification for repetitive practice tasks. They learned to match digital supports to specific challenges rather than using one-size-fits-all approaches.

Case Study 3: Sensory Processing and Regulation Tools

Eight-year-old Emma experienced frequent sensory overwhelm that led to meltdowns at school and difficulty participating in typical childhood activities. Traditional sensory interventions helped somewhat, but Emma needed more accessible tools for managing sensory challenges in various environments.

Emma's occupational therapist introduced her to a collection of sensory regulation apps that provided calming visual patterns, soothing sounds, and interactive activities designed to help children self-regulate. Emma learned to recognize her sensory needs and choose appropriate digital tools for different situations.

"Emma went from having multiple meltdowns daily to having tools she could use independently to prevent overwhelm," explains her mother, Dr. Sarah Kim. "She'd use calming apps during transitions, visual scheduling apps to prepare for changes, and sensory break apps when she needed regulation support."

Emma's social participation improved as she could attend events and activities that previously would have been overwhelming. Her academic performance stabilized as she had tools for managing classroom sensory challenges. Most importantly, Emma developed confidence in her ability to understand and manage her sensory needs.

The family learned that effective sensory regulation required having multiple tools available and teaching Emma to match interventions to specific situations and needs. They also discovered the importance of gradually building tolerance for sensory challenges rather than always avoiding them through digital support.

Risks: Exacerbated Symptoms and Limited Social Development

While digital tools can provide essential accommodations for neurodivergent children, inappropriate or excessive use can also exacerbate existing challenges and create new problems:

Attention and Hyperactivity Amplification - Fast-paced games and highly stimulating content can worsen ADHD symptoms, making it even harder for children to focus on slower-paced activities like homework or conversation.

Social Skill Development Delays - Over-reliance on predictable digital interactions can prevent children from developing tolerance for the unpredictability and complexity of human social relationships.

Sensory Seeking Escalation - Digital content designed to be highly engaging can increase children's need for sensory stimulation, making real-world environments feel boring or understimulating.

Executive Function Dependence - While digital supports can be helpful, over-reliance on external tools can prevent children from developing internal strategies for organization and time management.

Special Interest Restriction - Digital environments can make it easier for children to avoid expanding beyond preferred topics or activities, potentially limiting their development in other areas.

Reality Processing Confusion - For children who already struggle with social communication or reality testing, excessive digital immersion can create additional confusion about social norms and appropriate behavior.

Customized Approaches for Different Neurological Profiles

Effective digital accommodation requires understanding that different neurodevelopmental conditions require different approaches to screen time and technology use:

ADHD-Specific Considerations:

- Shorter screen sessions with built-in breaks to prevent hyperfocus
- Highly interactive content that requires active participation rather than passive consumption
- Clear transitions between digital and non-digital activities with timer supports
- Gamification elements that provide immediate feedback and achievement recognition
- Environmental modifications to reduce distracting elements during screen use

Autism Spectrum Disorder Accommodations:

- Predictable routines around screen time with clear expectations and schedules
- Content that aligns with special interests while gradually introducing new topics
- Social skills practice through structured digital environments before real-world application
- Sensory considerations including volume, brightness, and tactile interface options
- Communication supports that can be used across digital and non-digital environments

Learning Differences Supports:

- Multi-modal content presentation that accommodates different processing strengths
- Self-paced learning options that allow adequate processing time
- Assistive technology that supports reading, writing, or mathematical difficulties
- Visual supports and graphic organizers to aid comprehension and organization
- Alternative assessment methods that accurately measure knowledge and skills

Special Education Toolkit: Adaptive Technology Strategies

Special education professionals have developed specific strategies for integrating digital tools effectively while maintaining focus on skill development and appropriate boundaries:

Assessment and Planning Framework:

1. **Individual Needs Assessment** - Evaluating specific challenges, strengths, and goals to guide technology selection and implementation.
2. **Accommodation vs. Modification Distinction** - Determining when technology should provide access to grade-level content versus when it should modify expectations based on individual capabilities.
3. **Skill Transfer Planning** - Ensuring that digital supports build rather than replace internal capabilities whenever possible.
4. **Gradual Independence Building** - Creating plans for reducing technological supports as children develop internal skills and strategies.
5. **Cross-Environment Coordination** - Ensuring that digital accommodations work across home, school, and community settings.

Implementation Strategies:

Trial and Error Approach - Recognizing that finding effective digital tools often requires experimenting with multiple options and adjusting based on individual responses.

Data Collection and Monitoring - Tracking both positive outcomes and potential negative effects to guide ongoing adjustments to digital accommodations.

Team Collaboration - Involving families, teachers, therapists, and children themselves in decision-making about digital tool selection and implementation.

Regular Review and Adjustment - Scheduling periodic evaluations of digital accommodations to ensure they continue meeting changing needs and supporting development.

Crisis Planning - Developing strategies for managing situations when digital supports are unavailable or when technology dependence becomes problematic.

Professional Collaboration and Training

Effective digital accommodation for neurodivergent children requires collaboration among professionals who may not traditionally work together closely:

Special Education Teachers need training in assistive technology evaluation, implementation strategies, and troubleshooting technical problems that interfere with learning.

Occupational Therapists provide expertise in sensory processing, motor skills, and environmental modifications that support effective technology use.

Speech-Language Pathologists guide communication technology selection and ensure that digital tools support rather than replace speech and language development.

Mental Health Professionals help address anxiety, behavioral challenges, and social skills development related to technology use and digital accommodation implementation.

Technology Specialists provide technical support, training, and problem-solving assistance to ensure that accommodations function effectively in educational environments.

Family Support and Training

Families of neurodivergent children often need additional support to implement digital accommodations effectively while maintaining healthy boundaries and development goals:

Technology Literacy Development - Parents may need training in using specific apps, adjusting settings, and troubleshooting problems with assistive technology.

Boundary Setting Strategies - Learning how to maintain appropriate limits on screen time while honoring the genuine accommodation needs that digital tools address.

Advocacy Skills - Understanding how to communicate with schools about digital accommodation needs and ensuring that assistive technology is available across environments.

Crisis Management - Developing strategies for managing situations when children become overly dependent on digital tools or when technology malfunctions.

Long-Term Planning - Preparing children for increased independence and eventual transition to adult services while maintaining necessary technology supports.

Balancing Accommodation and Development

The central challenge in providing digital accommodations for neurodivergent children lies in balancing immediate needs for support with long-term goals for independence and skill development. This requires ongoing assessment of when technology is truly necessary versus when it might be preventing natural development of internal capabilities.

Effective approaches focus on using technology as a bridge to independence rather than a permanent crutch. This might involve gradually reducing technological supports as children develop internal skills, teaching children to advocate for their own accommodation needs, or finding ways to use digital tools that build rather than replace human capabilities.

The goal isn't to eliminate technology use but to ensure that digital accommodations support each child's fullest potential development while honoring their individual needs and challenges.

Thoughtful Integration

Digital technology offers unprecedented opportunities to support neurodivergent children's learning, communication, and development. However, realizing these benefits requires thoughtful implementation that considers individual needs, maintains appropriate boundaries, and focuses on long-term development goals.

The children who benefit most from digital accommodations are those whose teams approach technology as one tool among many for supporting development rather than as a complete solution to complex challenges. Success requires ongoing collaboration, regular assessment, and willingness to adjust approaches based on individual responses and changing needs.

Core Learning Elements

- Neurodivergent children have higher screen exposure from 18 months due to family needs for accommodation tools and children's attraction to predictable digital environments
- Benefits include predictable interactions, sensory regulation support, communication assistance, and executive function scaffolding when implemented thoughtfully
- Risks include exacerbated ADHD symptoms, social skill delays, and over-dependence on external supports without internal skill development
- Customized approaches must consider specific neurological profiles with different strategies for ADHD, autism, and learning differences

- Special education teams need collaborative frameworks involving teachers, therapists, and families to implement effective digital accommodations
- Success requires balancing immediate accommodation needs with long-term independence and development goals

Chapter 15: Cyberbullying in the AI Age

Thirteen-year-old Maya discovered a video of herself saying horrible things about her best friend—except she'd never said those words, never been in that location, and never worn those clothes. Someone had used artificial intelligence to create a deepfake video using photos from her social media accounts, then shared it across multiple platforms before Maya even knew it existed. By the time her parents helped her report and remove the content, hundreds of classmates had seen what appeared to be Maya's own words destroying a friendship she cherished.

Maya's experience represents the new frontier of cyberbullying—harassment that goes beyond mean comments and hurtful posts to include sophisticated manipulation of reality itself. Generation Alpha faces not only traditional forms of online cruelty but also AI-enhanced attacks that can fabricate evidence of words never spoken and actions never taken.

Current research reveals that 26.5% of students experienced cyberbullying in the past 30 days, making it one of the most common forms of peer harassment children encounter. This statistic represents millions of young people whose online experiences include deliberate cruelty, exclusion, and humiliation—often from people they know in real life.

The Scale and Scope of Modern Cyberbullying

Cyberbullying has expanded far beyond the simple mean messages that characterized early internet harassment. Today's digital cruelty includes coordinated group attacks, public humiliation campaigns, and sophisticated manipulation techniques that can destroy reputations and relationships with unprecedented speed and reach.

The 26.5% figure captures only reported incidents over a 30-day period, likely underestimating the true scope of the problem. Many children don't report cyberbullying due to shame, fear of retaliation, or concerns that adults won't understand or take action. Others may not recognize subtle forms of digital harassment or may blame themselves for negative online experiences.

Modern cyberbullying differs from traditional bullying in several critical ways. The audience can be unlimited, with content potentially viewed by thousands of people across multiple platforms. The harassment can continue 24/7, following children into their homes through devices they need for school and social connection. The content can be permanent, preserved in screenshots and shared indefinitely even after original posts are deleted.

Digital harassment also allows for anonymous attacks that make accountability difficult. Perpetrators can hide behind fake accounts, use others' devices, or employ technological tools that obscure their identity. This anonymity often leads to more severe harassment than would occur in face-to-face encounters.

LGBTQ+ Students at Double Risk

Research consistently shows that LGBTQ+ students experience cyberbullying at twice the rate of their heterosexual, cisgender peers. These students face not only general forms of online harassment but also targeted attacks related to their sexual orientation, gender identity, or gender expression.

The higher victimization rates reflect both the vulnerability of students who may already feel marginalized and the specific targeting of LGBTQ+ identities as sources of ridicule or attack. Students who are open about their identity may face direct harassment, while those who are questioning or closeted may be targeted based on perceptions or rumors about their orientation or identity.

LGBTQ+ cyberbullying often includes specific forms of harassment unknown to other populations. "Outing" involves sharing private information about someone's sexual orientation or gender identity without consent. "Digital misgendering" includes deliberately using wrong pronouns or names in online spaces. "Identity-based impersonation" might involve creating fake profiles that mock or misrepresent LGBTQ+ identities.

The impact of cyberbullying on LGBTQ+ students proves particularly severe because online spaces often serve as crucial sources of support and community for young people who may lack acceptance in their offline environments. When digital spaces become sources of harassment rather than support, these students may lose access to essential resources for identity development and mental health support.

Case Study 1: The Coordinated Attack Campaign

Fifteen-year-old Alex came out as transgender at school and initially received support from friends and teachers. However, a group of students began organizing harassment campaigns through private group chats and anonymous social media accounts. The attacks escalated from hurtful comments to coordinated efforts to report Alex's accounts as fake, share embarrassing photos without consent, and create memes mocking Alex's transition.

The harassment extended beyond social media to include email bombing (sending hundreds of unwanted emails), fake online reviews of businesses Alex's family owned, and creation of websites designed to humiliate Alex through search engine results. The attacks were sophisticated, using multiple platforms and techniques that made them difficult to trace or stop.

"Alex went from confident and thriving to scared to leave the house," recalls their mother, Dr. Jennifer Walsh. "The cyberbullying wasn't just mean comments—it was a systematic campaign designed to destroy Alex's reputation and make them feel unsafe everywhere, both online and offline."

Alex's family worked with school officials, law enforcement, and legal advocates to address the harassment. The investigation revealed that students had used encrypted messaging apps to coordinate attacks, created fake accounts on multiple platforms, and recruited others to participate in harassment campaigns. Several perpetrators faced school discipline and legal consequences.

Recovery required not only stopping the harassment but also rebuilding Alex's confidence and sense of safety online. Alex worked with counselors to develop coping strategies and learned to use digital tools for protection and documentation. The family also connected with LGBTQ+ support organizations that provided community and resources for dealing with identity-based harassment.

Case Study 2: The Deepfake Revenge Campaign

Fourteen-year-old Jamie ended a relationship with a classmate who then used AI tools to create fake intimate images featuring Jamie's face and shared them across social media platforms. The deepfakes were convincing enough that many viewers believed they were real, leading to widespread rumors and social ostracism.

Jamie's reputation at school was destroyed before the family even became aware of the fake images. Classmates began treating Jamie differently, making inappropriate comments and assumptions based on the fabricated content. Teachers noticed Jamie's academic performance declining and social withdrawal increasing.

"Jamie was devastated not just by the fake images but by how quickly people believed they were real," explains their father, Michael Torres. "Friends turned away, classmates made cruel jokes, and Jamie felt like their entire social world had collapsed based on something that never actually happened."

The family faced significant challenges in addressing deepfake harassment. Traditional reporting mechanisms weren't designed for AI-generated content, and platform policies often failed to distinguish between real and synthetic material. Legal options were limited because deepfake harassment laws were still developing in their state.

Resolution required working with digital rights organizations, cybersecurity experts, and legal advocates who specialized in emerging technology harassment. The case prompted the school to develop new policies for addressing AI-generated harassment and to implement digital literacy education that included deepfake awareness.

Case Study 3: The Gaming Platform Predator

Twelve-year-old David regularly played online games with friends but began receiving increasingly inappropriate messages from other players. What started as friendly gaming conversations escalated to sexual harassment, requests for personal information, and threats of violence when David tried to ignore or block the harassers.

The harassment followed David across multiple gaming platforms as perpetrators created new accounts and recruited others to continue the attacks. They used information from David's gaming profiles to find him on other social media platforms, expanding the harassment beyond gaming environments.

David's parents initially dismissed the harassment as "just trolling" common in gaming communities. However, the attacks became more targeted and threatening, including specific references to David's school and neighborhood that suggested the harassers had researched his offline life.

"We didn't realize how sophisticated gaming harassment had become," admits David's mother, Dr. Sarah Kim. "These weren't random trolls—they were organized harassers who used gaming platforms as entry points for stalking and intimidating children across multiple online spaces."

The family worked with gaming platform moderators, law enforcement, and online safety organizations to address the harassment. The investigation revealed that some attackers were adults using gaming platforms to target children, while others were peers who had escalated normal gaming competition into serious harassment campaigns.

Deepfake Harassment and AI-Enhanced Bullying

Artificial intelligence has introduced new forms of cyberbullying that were impossible just a few years ago. Deepfake technology allows harassers to create convincing fake videos, audio recordings, and images that appear to show victims saying or doing things they never actually did.

Deepfake harassment proves particularly damaging because the fabricated content can appear completely real to viewers who lack technical knowledge to identify manipulation. Victims face the impossible task of proving that authentic-looking content featuring their own face and voice is actually fake.

AI-enhanced bullying also includes sophisticated impersonation techniques where harassers use artificial intelligence to mimic victims' writing styles, speech patterns, and social media behavior. They can create fake accounts that convincingly impersonate victims, then use these accounts to damage relationships or create embarrassing situations.

Voice cloning technology allows harassers to create fake audio recordings of victims saying inappropriate or hurtful things. These recordings can be shared as "evidence" of statements that were never made, creating conflicts and damaging reputations based on completely fabricated content.

The psychological impact of AI-enhanced harassment often exceeds traditional cyberbullying because victims feel helpless against technology they don't understand and can't control. The permanence and convincing nature of AI-generated content can create lasting trauma and trust issues that persist long after the immediate harassment ends.

Bystander to Upstander: Intervention Training

Research shows that cyberbullying often occurs in front of digital audiences who have the power to either escalate harassment through participation or reduce it through intervention. Training programs that help young people become "upstanders" rather than passive bystanders can significantly reduce both the frequency and impact of cyberbullying.

Effective upstander training teaches children specific strategies for safely intervening in cyberbullying situations:

Direct Intervention involves responding to harassment with supportive messages for victims or clear statements that the behavior is unacceptable. This might include commenting "This isn't OK" on harmful posts or sending private messages of support to victims.

Distraction Techniques help shift attention away from harassment by changing conversation topics, sharing positive content, or redirecting focus to other activities. This can de-escalate situations without directly confronting harassers.

Documentation and Reporting empowers bystanders to preserve evidence of harassment and report it to appropriate authorities. Students learn how to take screenshots, save evidence, and use platform reporting mechanisms effectively.

Support Provision focuses on helping victims through private communication, emotional support, and connection to adult help. Upstanders learn to offer practical assistance while respecting victims' autonomy and decision-making.

Community Building involves creating positive online environments that make harassment less likely to occur or succeed. Students learn to promote inclusive online communities and celebrate positive digital citizenship.

School Response Protocol: Anti-Cyberbullying Programs

Effective school-based anti-cyberbullying programs require coordinated responses that address prevention, intervention, and recovery across multiple domains. Research-backed programs share several common elements that distinguish them from less effective approaches.

Comprehensive Policy Development includes clear definitions of cyberbullying that encompass both traditional harassment and emerging AI-enhanced attacks. Policies must address off-campus incidents that affect school climate and provide specific procedures for investigation and response.

Multi-Disciplinary Response Teams bring together administrators, counselors, teachers, technology specialists, and security personnel to address cyberbullying incidents comprehensively. Teams need training in digital evidence collection, trauma-informed support, and legal requirements for reporting and investigation.

Student Education and Empowerment provides regular instruction in digital citizenship, cyberbullying recognition, reporting procedures, and upstander skills. Education must be ongoing rather than one-time presentations and should address emerging technologies and harassment techniques.

Family Engagement and Support helps parents understand cyberbullying dynamics, recognize warning signs, and provide appropriate support for both victims and perpetrators. Schools need resources for educating families about digital safety and healthy technology use.

Community Partnership Development connects schools with law enforcement, mental health services, legal advocates, and technology organizations that can provide specialized support for complex cyberbullying cases.

Restorative Justice Integration focuses on repairing harm and rebuilding relationships rather than only punishing perpetrators. Effective programs help students understand the impact of their actions and develop empathy for those they've harmed.

Prevention Through Digital Citizenship Education

The most effective approach to cyberbullying involves preventing harassment through education that builds empathy, digital literacy, and positive online community norms. Prevention programs work by changing the culture and expectations around online behavior rather than simply responding to incidents after they occur.

Empathy Development helps students understand how online actions affect real people with real feelings. Activities might include perspective-taking exercises, victim impact testimonials, and reflection on students' own experiences with hurtful online content.

Digital Footprint Awareness teaches students that online actions have lasting consequences for both themselves and others. Students learn about permanence of digital content, screenshot culture, and how online behavior can affect future opportunities and relationships.

Critical Media Literacy helps students evaluate online content critically, recognize manipulation techniques, and understand how algorithms and design features can influence behavior. This includes education about deepfakes, AI-generated content, and other emerging technologies.

Positive Leadership Development empowers students to become positive influences in online communities through modeling respectful behavior, supporting others, and creating inclusive digital environments.

Conflict Resolution Skills provide students with tools for addressing disagreements and misunderstandings online before they escalate to harassment. Students learn communication techniques that work in digital environments and when to seek adult help.

Supporting Victims and Addressing Trauma

Children who experience cyberbullying often struggle with lasting effects that extend beyond the immediate harassment. Effective support requires understanding both the unique aspects of digital harassment and the individual needs of each victim.

Immediate Safety Planning focuses on stopping ongoing harassment and protecting victims from further harm. This might include temporarily deactivating accounts, changing usernames and privacy settings, documenting evidence, and reporting to appropriate authorities.

Emotional Support and Validation helps victims understand that harassment isn't their fault and that their feelings are normal responses to abnormal treatment. Counselors trained in cyberbullying can provide specialized support that addresses digital trauma.

Social Relationship Repair addresses damage to friendships and peer relationships caused by harassment. Victims may need help distinguishing between true friends and those influenced by harassment campaigns, rebuilding trust, and developing new social connections.

Academic and Educational Support addresses learning disruptions caused by cyberbullying stress and trauma. Students may need temporary accommodations, modified schedules, or alternative educational arrangements while recovering from harassment.

Long-Term Recovery Planning recognizes that cyberbullying effects can persist long after harassment ends. Ongoing support may include therapy, peer support groups, digital literacy education, and gradual reintegration into online activities.

Working with Perpetrators

Effective anti-cyberbullying programs must address the needs of students who engage in harassment behavior. Research shows that many cyber-perpetrators are also victims of bullying and may use digital harassment as a way to gain power or control in situations where they feel powerless.

Understanding Motivations helps identify why students engage in cyberbullying behavior. Common motivations include seeking revenge for perceived wrongs, gaining social status or attention, responding to peer pressure, or coping with their own victimization experiences.

Accountability and Responsibility involves helping perpetrators understand the real impact of their actions on victims. This might include victim impact statements, community service requirements, or restorative justice processes that focus on repairing harm.

Skill Building and Intervention addresses underlying issues that contribute to bullying behavior. Students may need help with emotion regulation, social skills, empathy development, or conflict resolution techniques.

Ongoing Monitoring and Support recognizes that behavior change takes time and requires consistent support. Perpetrators need ongoing guidance to develop positive online behavior patterns and avoid relapsing into harassment.

Building Resilient Online Communities

The ultimate goal of anti-cyberbullying efforts is creating digital environments where harassment is rare and quickly addressed by community members who share responsibility for maintaining positive online spaces.

Resilient online communities share several characteristics: clear behavioral expectations that are consistently enforced, active bystander intervention when problems arise, celebration of positive behavior and inclusive attitudes, regular education about digital citizenship and online safety, and strong connections between online and offline community relationships.

Success requires ongoing effort from all community members—students, families, educators, and community partners—working together to create and maintain positive digital environments that support all young people's healthy development.

Building Stronger Defenses

Cyberbullying in the AI age requires updated understanding, tools, and responses that address both traditional harassment and emerging technological threats. The children who will thrive online are those who develop both technical skills and human wisdom—understanding how to protect themselves while maintaining empathy for others.

Effective responses require coordination between families, schools, technology companies, and communities working together to create digital environments that support rather than undermine young people's wellbeing. This collaborative approach offers hope for reducing cyberbullying while preserving the positive potential of online connection and community.

Action-Oriented Takeaways

- 26.5% of students experienced cyberbullying in the past 30 days, with LGBTQ+ students facing double the risk due to identity-based targeting
- AI-enhanced bullying includes deepfakes, voice cloning, and sophisticated impersonation that creates new forms of harassment impossible to combat with traditional approaches
- Bystander intervention training transforms passive observers into active upstanders who can reduce harassment through direct support, distraction, and reporting
- School response protocols require multi-disciplinary teams, comprehensive policies, and partnerships with law enforcement and mental health services
- Prevention through digital citizenship education proves more effective than reactive responses, building empathy and positive online community norms
- Supporting victims requires immediate safety planning, emotional validation, and long-term recovery services that address digital trauma's unique characteristics

Chapter 16: Digital Citizenship Curriculum That Works

Mrs. Rodriguez watches her fifth-grade students collaborate on a multimedia project about climate change, seamlessly sharing documents, fact-checking sources, and creating presentations that will be viewed by their global partner classroom in Kenya. These same students who arrived in September posting thoughtless comments and sharing unverified information have transformed into thoughtful digital citizens who understand their responsibility in online communities.

This transformation didn't happen by accident. Mrs. Rodriguez's school implemented a research-backed digital citizenship curriculum that now reaches students in 88,000 schools across the United States through Common Sense Media's K-12 Digital Citizenship program. The curriculum's success lies not in teaching students to fear technology, but in empowering them to use it wisely, ethically, and effectively.

Digital citizenship education has moved from optional computer class add-on to core curriculum requirement as educators recognize that preparing students for academic and professional success requires teaching them to navigate online environments responsibly. The most effective programs integrate digital citizenship across all subjects rather than treating it as separate technology instruction.

Common Sense Media Reaching 88,000 US Schools

The scale of Common Sense Media's digital citizenship adoption reflects both the urgent need for this education and the program's demonstrated effectiveness. According to Education Week, the curriculum reaches over 50 million students annually, making it one of the most widely implemented educational programs in American schools.

The program's rapid adoption occurred because it addresses real problems teachers face daily: students sharing inappropriate content, falling for misinformation, struggling with online conflicts, and lacking basic understanding of digital privacy and safety. Traditional computer literacy education focused on technical skills but ignored the social and ethical dimensions of technology use.

Common Sense Media's approach differs by treating digital citizenship as a social-emotional learning curriculum that happens to use technology rather than a technology curriculum that mentions social skills. Students learn empathy, critical thinking, and ethical decision-making through digital contexts that feel relevant to their daily lives.

The curriculum's research foundation distinguishes it from programs based primarily on adult fears about technology. Lessons are designed around actual student experiences and challenges rather than hypothetical scenarios, making the content immediately applicable to students' online lives.

Six Core Competencies with 77% Student Success Rate

Research measuring the effectiveness of Common Sense Media's digital citizenship curriculum found that 77% of students demonstrated improved digital citizenship behaviors after completing the program. This success rate reflects the curriculum's focus on six core competencies that address the most common challenges students face online.

Digital Literacy and Media Literacy teaches students to evaluate information critically, identify bias and misinformation, understand how search algorithms work, and recognize persuasive techniques in online content. Students learn to ask questions like "Who created this content and why?" and "What evidence supports these claims?"

Privacy and Security helps students understand what personal information to protect, how to create strong passwords and use privacy settings, why companies collect user data and how it's used, and how to recognize and avoid scams and identity theft attempts.

Digital Communication and Collaboration focuses on respectful online communication, appropriate audience awareness for different platforms, conflict resolution in digital environments, and effective teamwork using digital tools.

Digital Ethics and Empathy builds understanding of how online actions affect real people, recognition of and response to cyberbullying and hate speech, respect for intellectual property and copyright, and consideration of diverse perspectives in online discussions.

Digital Health and Wellness addresses balanced technology use, recognition of problematic usage patterns, understanding of how technology affects mood and relationships, and strategies for maintaining physical health during screen time.

Digital Rights and Responsibilities teaches students about their rights to privacy and free expression online, responsibilities as digital community members, understanding of laws related to online behavior, and advocacy for positive change in digital spaces.

ISTE Standards and Global Adoption

The International Society for Technology in Education (ISTE) standards provide the framework that allows digital citizenship curricula to be implemented consistently across different schools, districts, and countries. These standards ensure that students develop essential skills regardless of their specific technology tools or platforms.

ISTE's Digital Citizen standard requires students to "recognize the rights, responsibilities and opportunities of living, learning and working in an interconnected digital world." This standard is broken down into specific performance indicators that help teachers assess student progress and adjust instruction based on individual needs.

Global adoption of ISTE standards reflects the international recognition that digital citizenship education is essential for preparing students for modern life and work. Countries including Canada,

Australia, Singapore, and the United Kingdom have implemented digital citizenship curricula based on similar frameworks, creating international consistency in digital literacy education.

The standards-based approach allows for local adaptation while maintaining core learning objectives. Schools can modify examples, activities, and contexts to reflect their specific communities while ensuring that all students develop essential digital citizenship competencies.

Case Study 1: Elementary Success Story

Washington Elementary School implemented digital citizenship education in kindergarten through fifth grade after experiencing problems with students sharing inappropriate content and engaging in online conflicts that carried over into classroom relationships. Principal Maria Santos wanted proactive education rather than reactive discipline.

The school integrated digital citizenship lessons into existing subjects rather than creating separate technology classes. In language arts, students analyzed online articles for bias and credibility. In social studies, they explored how different cultures use technology. In science, they discussed ethical implications of technological innovations.

"Students went from thoughtlessly clicking and sharing to asking critical questions about everything they encountered online," observes third-grade teacher Jennifer Kim. "They started fact-checking information before sharing it, thinking about how their comments might affect others, and helping classmates make better digital choices."

The school saw significant improvements in student behavior both online and offline. Incidents of cyberbullying decreased by 60% over two years. Students became more thoughtful about their digital footprints and began helping younger students develop positive online habits.

Parent feedback was overwhelmingly positive as families noticed children making better choices about screen time, sharing more appropriate content, and demonstrating increased awareness of online safety. Students also began educating family members about digital citizenship concepts they learned at school.

Case Study 2: Middle School Transformation

Jefferson Middle School faced increasing problems with social media conflicts affecting classroom dynamics and student wellbeing. Administrators implemented a school-wide digital citizenship program that addressed both individual skills and community culture change.

The program included weekly advisory lessons, subject-area integration, peer leadership opportunities, and family education components. Eighth-grade students served as digital citizenship ambassadors, helping younger students learn concepts while reinforcing their own understanding through teaching.

"The peer leadership component was crucial," explains school counselor David Rodriguez. "Students trust advice from older peers more than adult lectures. Having eighth-graders teach digital citizenship created a positive culture where good online behavior became 'cool' rather than restrictive."

The school developed partnerships with local businesses and organizations to provide real-world contexts for digital citizenship learning. Students created social media campaigns for nonprofit organizations, learned about digital marketing ethics, and explored career opportunities that require strong digital citizenship skills.

Academic performance improved as students developed better research skills, learned to collaborate effectively using digital tools, and became more engaged in learning through technology-enhanced projects. The school's climate surveys showed significant improvements in student relationships and sense of community.

Case Study 3: High School Digital Leadership

Roosevelt High School created a comprehensive digital citizenship program that prepared students for college and career success while addressing immediate social media challenges affecting student relationships and mental health.

The program included required freshman seminars, elective courses for advanced study, student leadership opportunities, and community service projects focused on digital citizenship advocacy. Students could earn digital citizenship certification that counted toward graduation requirements.

Advanced students created educational content for younger learners, developed policies for appropriate technology use, and served as consultants for local elementary and middle schools implementing digital citizenship programs. These leadership opportunities helped students see digital citizenship as empowerment rather than restriction.

"Students became advocates for positive change rather than just following rules," notes technology coordinator Sarah Walsh. "They started conversations about healthy social media use, challenged misinformation in their communities, and created resources to help peers navigate online challenges."

The school's college counselors reported that students were better prepared for digital aspects of college life, including online learning platforms, research skills, and professional online presence development. Graduates frequently returned to share how digital citizenship skills supported their college and career success.

Age-Appropriate Progression from K-12

Effective digital citizenship education requires developmental progression that matches instruction to students' cognitive abilities, technology access, and real-world online experiences. The most successful programs build concepts gradually while reinforcing core principles at every level.

Elementary Grades (K-5): Foundation Building Students learn basic concepts of kindness and respect in online environments, simple privacy rules like not sharing personal information, how to identify trusted adults for help with online problems, and beginning critical thinking about information sources.

Activities include role-playing online scenarios, creating class agreements for technology use, practicing password creation and privacy settings on age-appropriate platforms, and learning to identify reliable websites and sources.

Middle Grades (6-8): Skill Development and Application Students develop deeper understanding of digital footprints and their permanence, advanced evaluation of information credibility and bias, conflict resolution strategies for online disagreements, and beginning understanding of legal and ethical issues online.

Activities include analyzing social media posts for digital citizenship principles, creating multimedia projects that demonstrate proper attribution and copyright respect, researching controversial topics using multiple sources, and developing school-wide technology use agreements.

High School (9-12): Leadership and Real-World Application Students engage in complex ethical reasoning about technology issues, develop professional online presence and networking skills, understand legal implications of online behavior, and take leadership roles in promoting digital citizenship.

Activities include internships with technology companies or digital rights organizations, creation of digital citizenship resources for younger students, policy research and advocacy projects, and preparation for college and career digital responsibilities.

Educator's Manual: Implementing Digital Citizenship Across Subjects

Successful digital citizenship education requires integration across all subject areas rather than relegating it to computer or technology classes. This approach helps students understand that digital citizenship principles apply to all learning and working situations, not just designated "technology time."

English Language Arts Integration Students analyze online texts for bias and credibility, research topics using digital sources with proper attribution, write for authentic online audiences with appropriate tone and style, and explore literature themes related to technology and society.

Digital citizenship concepts include evaluating source reliability, understanding author perspective and bias, practicing respectful online communication, and recognizing the power of words in digital environments.

Social Studies Integration Students research historical events using primary and secondary digital sources, explore how technology affects different cultures and societies, analyze political campaigns and propaganda techniques online, and study digital rights and freedoms globally.

Digital citizenship concepts include understanding diverse perspectives, recognizing bias in historical and contemporary sources, developing civic engagement skills for digital environments, and understanding rights and responsibilities in democratic societies.

Science Integration Students use digital tools for data collection and analysis, explore ethical implications of scientific and technological innovations, collaborate with global partners on environmental or health projects, and evaluate scientific information online.

Digital citizenship concepts include understanding scientific method and evidence evaluation, considering ethical implications of technological development, practicing collaboration and communication in scientific communities, and distinguishing between reliable and unreliable scientific information online.

Arts Integration Students create original digital content while respecting copyright and fair use, explore how technology affects artistic expression and distribution, study digital art forms and their cultural impact, and develop creative projects that promote positive digital citizenship.

Digital citizenship concepts include intellectual property respect, understanding creative commons and licensing, exploring technology's impact on artistic careers and distribution, and using creativity to promote positive social change.

Professional Development and Teacher Support

Effective digital citizenship implementation requires ongoing professional development that helps educators develop both technical skills and pedagogical approaches for teaching digital citizenship concepts across subjects.

Foundation Training Teachers need basic understanding of digital citizenship concepts and their importance for student success, familiarity with age-appropriate curriculum resources and lesson plans, skills for facilitating discussions about sensitive online topics, and strategies for addressing cyberbullying and other digital conflicts.

Advanced Professional Learning Experienced educators benefit from training in advanced digital citizenship topics like artificial intelligence ethics, emerging technology trends and their educational implications, research-based approaches to digital wellness, and leadership skills for school-wide implementation.

Ongoing Support Systems Successful programs provide regular opportunities for educator collaboration and sharing, access to updated resources as technology and student needs change, coaching and mentoring for teachers new to digital citizenship education, and connections to broader communities of practice.

Family Engagement Training Educators need skills for communicating with families about digital citizenship goals and

181

strategies, resources for helping parents support digital citizenship learning at home, and approaches for addressing parent concerns about technology use in education.

Assessment and Evaluation Strategies

Measuring student progress in digital citizenship requires assessment approaches that go beyond traditional testing to include performance-based evaluation, self-reflection, and real-world application of skills.

Formative Assessment Approaches Teachers use observation of student online behavior and digital collaboration, analysis of student-created digital content for digital citizenship principles, student self-reflection surveys and goal-setting activities, and peer evaluation of digital citizenship demonstrations.

Summative Assessment Options Programs may include portfolio development showcasing digital citizenship growth over time, capstone projects that demonstrate comprehensive digital citizenship skills, certification or badge systems that recognize specific competency achievement, and authentic assessments using real-world digital citizenship challenges.

Program Evaluation Methods Schools track incident reports related to technology misuse and cyberbullying, conduct surveys of student attitudes and behaviors related to digital citizenship, monitor academic performance and engagement in technology-enhanced learning, and collect feedback from teachers, students, and families about program effectiveness.

Addressing Implementation Challenges

Common challenges in digital citizenship implementation include limited teacher confidence with technology, resistance from families concerned about screen time, insufficient technology access for hands-on learning, and competing priorities for curriculum time and resources.

Building Teacher Confidence Professional development programs focus on pedagogical approaches rather than technical skills, provide scaffolded learning opportunities that build gradually, create collaborative learning communities where teachers support each other, and recognize that effective digital citizenship teaching requires wisdom more than technical expertise.

Engaging Skeptical Families Schools communicate clearly about digital citizenship goals and their importance for student success, provide opportunities for families to experience digital citizenship lessons firsthand, share research evidence about program effectiveness, and emphasize that digital citizenship education prepares students to use technology wisely rather than promoting excessive use.

Maximizing Limited Resources Creative implementation strategies include using free online resources and open educational materials, leveraging existing devices and platforms rather than requiring new technology purchases, partnering with community organizations and businesses for support and expertise, and focusing on concepts that can be taught without technology when devices aren't available.

Future Directions and Emerging Needs

Digital citizenship education must continue adapting to address emerging technologies and evolving student needs. Future programs will need to address artificial intelligence ethics and interaction, virtual and augmented reality social norms, privacy and security in internet-of-things environments, and global digital citizenship as online communities become increasingly international.

The most successful future programs will maintain focus on fundamental principles—empathy, critical thinking, ethical reasoning, and responsible behavior—while adapting specific applications to new technological contexts and challenges.

Looking Forward

Digital citizenship education has moved from experimental program to essential curriculum as educators recognize its role in preparing students for success in learning, working, and living in connected communities. The programs that thrive focus on empowering students to make positive contributions to digital society rather than simply avoiding problems.

Success requires sustained commitment from educators, families, and communities working together to create cultures that value and practice good digital citizenship. The students who receive this education will be better prepared to harness technology's benefits while avoiding its pitfalls throughout their lives.

Essential Points for Implementation

- Common Sense Media's digital citizenship curriculum reaches 88,000 US schools with 77% student success rates through focus on six core competencies
- ISTE standards provide global framework for consistent digital citizenship education across schools and countries
- Age-appropriate progression from K-12 builds concepts gradually while reinforcing core principles at every developmental level
- Cross-curricular integration proves more effective than standalone technology classes for developing real-world digital citizenship skills
- Professional development and ongoing support systems are essential for successful teacher implementation and program sustainability
- Assessment strategies must include performance-based evaluation and real-world application rather than traditional testing approaches

Chapter 17: Online Predators and Protection Strategies

Sixteen-year-old Emma thought she had found her first real boyfriend. "Jake" was understanding, supportive, and seemed to truly care about her feelings in ways that her high school classmates didn't. They met on Discord, talked for hours every day, and shared intimate details about their lives. Jake was patient about meeting in person, understanding about her busy schedule, and generous with gifts and attention. Emma felt special, valued, and loved—until the day "Jake" demanded she send explicit photos and threatened to share their private conversations with her family if she refused.

Emma had spent six months building a relationship with someone who didn't exist. The person behind the "Jake" profile was a 35-year-old man who had carefully studied her social media presence, identified her vulnerabilities, and crafted a false identity designed to exploit her need for connection and validation. Emma's experience represents the sophisticated reality of modern online predation—a threat that has grown both in scale and complexity as predators adapt their methods to emerging technologies and platforms.

Recent data from the National Center for Missing & Exploited Children (NCMEC) reveals a 192% increase in online enticement reports, indicating that more predators are using digital platforms to target children and that these efforts are becoming more aggressive and sophisticated.

The 192% Increase in Enticement Reports

The dramatic rise in online enticement reports reflects several converging factors that have made internet predation both more common and more dangerous. The COVID-19 pandemic accelerated children's online presence, providing predators with increased access to potential victims who were spending more time in digital spaces with less adult supervision.

NCMEC's data shows that reports increased from approximately 15,000 annual cases in 2019 to over 44,000 cases in 2024. This figure represents only reported incidents—experts estimate that the true scope of online predation attempts is significantly higher, as many children don't report encounters due to shame, fear, or manipulation by predators.

The increase isn't just quantitative but qualitative. Modern predators use more sophisticated techniques, leverage artificial intelligence for deception, operate across multiple platforms simultaneously, and employ psychological manipulation strategies that make their approaches harder for children to recognize and resist.

Thorn, an organization that combats child sexual exploitation, notes that predators have adapted their methods to match how children actually use technology. Rather than relying on random contact through chat rooms, modern predators research potential victims through social media, gaming platforms, and online communities to craft personalized approaches that seem natural and appealing.

Financial Sextortion: 36 Teen Suicides Since 2021

One of the most alarming developments in online predation is the rise of financial sextortion—schemes where criminals trick teenagers into sharing nude or sexual images, then demand money to prevent the content from being shared with family, friends, or posted publicly. According to research by MissingKids.org, these schemes have led to at least 36 teen suicides since 2021.

Financial sextortion typically follows a predictable pattern. Criminals target teenage boys through social media or gaming platforms, often using attractive fake profiles of young women. They initiate friendly conversations, quickly move to private messaging, and begin romantic or sexual conversations. They may share fake nude images to encourage reciprocation or use video calls with pre-recorded attractive women to create the illusion of live interaction.

Once victims share intimate images, criminals reveal their true intent and demand payment—typically $300-1,500—to prevent image distribution. They often provide "proof" of their threat by showing that they've gathered contact information for the victim's family and friends. The extortion continues even after initial payments, with demands increasing over time.

Dr. John Shehan, Vice President of the National Center for Missing & Exploited Children, explains the psychological manipulation: "These criminals are expert at identifying vulnerable teenagers and exploiting their natural curiosity about sexuality and romance. They create artificial intimacy quickly, then use shame and fear to maintain control. Many victims feel trapped because they believe their lives will be ruined if anyone sees the images."

The devastating impact of financial sextortion reflects both the social stigma surrounding teen sexuality and the developmental reality that adolescents often lack perspective about long-term consequences. Victims may feel that suicide is preferable to facing perceived judgment from family and peers, not understanding that the crisis is temporary and support is available.

Case Study 1: The Gaming Platform Grooming Operation

Thirteen-year-old Marcus enjoyed playing Minecraft with friends but began receiving friend requests from players who claimed to be teenagers interested in collaborating on building projects. One player, "Alex," seemed particularly skilled and offered to teach Marcus advanced building techniques in a private server.

Over several weeks, Alex gradually shifted conversations from gaming topics to personal subjects. Alex claimed to be a 15-year-old from a nearby state dealing with family problems similar to Marcus's parents' recent divorce. Alex provided emotional support and understanding that felt genuine and helpful to Marcus during a difficult time.

Alex introduced Marcus to other "friends" who joined their private gaming sessions, creating a community that felt special and exclusive. These relationships provided Marcus with social support he wasn't finding at school, where he struggled with social anxiety and academic pressure.

"Marcus was spending hours every day in these private gaming sessions," recalls his mother, Dr. Lisa Rodriguez. "He seemed happier and more confident, and we were grateful that he was making friends. We didn't realize that he wasn't talking to other teenagers but to adults who were carefully manipulating his emotions and trust."

The grooming operation became apparent when Alex began asking for personal information—Marcus's real name, school, address, and family details. Alex also started requesting photos, initially innocent pictures that gradually became more personal. When Marcus began feeling uncomfortable, Alex used emotional manipulation, claiming that Marcus was abandoning him during a crisis.

The situation was discovered when Marcus's younger sister accidentally saw inappropriate messages on his computer. Investigation revealed that "Alex" and several other "friends" were the same adult predator using multiple accounts to create an illusion of peer community while isolating Marcus from real-world relationships and support.

Case Study 2: The Social Media Romance Scam

Fifteen-year-old Ashley met "Connor" through Instagram after he liked several of her photos and sent a friendly direct message complimenting her artistic posts. Connor claimed to be a 17-year-old from a neighboring city who was interested in photography and shared many of Ashley's interests in music and social causes.

Connor's profile appeared authentic with hundreds of photos spanning several years, friends who commented regularly, and interests that aligned perfectly with Ashley's. He was patient about meeting in person, understanding about her parents' restrictions on dating, and supportive during stressful periods with school and family conflicts.

The relationship developed over four months through daily messaging, phone calls, and video chats. Connor seemed mature, thoughtful, and genuinely caring in ways that boys at Ashley's school weren't. He listened to her problems, offered advice, and made her feel valued and understood.

"Ashley was glowing with confidence and seemed to be maturing emotionally," observes her father, Michael Torres. "She was making better choices about other relationships and seemed more self-assured. We were happy that she had found such a positive influence, even though we were cautious about the online nature of the relationship."

The deception became apparent when Connor began requesting increasingly intimate photos and information. He used Ashley's trust and emotional attachment to pressure her into compliance, threatening to end the relationship if she didn't demonstrate her love and commitment through sharing private images.

Investigation revealed that "Connor" was actually a 42-year-old man who had stolen photos and information from a real teenager to create an elaborate false identity. He was simultaneously operating multiple fake relationships with teenage girls across several states, using similar emotional manipulation techniques with each victim.

Case Study 3: The Platform-Hopping Predator

Twelve-year-old David first encountered "Ethan" on Roblox, where Ethan offered to give David rare virtual items and teach him advanced game strategies. Ethan seemed knowledgeable about gaming and claimed to be a 14-year-old who had been playing for years.

Ethan gradually introduced David to other platforms, claiming they could communicate more easily through Discord, share gaming videos through YouTube, and stay connected through Snapchat. Each platform offered different features that made their relationship seem more legitimate and comprehensive.

On Discord, Ethan introduced David to a gaming community with other "teenagers" who welcomed David and made him feel part of an exclusive group. On YouTube, Ethan shared gaming tutorials that demonstrated expertise and seemed to support his claims about his age and interests. On Snapchat, Ethan shared photos that appeared to show a teenager's daily life.

"Ethan seemed to be everywhere David was online," explains David's mother, Dr. Sarah Kim. "It felt like David had found a real friend who shared his interests and was available whenever David needed support or wanted to play games. We were relieved that David was socializing, since he struggled with friendships at school."

The predatory behavior escalated when Ethan began asking David to keep their friendship secret from parents and teachers, claiming that adults wouldn't understand their special connection. Ethan also started requesting personal information and photos, initially for innocent reasons that gradually became more inappropriate.

Discovery occurred when David's school counselor noticed behavioral changes including secrecy about online activities, anxiety when devices were taken away, and declining academic performance. Investigation revealed that "Ethan" was an adult predator who operated across multiple platforms to create comprehensive false identities and maintain contact with victims even when they were blocked or restricted on individual platforms.

AI Impersonation and Sophisticated Grooming Tactics

Artificial intelligence has dramatically increased predators' ability to create convincing false identities and maintain deceptive relationships with children. AI-powered tools can generate realistic photos of non-existent people, create consistent false biographical information, and even simulate age-appropriate communication styles.

Deepfake Profile Creation allows predators to generate unlimited realistic photos showing the same non-existent person in different settings, ages, and activities. These images can be used to create comprehensive social media profiles that appear to have years of authentic history.

AI-Generated Communication helps predators maintain consistent false identities by generating age-appropriate slang, interests, and communication patterns. AI can help adults simulate teenage communication styles they wouldn't naturally use.

Predictive Targeting uses AI analysis of children's social media posts to identify vulnerabilities, interests, and emotional needs that predators can exploit. AI can help predators craft approaches that seem naturally appealing to specific children.

Multi-Platform Coordination employs AI to maintain consistent false identities across multiple platforms simultaneously, ensuring that children encounter "evidence" of predators' false claims regardless of which platform they use to verify information.

Emotional Manipulation Enhancement uses AI analysis of victims' responses to optimize emotional manipulation techniques. AI can help predators identify which approaches are most effective with specific children and adjust their strategies accordingly.

Platform-Specific Safety Education

Different online platforms present different risks and require platform-specific safety education that addresses how predators operate within each environment's unique features and community norms.

Gaming Platforms (Roblox, Minecraft, Fortnite) Predators often use in-game gifts, rare items, or advanced skills to attract children's attention and create feelings of special treatment and obligation. Children need education about not accepting gifts from strangers, being suspicious of players who seem overly generous or helpful, and understanding that gaming skill doesn't indicate trustworthiness.

Social Media Platforms (Instagram, TikTok, Snapchat) Predators research children's interests, friends, and activities through public posts, then use this information to create seemingly natural connections. Children need education about privacy settings, recognizing when someone knows too much about them, and being cautious about friend requests from people they don't know in real life.

Communication Platforms (Discord, WhatsApp, Telegram) Predators use these platforms' privacy features to move conversations away from monitored or public spaces into private chats where manipulation can occur without oversight. Children need education about keeping conversations in public spaces, being suspicious of requests to move to private communication, and sharing concerning interactions with trusted adults.

Live Streaming Platforms (Twitch, YouTube Live, TikTok Live) Predators may pose as admirers or supporters, offering gifts or opportunities in exchange for private contact information or personal meetings. Children need education about not sharing personal information during live streams, being suspicious of viewers who offer special opportunities, and understanding that online attention doesn't equal real friendship.

Crisis Response Guide for Emerging Threats

When families discover that their child has been targeted by an online predator, immediate and coordinated response is essential to protect the child, preserve evidence, and prevent further victimization.

Immediate Safety Steps:

1. Ensure the child's physical safety and emotional support
2. Preserve all evidence including screenshots, messages, and account information
3. Report to local law enforcement and NCMEC's CyberTipline
4. Contact platform providers to report accounts and preserve evidence

5. Consider temporary restrictions on the child's online activities if necessary for safety

Evidence Preservation Protocol:

- Take screenshots of all communications, profiles, and relevant content
- Document dates, times, and platforms where contact occurred
- Save any files, images, or videos received from the predator
- Record the predator's usernames, account information, and any personal details shared
- Preserve the child's device if it contains relevant evidence

Law Enforcement Coordination:

- Contact local police and FBI if the predator crossed state lines
- Provide comprehensive evidence packages to investigators
- Follow law enforcement guidance about continued contact with predators
- Understand that investigations may take time and require the child's cooperation
- Connect with victim services for ongoing support during the investigation process

Child Support and Recovery:

- Provide immediate emotional support and reassurance that the child isn't at fault
- Connect with mental health professionals experienced in online victimization
- Address the child's concerns about privacy, embarrassment, and social consequences
- Develop safety plans for the child's return to online activities
- Consider support groups for families dealing with online predation

Prevention Through Education and Awareness

Effective prevention requires ongoing education that helps children recognize grooming tactics, understand predatory behavior patterns, and feel comfortable seeking help when they encounter concerning situations online.

Age-Appropriate Predator Education: Elementary Ages (6-10): Teaching about appropriate vs. inappropriate adult interest in children, the concept that adults shouldn't ask children to keep secrets, and the importance of telling trusted adults about uncomfortable online experiences.

Middle School Ages (11-13): Understanding more sophisticated grooming tactics including gift-giving, emotional manipulation, and gradual boundary pushing. Learning to recognize when online relationships are moving too fast or becoming too intimate.

High School Ages (14-18): Comprehensive education about predatory psychology, financial sextortion schemes, AI-generated deception, and the legal and emotional consequences of predatory relationships.

Building Protective Factors:

- Strong relationships with trusted adults who children can approach with problems
- Healthy offline social connections that reduce reliance on online relationships for emotional support
- Critical thinking skills for evaluating online relationships and recognizing manipulation
- Understanding of privacy settings and safe online communication practices
- Knowledge of reporting mechanisms and support resources

Technology Industry Responsibility

Protecting children from online predators requires cooperation from technology companies, law enforcement, educators, and families working together to create safer online environments.

Platform Design Improvements:

- Enhanced age verification and identity confirmation systems
- AI-powered detection of grooming behavior patterns
- Improved reporting mechanisms that respond quickly to predator accounts
- Default privacy settings that protect children from unwanted contact
- Better integration with law enforcement for evidence preservation and investigation

Industry Collaboration:

- Information sharing about known predators across platforms
- Coordinated response to ban predators from all associated services
- Investment in research and development of predator detection technology
- Support for organizations working to combat online child exploitation
- Transparency about platform safety measures and their effectiveness

Building Community Resilience

Protecting children from online predators requires community-wide awareness and response capabilities that support both prevention and recovery from victimization.

Community Education Programs:

- Regular workshops for parents about online predator tactics and warning signs
- School programs that educate children about online safety without creating excessive fear
- Training for educators, coaches, and youth workers about recognizing signs of online victimization

- Community partnerships with law enforcement for education and response

Support System Development:

- Victim services specifically trained in online predation cases
- Support groups for families dealing with online victimization
- Resource networks connecting families with legal, mental health, and educational support
- Peer support programs that help children recover from predatory relationships

The fight against online predators requires sustained vigilance, ongoing education, and coordinated response from all adults responsible for children's safety. Success depends on creating cultures where children feel safe reporting concerning online interactions and where adults have the knowledge and resources to respond effectively.

Staying Vigilant

Online predators represent one of the most serious threats facing Generation Alpha, but they are not an inevitable aspect of digital life. Through education, prevention, and coordinated response, families and communities can significantly reduce both the likelihood of victimization and the impact when predatory contact occurs.

The children who are safest online are those who have strong offline relationships, understand predatory tactics, and feel comfortable seeking help from trusted adults. Building these protective factors requires ongoing effort but provides essential protection in an increasingly connected world.

Strategic Protection Principles

- NCMEC reports show a 192% increase in online enticement cases, with financial sextortion leading to 36 teen suicides since 2021

- Modern predators use AI for sophisticated identity creation, multi-platform coordination, and emotional manipulation enhancement
- Gaming, social media, and communication platforms each present unique risks requiring platform-specific safety education
- Crisis response requires immediate safety measures, evidence preservation, law enforcement coordination, and comprehensive child support
- Prevention through age-appropriate education and building protective factors proves more effective than reactive responses
- Community-wide awareness and coordinated response from families, schools, technology companies, and law enforcement are essential for child protection

Chapter 18: Privacy, Data, and Your Child's Digital Footprint

Eight-year-old Sophie loves taking selfies with fun filters and sharing videos of her dance routines on her family's social media accounts. Her parents think it's harmless—just cute moments shared with grandparents and close friends. They don't realize that these innocent posts are creating a detailed digital dossier about Sophie that includes biometric data, location information, behavioral patterns, and personal preferences that could follow her for the rest of her life.

By the time Sophie reaches high school, artificial intelligence systems will have analyzed thousands of her photos to track physical development, facial recognition databases will have catalogued her appearance across hundreds of posts, and data brokers will have compiled comprehensive profiles of her interests, relationships, and activities. College admissions officers, future employers, and even romantic partners may make decisions about Sophie based on data collected during her childhood—decisions she had no ability to influence or control.

Sophie's situation reflects a fundamental shift in how privacy affects children. Previous generations could expect that childhood mistakes and embarrassing moments would fade from memory and disappear from public awareness. Generation Alpha children are creating permanent digital records from birth, often without their knowledge or consent, that could affect their opportunities and relationships throughout their lives.

COPPA Updates 2025: Expanded Protections and Definitions

The Children's Online Privacy Protection Act (COPPA) underwent significant updates in 2025 that reflect both technological advances and growing awareness of children's privacy vulnerabilities. According to analysis by Goodwin law firm and other legal experts, the updated regulations expand protections far beyond the original 1998 framework.

The 2025 COPPA updates broaden the definition of "personal information" to include biometric data collected through facial recognition, voice prints from smart speakers and voice assistants, location tracking data from mobile devices and apps, behavioral profiles created through AI analysis of online activities, and inferences about children's characteristics, preferences, or future behavior based on data analysis.

These expansions reflect the reality that modern technology collects far more personal information than legislators anticipated when COPPA was originally drafted. Children using seemingly innocent apps or devices may unknowingly share data that reveals intimate details about their personalities, family relationships, health conditions, and future prospects.

The updated regulations also strengthen parental consent requirements by requiring explicit, specific consent for each type of data collection rather than general permission. Companies must provide clear explanations of how children's data will be used, stored, and shared in language that parents can easily understand. The regulations also expand parents' rights to access, correct, and delete their children's personal information.

Enforcement mechanisms were significantly strengthened with increased penalty amounts for violations—up to $50,000 per child affected by violations. The Federal Trade Commission gained expanded authority to investigate violations and implement corrective measures. State attorneys general can now bring enforcement actions for violations affecting children in their states.

State-Level Age Appropriate Design Codes

Individual states have implemented additional protections through Age Appropriate Design Codes that require technology companies to consider children's developmental needs and privacy rights when designing products and services. California's code, which serves as a model for other states, requires companies to configure privacy settings to provide the highest level of protection by default for users under 18.

The design codes require companies to conduct "child impact assessments" before launching products likely to be used by minors. These assessments must evaluate how products might affect children's physical and mental health, how data collection practices might harm children's privacy, and what measures can be implemented to minimize risks while preserving beneficial features.

Companies must also implement "age assurance" mechanisms to verify users' ages and apply appropriate protections. This might include using artificial intelligence to analyze behavior patterns, requiring identity verification for certain features, or implementing graduated permissions based on assessed user age.

The codes prohibit certain practices that are particularly harmful to children including using dark patterns to encourage data sharing or extended usage, collecting location data unless strictly necessary for service provision, using children's personal data for advertising or marketing purposes, and sharing children's data with third parties without explicit parental consent.

Teaching Permanence of Digital Actions

One of the most challenging concepts for Generation Alpha children to understand is the permanence of digital actions. Unlike previous generations who could expect that childhood mistakes would eventually be forgotten, today's children must learn that digital content can persist indefinitely and potentially affect their future opportunities.

Effective privacy education helps children understand that digital content can be copied, saved, and shared by others even after they delete the original. Screenshots can preserve embarrassing posts long after accounts are deactivated. Search engines may cache content that remains accessible even when original websites remove it.

Children need concrete examples of how permanent digital records affect real people. This might include stories of college applicants whose admission offers were rescinded due to social media posts, employees who lost jobs due to inappropriate online content, or relationships that ended due to digital discoveries about past behavior.

Age-appropriate privacy education progresses from simple concepts like "don't share personal information with strangers" in elementary years to sophisticated understanding of data collection, algorithmic profiling, and long-term reputation management in high school years.

Case Study 1: The Social Media Time Bomb

Sixteen-year-old Michael had been posting on social media since middle school, sharing typical teenage content including complaints about teachers, photos from parties, and jokes that seemed funny at the time but might appear offensive to adults. His parents monitored his accounts occasionally but focused on obvious safety concerns rather than long-term reputation implications.

Michael's digital footprint became problematic when he applied for a prestigious summer internship program. The selection committee found several posts that raised concerns about his judgment and maturity, including photos from parties where underage drinking appeared to be occurring and comments that could be interpreted as disrespectful toward authority figures.

"Michael was devastated when he didn't get the internship, especially after learning that his social media presence had influenced the decision," recalls his mother, Dr. Jennifer Walsh. "He had no idea that posts from years earlier would be evaluated by adults making decisions about his future. It was a harsh lesson about digital permanence."

The family worked with Michael to conduct a comprehensive audit of his digital footprint, removing problematic content where possible and creating more positive online content that better represented his character and accomplishments. They also developed strategies for future online behavior that considered long-term reputation implications.

Michael's experience prompted his family to implement regular digital footprint reviews for all their children and to discuss reputation management as an ongoing life skill rather than a one-time conversation about online safety.

Case Study 2: The Identity Theft Aftermath

Twelve-year-old Emma's parents had shared photos and information about her online since birth, creating a comprehensive digital record of her development, interests, and activities. They thought they were being careful by using privacy settings and sharing only with friends and family.

However, a data breach at a popular parenting app exposed personal information about thousands of children, including Emma's full name, birthdate, address, school, and detailed behavioral information collected through the app's development tracking features. This information was subsequently sold on dark web marketplaces.

Emma's identity was used to open credit accounts, apply for government benefits, and create fake social media profiles that were used to catfish other children. The family discovered the identity theft only when Emma's mother received collection notices for accounts Emma had supposedly opened.

"The identity theft nightmare lasted for over a year and required constant vigilance to prevent new fraudulent accounts," explains Emma's father, Michael Torres. "We never imagined that sharing innocent developmental milestones could lead to such serious consequences for Emma's financial future."

The family learned that children's identities are particularly valuable to criminals because the theft often goes undetected for years, allowing fraudulent accounts to age and become more valuable. They also discovered that many companies don't have procedures for handling identity theft involving minors.

Recovery required working with credit agencies, law enforcement, and legal advocates to clean up Emma's credit history and implement monitoring systems to detect future fraud attempts. The experience taught the family to be much more cautious about sharing children's personal information online.

Case Study 3: The AI Profiling Discovery

Fourteen-year-old Alex was rejected for a teen leadership program despite having strong qualifications and enthusiasm for the opportunity. The family later discovered that the selection process included analysis of applicants' "digital maturity" based on AI analysis of their online behavior and content.

The AI system had analyzed Alex's social media posts, online comments, gaming behavior, and even family members' social media content to create a "risk profile" that suggested Alex might not be a good fit for the leadership program. The analysis flagged Alex's interest in certain video games, friendship with peers who had posted controversial content, and family political affiliations.

"Alex was essentially rejected by an algorithm that made judgments about character based on data points that seemed completely unrelated to leadership potential," observes their mother, Dr. Sarah Kim. "It was terrifying to realize that AI systems were making decisions about our child's opportunities based on analysis we couldn't see or challenge."

The family challenged the decision and eventually learned that the AI system had incorrectly categorized several of Alex's activities and interests. However, they also discovered that many organizations were beginning to use similar AI analysis for selection processes without disclosing this practice to applicants or their families.

The experience led the family to research how AI systems analyze online behavior and to make strategic changes to Alex's digital presence to avoid similar problems in the future. They also became advocates for transparency in AI-based selection processes affecting children.

Building Positive Online Presence for Future Opportunities

While protecting privacy is essential, children also need guidance in creating positive digital footprints that can support their future goals and opportunities. This requires balancing privacy protection with strategic online presence development.

Academic and Professional Portfolio Development Students can create positive digital content that showcases their academic achievements, community service, creative projects, and leadership experiences. This might include blogs about academic interests, portfolios of creative work, documentation of volunteer activities, and participation in positive online communities.

Digital Leadership and Citizenship Young people can build reputations as thoughtful digital citizens by participating constructively in online discussions, creating educational content for peers, advocating for positive causes, and demonstrating ethical online behavior that serves as a model for others.

Professional Network Building Older students can begin building professional networks through platforms like LinkedIn, participation in industry-specific online communities, engagement with potential mentors and role models, and creation of content that demonstrates expertise in areas of interest.

Creative and Entrepreneurial Expression Students can use digital platforms to develop and share creative work, build audiences for artistic or entrepreneurial projects, collaborate with peers on innovative initiatives, and demonstrate skills that might not be apparent through traditional academic metrics.

Legal Primer: Understanding Your Child's Privacy Rights

Parents need basic legal literacy about their children's privacy rights and their own responsibilities as digital guardians to make informed decisions about data sharing and privacy protection.

Parental Rights and Responsibilities Parents have broad authority to make decisions about their children's data privacy, including controlling what personal information is shared online. However, they also have responsibilities to consider their children's future interests and to respect their developing autonomy as they mature.

As children age, their own privacy preferences should be increasingly considered in family decision-making about data sharing and online presence management. Teenagers may have legitimate reasons for wanting to control their own privacy settings and online content.

Children's Independent Privacy Rights While parents generally control privacy decisions for young children, teenagers have some independent privacy rights that vary by state and context. Children may be able to request removal of content they posted themselves, control their own privacy settings on platforms they use independently, and make decisions about sharing personal information with certain service providers.

Data Protection Under Federal Law COPPA provides baseline protections for children under 13, but teenagers have fewer specific privacy protections under federal law. The Family Educational Rights and Privacy Act (FERPA) protects educational records, and various state laws provide additional protections for minors' personal information.

Remedies for Privacy Violations Families have several options when children's privacy rights are violated, including filing complaints with the Federal Trade Commission for COPPA violations, contacting state attorneys general about violations of state privacy laws, pursuing legal action against companies that misuse children's data, and working with privacy advocacy organizations for support and resources.

Practical Privacy Protection Strategies

Protecting children's digital privacy requires ongoing attention and adaptation as technologies and threats change. Families need practical strategies that balance protection with allowing children to benefit from digital opportunities.

Information Sharing Guidelines Families should develop clear guidelines about what personal information can be shared online, including restrictions on full names, birth dates, addresses, school names, and specific location information. Photos should be carefully considered for what background information they might reveal about family routines, locations, and personal details.

Privacy Settings and Digital Hygiene Regular review and adjustment of privacy settings across all platforms and devices ensures that personal information remains as protected as possible. Children should learn to evaluate app permissions before installation and to understand what data different services collect and how it's used.

Digital Footprint Auditing Families should conduct regular reviews of children's digital footprints by searching for their names online, reviewing social media posts and interactions, checking what information appears in family members' posts that might affect children, and monitoring for signs of identity theft or unauthorized use of personal information.

Future-Focused Decision Making Privacy decisions should consider not just current risks but future implications of data sharing and online content creation. This includes thinking about how current posts might be viewed by future college admissions officers or employers, considering whether childhood interests and activities should be permanently associated with children's names, and evaluating what data collection practices might affect children's future autonomy and opportunities.

Technology Industry Accountability

Protecting children's privacy requires sustained pressure on technology companies to prioritize child welfare over profit maximization in their product design and data practices.

Advocacy and Consumer Pressure Families can support organizations advocating for stronger child privacy protections, choose products and services from companies with strong child privacy policies, and voice concerns directly to companies about problematic practices affecting children.

Policy and Regulatory Support Supporting legislators who prioritize child privacy protection, staying informed about proposed privacy regulations and their implications for children, and participating in public comment processes for new privacy rules helps advance systemic change.

Education and Awareness Sharing knowledge about privacy risks and protection strategies with other families, advocating for privacy education in schools, and supporting research into children's privacy needs and effective protection strategies contributes to broader cultural change around child privacy protection.

Preparing for an Uncertain Future

The privacy challenges facing Generation Alpha will continue changing as new technologies emerge and data collection practices become more sophisticated. Preparing children for this uncertain future requires building adaptable privacy awareness rather than focusing only on current threats.

Children need to understand fundamental privacy principles that apply regardless of specific technologies: the value of personal information and why it should be protected, how to evaluate privacy tradeoffs when using new services, the importance of reading and understanding privacy policies, and when to seek help with privacy decisions they're not prepared to make independently.

Securing Tomorrow's Privacy

Children's digital privacy represents one of the most complex challenges facing families, requiring both immediate protection strategies and long-term planning for an uncertain technological future. Success requires understanding legal protections, implementing practical privacy measures, and building children's own privacy awareness and decision-making skills.

The children who will thrive in the future are those who understand both the benefits and risks of digital participation, who can make informed decisions about privacy tradeoffs, and who have adults in their lives committed to protecting their interests while respecting their developing autonomy.

Privacy Protection Fundamentals

- COPPA updates in 2025 expand protections to include biometric data, voice prints, location tracking, and AI-generated behavioral profiles
- State-level Age Appropriate Design Codes require companies to provide highest privacy protection by default for users under 18
- Digital permanence education must help children understand that online actions can have lasting consequences for future opportunities
- Building positive digital presence requires balancing privacy protection with strategic creation of content that supports future goals
- Legal literacy about children's privacy rights helps families make informed decisions about data sharing and protection strategies
- Industry accountability through advocacy, consumer pressure, and policy support is essential for systemic privacy protection improvements

Chapter 19: Family Media Plans That Actually Work

The Martinez family sits around their kitchen table on a Sunday afternoon, laptops and phones scattered among them, working together to create what they hope will finally be a technology agreement that everyone can live with. Their previous attempts at "screen time rules" had devolved into daily battles, secret device usage, and family conflicts that made everyone miserable. This time, they're trying something different—a collaborative approach that treats technology as a family issue requiring everyone's input and commitment.

"What if we could use technology to bring us together instead of drive us apart?" asks 14-year-old Sofia, surprising her parents with her insight. Her question captures the shift that successful Family Media Plans represent—from viewing technology as a problem to be controlled to seeing it as a tool that can either support or undermine family goals depending on how it's integrated into daily life.

The American Academy of Pediatrics' updated Family Media Plan tool has moved away from rigid time limits toward collaborative approaches that consider each family's unique circumstances, values, and needs. Research published by Reach Out and Read and other organizations shows that families who develop media agreements together experience better compliance, fewer conflicts, and more positive technology relationships than those who rely on top-down rule enforcement.

AAP's Updated Family Media Plan Tool

The American Academy of Pediatrics revolutionized family technology guidance by replacing their controversial screen time limits with a collaborative Family Media Plan framework that recognizes the complexity of modern family life and technology integration. The updated tool shifts focus from controlling technology to using it intentionally in ways that support family wellbeing and individual development.

The new framework acknowledges that technology serves many legitimate functions in family life including education, communication with extended family, creative expression, and reasonable entertainment. Rather than treating all screen time as equivalent, the plan helps families distinguish between beneficial and problematic technology use while building skills for making these distinctions independently.

The collaborative approach proves more effective than authoritarian rule-setting because it engages children as partners in problem-solving rather than subjects of parental control. When children participate in creating family agreements, they develop ownership of the guidelines and better understanding of the reasoning behind technology boundaries.

The AAP tool provides templates and discussion guides that help families address key areas including device-free times and spaces, content quality standards, technology's role during family time, individual and shared technology goals, and procedures for addressing conflicts about technology use.

Collaborative Rule-Setting for Better Compliance

Research published in Manochikitsa and PubMed Central demonstrates that family technology agreements developed through collaborative processes show significantly higher compliance rates than rules imposed by parents alone. Children who participate in creating family media plans report feeling more respected, better understanding the reasoning behind guidelines, and greater motivation to follow agreements they helped design.

Collaborative rule-setting requires a fundamental shift in how families approach technology conflicts. Instead of parents dictating terms, families work together to identify problems, generate solutions, and design systems that work for everyone involved. This process takes more time initially but reduces ongoing conflicts and power struggles.

The collaborative approach begins with family discussions about technology's current role in daily life and its effects on individual and family wellbeing. Everyone shares observations about when technology feels helpful versus problematic, what activities or relationships might be suffering due to technology use, and what positive changes they'd like to see in family technology habits.

From these discussions, families develop shared goals that reflect everyone's input and priorities. These might include spending more quality time together, improving sleep routines, enhancing academic performance, or creating better balance between online and offline activities.

Case Study 1: The Collaborative Success Story

The Thompson family had struggled with technology conflicts for over a year before deciding to try a collaborative approach to their family media agreement. Parents Jennifer and Mark felt like they were constantly policing their three children's device usage, while the children—ages 8, 11, and 15—resented the restrictions and found ways to circumvent parental controls.

The family began by spending a week tracking everyone's technology use without judgment or restrictions, simply gathering data about current patterns. They discovered that technology problems weren't limited to the children—parents were also struggling with work-life boundaries and modeling behaviors they wanted to change.

"The tracking week was eye-opening for all of us," recalls Jennifer Thompson. "We realized that our technology use was affecting our family relationships in ways we hadn't recognized. The kids were more aware of technology's impact than we'd given them credit for, and they had good insights about solutions."

The family held three planning sessions where everyone contributed ideas for technology guidelines, family activities, and problem-solving strategies. The children suggested device-free meal times and family game nights, while parents proposed homework completion requirements before recreational screen time.

The final agreement included both boundaries and positive goals: device-free family dinner and one evening activity per week, homework completion before recreational screen time, no devices in bedrooms during sleep hours, weekly family discussions about technology experiences, and monthly reviews of the agreement with adjustments as needed.

Six months later, the family reported significantly fewer technology-related conflicts, improved communication about online experiences, and better balance between digital and analog activities. The children felt more respected in family decision-making, while parents felt more confident about technology's role in family life.

Case Study 2: Managing Multi-Device Households

The Chen family faced unique challenges managing technology across multiple devices and platforms used by parents Dr. Lisa Chen and Michael Chen and their children ages 7, 10, and 13. Each family member had smartphones, tablets, gaming devices, and access to shared computers, creating complexity that simple time limits couldn't address.

The family's initial approach of trying to monitor all devices individually proved overwhelming and ineffective. The children found ways to migrate between devices when one was restricted, and parents struggled to keep track of usage across platforms.

"We realized we were playing whack-a-mole with devices instead of addressing the underlying issues," explains Dr. Chen. "The children were following the letter of our rules while violating the spirit, and we were spending more time managing technology than enjoying family relationships."

The family redesigned their approach around principles rather than device-specific rules. They establishe

The family redesigned their approach around principles rather than device-specific rules. They established "zones and times" that applied regardless of which device was being used: mornings were device-free until everyone was ready for school, family time meant no individual devices for any family member, bedtime routines excluded all screens for everyone, and homework/work time limited devices to necessary functions only.

The family also implemented a "one screen rule" where family members could only use one type of device at a time, preventing the device-hopping that had made previous limits ineffective. They created shared charging stations outside bedrooms and established "device parking" areas during family meals and activities.

"The principles-based approach worked because it addressed our actual goals rather than trying to micromanage specific devices," notes Michael Chen. "The children understood that we wanted focused attention during family time and better sleep habits, which made more sense than arbitrary time limits on specific devices."

The family developed systems for self-monitoring where each person tracked their own technology use and reflected on whether it supported their personal and family goals. Monthly family meetings provided opportunities to discuss challenges and adjust strategies based on what was working well.

Case Study 3: Cultural Considerations in Implementation

The Rodriguez family needed to balance their traditional Mexican cultural values with their children's American social environment, creating unique challenges for their family media plan. Extended family members had strong opinions about technology use, while the children felt pressure to keep up with American peers' digital activities.

Parents Maria and Carlos Rodriguez valued family connection, respect for elders, and community engagement, but they also wanted their children to succeed in a digital world. They struggled to create technology guidelines that honored their cultural values while preparing their children for academic and social success.

"We had to figure out how to maintain our family's cultural identity while helping our children navigate American digital culture," explains Maria Rodriguez. "Our extended family thought we were too permissive with technology, while our children's friends thought our restrictions were too strict."

The family incorporated cultural values directly into their media plan by emphasizing technology use that supported family connections, community engagement, and cultural identity development. They prioritized video calls with extended family in Mexico, research projects about Mexican history and culture, and Spanish-language content that supported bilingual development.

The plan also included specific accommodations for cultural differences such as later dinner times to accommodate extended family video calls, flexibility during cultural holidays and celebrations, and respect for extended family opinions while maintaining parental authority over household decisions.

The children learned to explain their family's technology choices to peers and to find ways to maintain friendships while honoring family values. The family discovered that their cultural approach to technology actually provided advantages in terms of family cohesion and community connection.

Managing Multi-Device Households

Modern families often struggle with the complexity of managing technology across multiple devices, platforms, and family members.

Research published in Embracingjoy and other sources indicates that successful multi-device management requires systemic approaches rather than device-by-device restrictions.

Device Integration Strategies Effective families treat all devices as part of a connected ecosystem rather than separate entities requiring individual management. This might involve using parental control systems that work across multiple devices, establishing consistent rules that apply regardless of which device is being used, and creating family protocols for sharing devices and managing conflicts over device access.

Platform-Agnostic Guidelines Rather than creating different rules for each app or platform, successful families develop principles that apply across all digital activities. These might include guidelines about appropriate content regardless of platform, time boundaries that apply to total screen time rather than specific devices, and communication standards that govern all online interactions.

Family Technology Infrastructure Well-organized families create physical and digital infrastructure that supports their media plan goals. This includes centralized charging stations that prevent devices from migrating to bedrooms, shared family calendars that coordinate device-free times, and network-level controls that support family agreements about internet access.

Cultural Considerations in Digital Parenting

Research published in Taylor & Francis Online highlights the importance of considering cultural factors when developing family media plans. Different cultural backgrounds bring varying perspectives on authority, family relationships, technology adoption, and childhood development that affect how families approach digital parenting.

Individualistic vs. Collectivistic Approaches Families from individualistic cultures may emphasize personal choice and self-regulation in technology use, while families from collectivistic cultures may prioritize family harmony and community standards. Effective media plans accommodate these different value systems while addressing practical technology challenges.

Intergenerational Perspectives Extended family members may have strong opinions about technology use that conflict with parents' approaches or children's social needs. Successful families find ways to honor elder perspectives while maintaining practical family functioning in digital environments.

Language and Communication Patterns Multilingual families may need to consider how technology affects language development and cultural identity maintenance. Media plans might include specific provisions for native language content, communication with extended family, and balance between heritage culture and mainstream cultural participation.

Economic and Access Considerations Family economic circumstances affect device availability, internet access quality, and technology upgrade capabilities. Media plans should be realistic about family resources while ensuring that economic limitations don't prevent children from developing necessary digital skills.

Template Library: Customizable Family Agreements

Successful family media plans typically include several key components that can be adapted to different family circumstances and values:

Family Values and Goals Section This foundational element articulates why the family is creating a media plan and what they hope to achieve. It might include statements about family priorities, individual development goals, and how technology can support rather than undermine family values.

Device-Free Times and Spaces Most successful plans designate specific times and locations where devices are not used by any family members. Common examples include family meals, bedtime routines,

216

family meeting times, and specific rooms like bedrooms or dining areas.

Content Standards and Guidelines Families need shared understanding about appropriate content for different family members. This might include age-based content restrictions, guidelines for evaluating new apps or games, and procedures for addressing inappropriate content discoveries.

Communication and Conflict Resolution Plans should include procedures for discussing technology concerns, addressing violations of family agreements, and modifying rules based on changing circumstances or family needs.

Individual Accommodations Recognition that different family members may have different technology needs and capabilities, with specific accommodations for children with special needs, varying academic requirements, or different social circumstances.

Review and Revision Procedures Successful plans include regular opportunities to evaluate effectiveness and make adjustments based on family experience and changing needs.

Implementation Strategies That Work

Creating a family media plan is only the first step—successful implementation requires ongoing attention and adaptation based on family experience and changing circumstances.

Gradual Implementation Rather than implementing all aspects of a media plan simultaneously, many families find success with gradual rollout that allows everyone to adjust to changes without overwhelming the family system. This might involve implementing one new guideline per week or focusing on specific times of day before expanding to other periods.

Positive Reinforcement Successful implementation focuses more on celebrating successes than punishing violations. Families might acknowledge when family members demonstrate good digital citizenship, recognize improvements in family communication or relationships, and celebrate achieving family technology goals.

Flexibility and Adaptation Rigid adherence to initial agreements often leads to failure when circumstances change or when initial plans prove unrealistic. Successful families build flexibility into their agreements and regularly evaluate whether modifications are needed.

Modeling and Leadership Parents' own technology behavior significantly influences children's compliance with family agreements. Successful implementation requires parents to model the behavior they expect from children and to acknowledge when their own technology use needs adjustment.

Addressing Common Implementation Challenges

Even well-designed family media plans encounter predictable challenges that require specific strategies and ongoing problem-solving.

Resistance and Pushback Children may initially resist new guidelines, especially if they perceive them as restrictive compared to previous arrangements. Successful families address resistance through discussion rather than force, acknowledge children's concerns while maintaining family boundaries, and emphasize the collaborative nature of the agreement.

Inconsistent Enforcement Busy family schedules and competing priorities can lead to inconsistent implementation of media plans. Successful families build accountability systems that don't rely solely on parental monitoring, create environmental supports that make compliance easier, and focus on building habits rather than requiring constant decision-making.

Changing Circumstances Family circumstances change due to school schedules, work demands, health issues, or other factors that affect technology use patterns. Successful plans include procedures for temporary modifications and regular review processes that allow for permanent adjustments when needed.

Peer Pressure and Social Comparison Children may feel that their family's media plan puts them at social disadvantage compared to peers with different technology rules. Successful families help children understand and articulate their family's values, find ways to maintain friendships within family guidelines, and adjust plans when social isolation becomes a genuine concern.

Technology Tools That Support Family Plans

Various technology tools can support family media plan implementation by providing structure, monitoring, and communication features that reduce the burden of manual oversight.

Parental Control Software These tools can help implement time limits, content restrictions, and device access controls that support family agreements. However, they work best when used to support collaborative agreements rather than impose unwanted restrictions.

Family Scheduling and Communication Apps Shared calendars, communication platforms, and task management tools can help families coordinate device-free times, track individual and family goals, and maintain communication about technology experiences.

Screen Time Monitoring Tools Built-in screen time tracking features and third-party apps can provide objective data about technology use patterns, help family members understand their usage habits, and track progress toward family goals.

Educational and Wellness Apps Technology can also support family wellness goals through meditation apps, educational content, creative tools, and fitness applications that promote positive technology use.

Professional Support for Complex Situations

Some families benefit from professional guidance when developing or implementing family media plans, particularly when technology conflicts are severe or when family members have special needs that complicate technology management.

Family Counselors can help address underlying relationship issues that contribute to technology conflicts and facilitate productive family discussions about technology boundaries and goals.

Digital Wellness Coaches specialize in helping families develop healthy technology relationships through structured programs and ongoing support.

Educational Professionals can provide guidance about age-appropriate technology use and academic technology requirements that should be considered in family planning.

Mental Health Professionals can address individual mental health issues that affect technology use and provide specialized strategies for children with ADHD, anxiety, or other conditions that influence technology relationships.

Long-Term Success and Family Growth

The most successful family media plans view technology management as an ongoing aspect of family life rather than a problem to be solved once and forgotten. Families that thrive with technology over time develop several characteristics:

They maintain focus on family relationships and individual wellbeing rather than technology control for its own sake. They adapt their approaches as children mature and family circumstances change. They model healthy technology use rather than just setting rules for children. They celebrate positive technology experiences alongside managing potential problems.

Most importantly, they recognize that the goal isn't to eliminate technology but to ensure that it supports rather than undermines the family's deeper values and goals.

The Foundation for Digital Wisdom

Family media plans represent more than technology management—they provide frameworks for developing digital wisdom that will serve family members throughout their lives. The children who grow up in families with thoughtful, collaborative approaches to technology learn skills for intentional technology use, critical evaluation of digital experiences, and balance between online and offline activities.

These skills become increasingly important as technology continues advancing and children face new platforms, devices, and digital challenges throughout their development. The families who invest time in developing collaborative approaches to technology create foundations for lifelong healthy relationships with digital tools.

Key Elements for Family Success

- AAP's updated Family Media Plan tool emphasizes collaboration over control, leading to better compliance and fewer family conflicts
- Collaborative rule-setting engages children as partners in problem-solving rather than subjects of parental control
- Multi-device households require systemic approaches and principles-based guidelines rather than device-specific restrictions
- Cultural considerations including individualistic vs. collectivistic values significantly influence effective family media plan design
- Implementation requires gradual rollout, positive reinforcement, flexibility, and consistent parental modeling of desired behaviors
- Professional support helps families address complex technology conflicts and accommodate special needs within media planning

Chapter 20: The Professional's Toolkit

Dr. Sarah Martinez sits in her pediatric office, looking at her appointment schedule and noting how many of today's concerns relate to screen time, social media anxiety, gaming conflicts, and digital-age behavioral issues. Ten years ago, these topics rarely came up during well-child visits. Now they dominate parent concerns and require clinical responses that traditional medical training never addressed.

Dr. Martinez represents thousands of professionals across healthcare, education, and mental health who need new tools and approaches for addressing digital-age challenges affecting children and families. This professional convergence reflects the reality that technology's impact on child development crosses traditional disciplinary boundaries and requires coordinated responses from multiple professional perspectives.

The most effective interventions combine clinical expertise with digital literacy, traditional therapeutic approaches with technology-informed strategies, and individual treatment with family and community support systems. Professionals who succeed in this new environment learn to adapt their existing skills while developing new competencies specific to digital-age challenges.

For Pediatricians: Screening Protocols and Referral Pathways

Primary care pediatricians serve as the first line of detection for many digital-age mental health and developmental issues. However, traditional medical training provides limited preparation for assessing technology-related problems or distinguishing between normal digital behavior and concerning patterns requiring intervention.

Comprehensive Digital Health Screening Effective pediatric screening integrates technology-related questions into routine well-child visits rather than treating digital health as a separate issue. This includes asking about screen time patterns and their effects on sleep, mood, and family relationships; social media use and any experiences with cyberbullying or inappropriate content; gaming habits and signs of problematic usage patterns; and physical symptoms that might be related to excessive screen time including headaches, eye strain, neck pain, or sleep disruption.

The screening process should also assess positive aspects of technology use including educational applications, creative projects, social connections with distant family or friends, and assistive technology for children with special needs. This balanced approach helps identify both problems requiring intervention and strengths that can be built upon.

Age-Appropriate Assessment Tools Different developmental stages require different screening approaches. Preschool children need assessment of developmental milestones in the context of screen exposure, parent-child interaction patterns during technology use, and whether screen time is displacing essential activities like physical play or social interaction.

School-age children require evaluation of academic performance relationships to technology use, peer interaction patterns both online and offline, and emerging signs of anxiety or depression that might be technology-related.

Adolescents need assessment of social media's impact on self-esteem and body image, romantic relationship development in digital contexts, and risk-taking behaviors that might be facilitated by technology use.

Referral Pathways and Collaborative Care Pediatricians need clear protocols for when digital-age concerns require specialized intervention and established relationships with mental health professionals, educational specialists, and family counselors who understand technology-related issues.

Effective referral requires understanding which problems can be addressed through brief interventions in primary care versus those requiring specialized treatment. Mild screen time concerns might be addressed through family education and goal-setting, while significant gaming addiction or cyberbullying trauma requires mental health referral.

For Therapists: CBT Adaptations for Digital Issues

Mental health professionals need therapeutic approaches that address both traditional psychological issues and their digital manifestations. Cognitive Behavioral Therapy (CBT) provides an excellent framework for addressing digital-age mental health concerns but requires adaptation for technology-specific challenges.

Technology-Informed Assessment Therapeutic assessment must include detailed exploration of clients' digital lives including which platforms they use and how these affect their mood, thought patterns related to social media comparison and validation-seeking, and relationships between online experiences and offline functioning.

Therapists need to understand specific technologies their clients use rather than treating all "screen time" as equivalent. The therapeutic implications of creative gaming differ significantly from passive social media consumption, and treatment approaches should reflect these distinctions.

CBT Adaptations for Digital Anxiety Traditional CBT techniques can be modified to address technology-specific anxiety patterns. Thought challenging exercises can focus on social media comparison thoughts and FOMO-related catastrophizing. Behavioral experiments might involve gradually reducing social media checking or testing feared consequences of posting less frequently.

Exposure therapy can help clients who have developed anxiety about offline social situations due to over-reliance on digital communication. Gradual exposure to face-to-face social interaction helps rebuild confidence in non-digital social skills.

Mindfulness Integration Mindfulness practices prove particularly effective for digital-age issues by helping clients develop awareness of technology's effects on their mood, attention, and behavior. Mindful technology use exercises teach clients to notice urges to check devices without automatically acting on them.

Body awareness practices help clients recognize physical tension, eye strain, or fatigue associated with excessive screen time. Mindful transitions help clients shift attention between digital and offline activities more effectively.

Case Study 1: Pediatric Intervention Success

Dr. Jennifer Walsh, a pediatrician in suburban Chicago, noticed increasing numbers of families reporting sleep problems, academic decline, and family conflicts related to children's technology use. She implemented a systematic screening protocol that integrated digital health assessment into routine visits.

During eight-year-old Marcus's well-child visit, Dr. Walsh's screening revealed that he was spending 6-7 hours daily on devices, experiencing frequent headaches and neck pain, and having nightly battles with parents about bedtime screen time. His academic performance had declined over the past year.

"The screening helped me see patterns I hadn't connected before," explains Marcus's mother, Dr. Lisa Rodriguez. "We thought the headaches were vision problems, the academic issues were just a difficult teacher, and the bedtime battles were normal childhood resistance. Dr. Walsh helped us see how these were all connected to Marcus's screen time patterns."

Dr. Walsh provided the family with specific strategies for gradual screen time reduction, sleep hygiene improvements, and alternative activities for Marcus. She also referred them to a family counselor who specialized in technology-related issues for additional support with implementation.

Follow-up visits showed significant improvements in Marcus's physical symptoms, academic performance, and family relationships. The systematic approach helped address multiple related issues rather than treating symptoms separately.

Case Study 2: Therapeutic Innovation for Social Media Anxiety

Fifteen-year-old Emma sought therapy for increasing anxiety and depression that seemed to worsen during the school year. Traditional anxiety treatment approaches helped somewhat, but her therapist, Dr. Michael Torres, noticed that Emma's mood fluctuations correlated with her social media usage patterns.

Dr. Torres adapted CBT techniques to focus specifically on Emma's social media experiences. They identified thought patterns like "Everyone else is having more fun than me" and "I must not be likeable if my posts don't get many likes" that were triggered by specific online experiences.

"The therapy helped me realize how much my mood was being controlled by social media algorithms and other people's highlight reels," recalls Emma. "I learned to question the thoughts that Instagram triggered and to find other ways to feel good about myself that didn't depend on online validation."

Treatment included behavioral experiments where Emma tested her predictions about what would happen if she posted less frequently or didn't check her phone immediately when she received notifications. She discovered that her feared consequences rarely occurred and that reducing social media use actually improved her mood and relationships.

Emma also learned mindfulness techniques for noticing when social media was affecting her mood and strategies for using platforms more intentionally rather than compulsively. Her anxiety decreased significantly as she developed healthier relationships with technology.

Case Study 3: Educational Intervention for Gaming Issues

Twelve-year-old David's teacher, Mrs. Patricia Kim, noticed that his academic performance and social interactions had declined significantly over several months. He appeared tired and distracted during class, had difficulty concentrating on assignments, and seemed to have lost interest in activities he previously enjoyed.

Mrs. Kim implemented classroom strategies designed to address attention and engagement issues while also communicating with David's family about her observations. She discovered that David was gaming until 2-3 AM on school nights and had become isolated from previous friend groups.

"Mrs. Kim approached the situation with curiosity rather than judgment," explains David's father, Carlos Martinez. "She helped us see that David's classroom struggles were connected to his gaming habits and worked with us to develop strategies that supported him both at home and school."

Mrs. Kim modified David's classroom environment to include more movement breaks, hands-on learning activities, and opportunities for social interaction that helped him stay engaged despite fatigue from late-night gaming. She also coordinated with the school counselor to provide David with additional support.

The collaborative approach between home and school helped David gradually reduce his gaming time while building alternative sources of engagement and social connection. His academic performance improved as his sleep patterns normalized and his attention capabilities recovered.

For Educators: Classroom Management in the Digital Age

Teachers need new strategies for managing classrooms where students have varying relationships with technology and may struggle with attention, social skills, or emotional regulation related to their digital experiences outside school.

Attention and Engagement Strategies Students who spend significant time with fast-paced digital content may struggle with traditional classroom pacing and teaching methods. Effective strategies include incorporating movement and hands-on activities into lessons, using varied teaching modalities that match different learning preferences, and building in frequent opportunities for interaction and participation.

Teachers can also help students develop attention regulation skills through mindfulness exercises, explicit instruction in focus strategies, and gradual building of sustained attention capabilities through progressively longer activities.

Social Skills Support Students who spend significant time in digital social environments may need explicit instruction and practice in face-to-face social skills. This includes teaching nonverbal communication reading, conflict resolution in person rather than through text, and collaboration skills that don't rely on digital mediation.

Digital Citizenship Integration Rather than treating digital citizenship as separate curriculum, effective teachers integrate these concepts across all subjects. This helps students understand that digital citizenship principles apply to all learning and working situations.

For School Counselors: Crisis Intervention Strategies

School counselors increasingly encounter crises related to cyberbullying, online predation, social media harassment, and technology addiction. These situations require specialized response protocols that address both immediate safety and long-term recovery.

Crisis Assessment Protocols Counselors need frameworks for quickly assessing the severity of technology-related crises and determining appropriate response levels. This includes evaluating immediate safety concerns, identifying support systems and resources, and determining when situations require law enforcement involvement or specialized professional intervention.

Immediate Support Strategies Crisis intervention often requires helping students feel safe and supported while practical issues are addressed. This might include temporarily removing students from triggering online environments, connecting them with trusted adults and support systems, and providing coping strategies for managing acute stress and anxiety.

Long-Term Recovery Planning Recovery from technology-related crises often requires ongoing support that addresses both the immediate trauma and underlying vulnerabilities that made students susceptible to harmful online experiences. This includes therapeutic support for trauma recovery, skill building for healthier technology relationships, and environmental modifications that support continued safety and growth.

Evidence-Based Approaches and Outcome Measurement

Professional interventions for digital-age issues need to be grounded in research evidence and include systematic outcome measurement to ensure effectiveness and guide program improvements.

Assessment Tools and Metrics Professionals need valid and reliable tools for assessing technology-related problems and measuring intervention effectiveness. This includes standardized questionnaires about screen time, mood, and functioning; behavioral observation protocols for classroom and clinical settings; and objective measures like academic performance, sleep quality, and social relationship quality.

Research-Informed Practice Effective professionals stay current with research about technology's effects on child development and evidence-based interventions for digital-age issues. This includes understanding which interventions have research support versus those that are based primarily on clinical experience or theoretical approaches.

Collaborative Care Models The most effective interventions often involve collaboration among multiple professionals rather than isolated individual treatment. This includes coordinated care teams that include medical, mental health, and educational professionals; regular communication among providers to ensure consistent approaches; and family involvement in all aspects of assessment and intervention planning.

Professional Development and Training Needs

Healthcare, education, and mental health professionals need ongoing training to develop competencies for addressing digital-age challenges affecting children and families.

Core Competency Development All professionals working with children need basic literacy about technology's effects on development, assessment skills for identifying technology-related problems, and intervention strategies appropriate to their professional role and setting.

Specialized Training Programs Some professionals benefit from intensive training in specialized areas like gaming addiction treatment, cyberbullying intervention, or therapeutic use of technology. These programs provide in-depth knowledge and advanced skills for addressing complex technology-related issues.

Interdisciplinary Collaboration Skills Effective response to digital-age challenges often requires collaboration among professionals from different disciplines. Training programs should include communication skills, understanding of different professional perspectives, and protocols for coordinated care.

Building Effective Professional Networks

Professionals addressing digital-age issues benefit from networks that provide consultation, support, and ongoing learning opportunities. These networks help individual professionals stay current with rapidly changing technology trends and intervention approaches.

Professional Organizations and Communities Joining professional organizations focused on digital wellness, child development, or technology-related mental health provides access to resources, training, and consultation opportunities.

Local Collaborative Networks Building relationships with other professionals in the local community creates referral networks and consultation opportunities that benefit both professionals and the families they serve.

Research and Academic Partnerships Connecting with researchers and academic institutions provides access to cutting-edge knowledge and opportunities to contribute to the evidence base for digital-age interventions.

Future Directions and Emerging Needs

Professional practice for digital-age issues will continue evolving as technology advances and new challenges emerge. Effective professionals maintain flexibility and commitment to ongoing learning while focusing on fundamental principles of child development and family wellbeing.

Emerging Technology Challenges Professionals need to prepare for challenges related to artificial intelligence, virtual reality, and other emerging technologies that will affect children's development in new ways.

Prevention and Early Intervention Growing emphasis on prevention and early intervention requires professionals to develop skills for identifying risk factors and implementing preventive strategies before serious problems develop.

Cultural Competency and Equity Addressing digital-age issues effectively requires understanding how technology affects different communities and adapting interventions to be culturally responsive and accessible to diverse populations.

Professional Wisdom in Practice

The professionals who succeed in addressing digital-age challenges combine traditional clinical skills with new technology literacy, individual intervention capabilities with systems thinking, and evidence-based practice with creative adaptation to novel situations.

Success requires ongoing learning, collaboration with colleagues from different disciplines, and commitment to placing child and family wellbeing at the center of all intervention decisions. The children and families who benefit most from professional support are those who encounter professionals prepared to address both traditional developmental challenges and their digital-age manifestations.

Professional Implementation Essentials

- Pediatricians need integrated digital health screening protocols and clear referral pathways for technology-related concerns
- Mental health professionals require CBT adaptations that address social media anxiety, gaming issues, and digital-age thought patterns
- Educators need classroom management strategies for students with technology-related attention and social skill challenges
- School counselors require crisis intervention protocols for cyberbullying, online predation, and technology addiction situations
- Evidence-based practice demands valid assessment tools, research-informed interventions, and systematic outcome measurement
- Professional development must include interdisciplinary collaboration skills and ongoing education about emerging technology challenges

Chapter 21: Physical Health in the Digital Age

Fourteen-year-old Jason sits hunched over his gaming setup, neck craned forward at an unnatural angle, shoulders rounded inward, eyes fixed on the screen just eighteen inches from his face. He's been in this position for four hours straight, pausing only to grab snacks and use the bathroom. His mother notices him rubbing his neck and complaining of headaches, but she assumes it's just growing pains—until their pediatrician explains that Jason is developing "text neck" and chronic eye strain that could affect his physical development for years to come.

Jason represents millions of Generation Alpha children whose bodies are adapting to unprecedented amounts of screen time during crucial developmental years. Unlike previous generations who developed musculoskeletal systems through varied physical activities, these children spend formative hours in static positions that challenge their bodies in ways human physiology never anticipated.

The physical health consequences of digital-age childhood extend far beyond simple fatigue or occasional discomfort. Children are developing chronic pain conditions, vision problems, sleep disorders, and movement patterns that affect their long-term health and physical capabilities. Healthcare providers report seeing conditions in children that were previously observed only in adults with decades of desk work behind them.

Posture Problems and the Text Neck Epidemic

"Text neck" has become so common among Generation Alpha that physical therapists now consider it a normal part of pediatric practice rather than an unusual condition. The term describes the forward head posture and rounded shoulders that develop from looking down at devices for extended periods.

234

The human head weighs approximately 10-12 pounds when properly positioned over the spine. However, when the head tilts forward to look at a screen, the effective weight on the cervical spine increases dramatically. At a 15-degree forward tilt, the head effectively weighs 27 pounds. At 45 degrees—common when looking at smartphones—the spine bears the equivalent of 49 pounds.

Children's developing musculoskeletal systems are particularly vulnerable to these forces. Their bones, muscles, and ligaments are still forming and adapting to habitual positions and movements. Prolonged poor posture during these developmental years can lead to permanent structural changes that affect physical capabilities throughout life.

Dr. Erik Peper, a research scientist who studies technology's effects on posture, explains: "Children who spend hours daily in forward head posture are essentially training their bodies to maintain these positions. The muscles adapt, the spine adapts, and what starts as a temporary position becomes a permanent physical pattern."

The consequences extend beyond appearance. Poor posture affects breathing capacity, as rounded shoulders compress the chest cavity and reduce lung expansion. It can cause chronic neck and shoulder pain, headaches, and even affect mood and energy levels through its impact on circulation and nervous system function.

Vision Protection Beyond the 20-20-20 Rule

The 20-20-20 rule—looking at something 20 feet away for 20 seconds every 20 minutes—has become standard advice for reducing eye strain, but Generation Alpha children need more robust vision protection strategies given their intensive screen use patterns.

Digital eye strain affects up to 90% of people who use screens for more than three hours daily, and children often exceed this threshold significantly. Symptoms include dry eyes, blurred vision, headaches, neck and shoulder pain, and difficulty focusing. These symptoms occur because screens demand sustained focus at close distances while reducing natural blinking rates.

Children's eyes are particularly vulnerable because their visual systems are still developing. Extended close-up focus during childhood can contribute to the development of myopia (nearsightedness), which has increased dramatically among children in countries with high screen usage rates.

Enhanced Vision Protection Strategies

Beyond the basic 20-20-20 rule, children need comprehensive approaches to protect their developing vision. Screen positioning should place the top of the monitor at or slightly below eye level, with the screen 20-26 inches from the eyes for computer work and arms' length for mobile devices.

Lighting considerations include reducing glare through proper room lighting and screen positioning, using devices with adjustable brightness that matches surrounding light levels, and avoiding screen use in completely dark rooms which increases eye strain.

Blinking exercises become necessary because screen use reduces natural blinking rates from 15-20 blinks per minute to as few as 5 blinks per minute. Children need reminders to blink fully and frequently, and eye exercises that promote moisture distribution across the eye surface.

Case Study 1: The Gaming Posture Crisis

Twelve-year-old Marcus began experiencing severe neck pain and headaches that interfered with his sleep and school performance. His parents initially attributed the symptoms to stress from academic pressure, but a pediatric physical therapist identified significant postural problems related to his gaming setup.

Marcus spent 4-6 hours daily gaming on a computer placed on a desk designed for adult height. His chair didn't support proper posture, and his monitor was positioned too low, forcing him to crane his neck downward. Over months, he developed forward head posture, rounded shoulders, and tight chest muscles that pulled his upper body into an unhealthy position.

"Marcus looked like a completely different kid when he stood up straight," recalls his mother, Dr. Jennifer Walsh. "His shoulders were so rounded that he appeared to have a hunched back. The physical therapist said he had the posture of someone who'd worked at a desk for 20 years, not a child who should be developing strong, straight posture."

Treatment required both addressing the immediate physical problems and modifying Marcus's gaming environment. Physical therapy focused on stretching tight muscles, strengthening weak postural muscles, and teaching Marcus proper body awareness. Environmental changes included adjusting his desk and chair heights, repositioning his monitor, and implementing regular movement breaks.

Recovery took several months of consistent effort, but Marcus's pain resolved and his posture improved significantly. The family learned that preventing postural problems requires ongoing attention to ergonomics and movement, not just treating symptoms after they develop.

Case Study 2: The Vision Deterioration Story

Ten-year-old Emma had perfect vision during her kindergarten screening but began squinting and complaining of headaches by third grade. Her parents scheduled an eye exam expecting she might need glasses for a minor vision problem, but discovered she had developed significant myopia that required strong corrective lenses.

Emma's vision changes coincided with increased screen time for remote learning during the pandemic, followed by continued heavy device use for homework and entertainment. She often read on a tablet held close to her face and spent hours daily focusing on screens at close distances.

"Emma went from perfect vision to needing strong glasses in just two years," explains her father, Michael Torres. "The eye doctor said her myopia was progressing faster than normal and that extended close-up focus was likely contributing to the problem. We had no idea that screen time could affect vision development so dramatically."

Treatment included corrective lenses and strategies to slow myopia progression including increased outdoor time which helps regulate eye growth, regular distance vision activities like looking across playing fields or parks, and modified screen use with larger fonts and increased viewing distances.

The family implemented the 20-20-20 rule consistently and made environmental changes including better lighting for homework areas, larger external monitors for computer work, and regular vision breaks during extended study sessions.

Case Study 3: The Sleep Disruption Cascade

Eight-year-old David had been a good sleeper until he began using a tablet for educational games and videos. Over several months, his parents noticed he was taking longer to fall asleep, waking more frequently during the night, and seeming tired and irritable during the day.

David's sleep problems created a cascade of physical health issues including increased susceptibility to colds and infections, difficulty concentrating at school, and behavioral problems that hadn't existed previously. His pediatrician initially looked for medical causes but eventually connected the sleep disruption to his evening screen use.

"David's sleep problems seemed to come out of nowhere," recalls his mother, Dr. Sarah Kim. "We didn't connect them to his tablet use because he was using educational apps that seemed beneficial. We learned that even educational screen time can disrupt sleep if it happens too close to bedtime."

Blue light exposure from screens interferes with melatonin production, the hormone that regulates sleep cycles. Children's developing circadian rhythms are particularly sensitive to this disruption, and the effects can persist even after screen use ends.

Resolution required establishing a technology curfew two hours before bedtime, replacing evening screen time with quiet activities like reading or puzzles, and creating a consistent bedtime routine that supported natural sleep patterns. David's sleep quality improved within two weeks, and his daytime behavior and health returned to normal.

Sleep Hygiene and Managing Blue Light Exposure

Sleep disruption represents one of the most serious physical health consequences of excessive screen time, particularly for children whose developing brains require adequate rest for proper growth and function. Research from the Child Mind Institute and other organizations demonstrates clear connections between evening screen use and sleep quality problems.

Blue light exposure from screens suppresses melatonin production more effectively than other light wavelengths, essentially telling the brain to stay awake when it should be preparing for sleep. Children's eyes are more susceptible to blue light effects because their lenses filter less blue light than adult eyes.

Effective Sleep Hygiene Strategies

Creating technology curfews at least one hour before bedtime allows melatonin production to begin naturally. However, two hours proves more effective for children who have been experiencing sleep problems related to screen use.

Bedroom environment modifications include removing all screens from children's bedrooms, using blackout curtains to create darkness that supports natural sleep cycles, and maintaining cool temperatures that promote restful sleep.

Alternative evening activities help children wind down without screens. Reading physical books, gentle stretching or yoga, quiet music or audiobooks, and family conversation all support natural transitions to sleep without the stimulating effects of screen interaction.

Morning light exposure helps regulate circadian rhythms by providing natural cues about wake times. Children benefit from outdoor light exposure within an hour of waking, which helps establish healthy sleep-wake cycles that make evening sleep transitions easier.

Movement Integration and Active Gaming

The sedentary nature of most screen activities contributes to decreased physical activity levels that affect children's cardiovascular health, muscle development, and motor skill acquisition. However, some technology applications can actually promote movement and physical activity when used thoughtfully.

Active Gaming Applications

Motion-controlled games and virtual reality applications can provide genuine physical activity while maintaining the engaging aspects of gaming that children enjoy. Dance games, sports simulations, and adventure games that require physical movement offer alternatives to sedentary screen time.

However, active gaming works best as a supplement to rather than replacement for traditional physical activities. Children still need outdoor play, sports, and unstructured movement that develop different motor skills and provide social interaction opportunities.

Movement Break Integration

Regular movement breaks during extended screen sessions help counteract the physical effects of static positioning. Simple exercises like neck rolls, shoulder shrugs, spinal twists, and standing stretches can be performed between gaming sessions or homework periods.

Transition activities help children shift from sedentary screen time to active pursuits. Brief walks, jumping jacks, or dance breaks can serve as physical and mental transitions that prepare children for different types of activities.

Health Professional Guide for Addressing Physical Impacts

Healthcare providers need systematic approaches for assessing and addressing the physical health consequences of digital-age childhood. Many traditional pediatric assessments don't account for technology-related health problems, requiring expanded evaluation approaches.

Physical Assessment Protocols

Posture evaluation should include observation of standing and sitting positions, assessment of head and neck positioning, shoulder alignment evaluation, and range of motion testing for neck and shoulder movements.

Vision screening needs enhancement beyond standard acuity testing to include close-up focusing ability, eye movement coordination, evaluation of eye strain symptoms, and assessment of visual comfort during near work.

Sleep quality assessment includes questions about bedtime routines and screen use, evaluation of daytime fatigue and attention problems, and assessment of sleep duration and quality patterns.

Intervention Strategies for Healthcare Providers

Ergonomic education helps families create physical environments that support healthy posture and reduce strain during necessary screen use. This includes guidance about appropriate furniture, monitor positioning, and workspace setup.

Exercise prescription for children needs modification to address technology-related physical problems including specific exercises for postural muscles, eye exercises for visual health, and movement recommendations that counteract sedentary screen time.

Family education about recognizing early signs of technology-related physical problems helps prevent minor issues from becoming chronic conditions requiring extensive treatment.

Prevention Through Environmental Design

Creating physical environments that support healthy technology use proves more effective than trying to modify behavior within problematic setups. Environmental design considers both the immediate workspace and broader activity patterns.

Workspace Optimization

Proper furniture sizing ensures that children can use technology with good posture rather than adapting their bodies to inappropriate setups. This includes adjustable chairs that support feet flat on the floor, desks at appropriate heights for elbow positioning, and monitor stands that allow proper head and neck alignment.

Lighting design reduces eye strain through appropriate room lighting that matches screen brightness, positioning screens to avoid glare from windows or overhead lights, and providing task lighting for reading and homework that doesn't create harsh contrasts.

Activity Space Integration

Homes need designated areas for different types of activities including quiet spaces for reading and homework, active areas for movement and exercise, and technology zones that are separate from sleeping and eating areas.

Outdoor access and encouragement help children maintain connection to natural environments and activities that support physical development in ways that indoor screen time cannot provide.

Long-Term Physical Development Considerations

The physical habits children develop during their formative years often persist into adulthood, making childhood intervention efforts particularly important for long-term health outcomes. Children who learn healthy technology habits and physical awareness during development are more likely to maintain these patterns throughout their lives.

Motor Skill Development

Traditional childhood activities like climbing, running, jumping, and manipulating objects develop motor skills that extensive screen time cannot provide. Children need diverse physical experiences to develop full ranges of movement and coordination.

Strength and Endurance Building

Physical fitness during childhood establishes patterns and capabilities that affect adult health outcomes. Regular physical activity during development builds bone density, muscle strength, and cardiovascular capacity that provide health benefits throughout life.

Body Awareness and Self-Care

Children who learn to notice physical discomfort and respond appropriately develop self-care skills that help them maintain physical health independently. This includes recognizing when they need movement breaks, adjusting postures when experiencing discomfort, and seeking help for physical problems before they become severe.

Creating Sustainable Physical Health Habits

Long-term success requires building habits and environmental supports that make healthy choices easier than unhealthy ones. This involves both individual behavior change and family system modifications.

Habit Integration

Successful families build movement and postural awareness into daily routines rather than treating them as separate health requirements. This might include stretching during TV commercial breaks, taking family walks after dinner, or doing exercises together during technology breaks.

Environmental Cues

Physical environments can prompt healthy choices through visual reminders about posture, timers that signal movement breaks, and activity options that are easily accessible when children need alternatives to screen time.

Social Support

Family members who support each other's physical health goals through shared activities, gentle reminders about posture and movement, and celebration of healthy choices create cultures that maintain good habits over time.

Perspective on Physical Wellness

The physical health challenges facing Generation Alpha require proactive responses that address both immediate symptoms and long-term development patterns. Children who develop awareness of their physical needs and habits for maintaining health while using technology will be better prepared for lifelong wellness in an increasingly screen-based world.

Success requires collaboration between families, healthcare providers, educators, and technology designers to create environments and habits that support rather than undermine children's physical development. The goal isn't to eliminate technology but to ensure that its use enhances rather than compromises physical health and capabilities.

Health Maintenance Fundamentals

- Text neck and postural problems affect millions of children due to prolonged forward head positioning during screen use
- Vision protection requires strategies beyond the 20-20-20 rule including proper screen positioning, lighting optimization, and regular eye exercises
- Sleep hygiene demands technology curfews and blue light management to protect children's developing circadian rhythms

- Movement integration through active gaming and regular breaks helps counteract sedentary screen time effects
- Healthcare providers need enhanced assessment protocols and intervention strategies for technology-related physical health problems
- Environmental design and habit formation create sustainable approaches to maintaining physical health during necessary technology use

Chapter 22: Cultural Adaptation and Inclusive Digital Parenting

The Patel family gathers around their dinner table, three generations sharing a meal while navigating vastly different relationships with technology. Grandmother Priya expresses concern about her grandchildren's screen time, drawing on traditional Indian values about family connection and respect for elders. Parents Raj and Meera struggle to balance their heritage culture with American digital norms that their children encounter at school. Meanwhile, ten-year-old Arjun and twelve-year-old Kavya feel caught between their grandmother's expectations and their peers' digital activities.

This scene plays out in millions of households where cultural values, economic circumstances, and digital realities intersect in complex ways that traditional parenting advice doesn't address. Generation Alpha families represent unprecedented cultural diversity, with children growing up in households where multiple cultural frameworks, languages, and value systems shape their understanding of technology's appropriate role in daily life.

Research published in PubMed Central and Taylor & Francis Online reveals significant variations in how different cultural groups approach digital parenting, with implications for children's development that extend far beyond simple screen time considerations. Understanding these cultural dimensions proves essential for creating inclusive approaches to digital wellness that respect diverse values while protecting children's wellbeing.

Individualistic vs. Collectivistic Approaches to Digital Parenting

Cultural orientation toward individualism versus collectivism fundamentally shapes how families approach technology use, privacy, and digital development. These differences affect everything from social media policies to educational technology choices and require tailored approaches rather than one-size-fits-all solutions.

Individualistic Cultural Frameworks

Families from individualistic cultures typically emphasize personal choice, self-expression, and individual achievement in their approach to technology. Children may be encouraged to use technology for creative projects, personal exploration, and individual skill development. Privacy is often viewed as an individual right, with children gaining increasing control over their digital lives as they mature.

These families might prioritize technology that supports individual learning styles, allows for personal creative expression, and prepares children for independent decision-making about digital choices. Conflicts often center on balancing individual freedom with family values and safety concerns.

Collectivistic Cultural Frameworks

Families from collectivistic cultures often emphasize family harmony, respect for authority, and community connection in their technology approaches. Technology use might be viewed through the lens of how it affects family relationships, cultural identity maintenance, and community involvement.

These families may prioritize technology that supports family communication, cultural learning, and community connections. Privacy might be viewed as less important than family oversight and protection. Children may be expected to defer to parental and elder judgment about technology choices even as they mature.

The collectivistic approach might include shared family devices rather than individual ownership, family discussions about appropriate technology use, and emphasis on technology that brings families together rather than isolating individuals.

Case Study 1: The Multigenerational Technology Divide

The Kim family includes grandmother Hae-sook, who emigrated from South Korea fifty years ago, parents Min-jun and Soo-jin, who arrived as young adults, and their children Jennifer (16) and David (13), who were born in the United States. Each generation holds different perspectives on technology's appropriate role in family life.

Grandmother Hae-sook values face-to-face communication, family meals without distractions, and respect for elder wisdom. She views her grandchildren's device use as disrespectful and worries that technology is undermining traditional Korean values about family hierarchy and connection.

Parents Min-jun and Soo-jin appreciate technology's educational benefits and understand its necessity for their children's academic and social success in American culture. However, they also want to maintain Korean cultural values and language within their family.

Jennifer and David feel pressure to maintain Korean traditions while fitting in with American peer culture that revolves heavily around social media, gaming, and digital communication. They struggle to explain to their grandmother why technology is important for their social relationships and academic success.

"Every family dinner became a battle about phones and respect," recalls mother Soo-jin. "Grandmother felt disrespected when the children checked devices, but the children felt restricted compared to their friends. We needed to find ways to honor our Korean values while allowing the children to participate in American digital culture."

The family worked with a counselor familiar with Korean culture to develop technology agreements that respected all three generations' perspectives. They established device-free family meal times and implemented Korean language technology use that helped maintain cultural connections. The children taught their grandmother about their digital world while learning to appreciate her concerns about family connection.

Case Study 2: Economic Access and Digital Equity

The Rodriguez family includes parents Maria and Carlos, who work multiple jobs to support their three children in a low-income neighborhood where reliable internet access is expensive and devices are shared among family members. Their technology challenges differ significantly from families with greater economic resources.

Eight-year-old Sofia, ten-year-old Miguel, and thirteen-year-old Ana must share two older smartphones and one tablet among them for both educational and recreational purposes. The family's internet connection is often slow or unreliable, making online homework assignments difficult to complete.

The children feel embarrassed about their older devices and limited connectivity compared to classmates who have individual phones and unlimited data plans. They sometimes struggle to participate in class discussions about online content or digital projects that assume reliable technology access.

"The children's teachers assigned homework that required internet research and online submissions, but our internet would cut out when too many neighbors were online," explains mother Maria. "Sofia would cry because she couldn't watch the educational videos her teacher recommended, while Ana felt left out of social media conversations that her friends took for granted."

The family connected with community organizations that provided discounted internet access and refurbished devices for low-income families. They also worked with the children's schools to ensure that technology-based assignments had offline alternatives or could be completed using school resources.

The experience taught the family to advocate for digital equity in their community and helped the children develop empathy for others facing similar economic challenges with technology access.

Case Study 3: Religious Values and Technology Integration

The Ahmad family practices Islam and must navigate how their religious values intersect with their children's participation in American digital culture. Parents Fatima and Omar want their children to benefit from technology while maintaining Islamic principles about modesty, community, and spiritual development.

Fifteen-year-old Amina and twelve-year-old Hassan face conflicts between their family's religious expectations and peer pressure around social media use, gaming content, and online social activities. They struggle to explain to friends why they can't participate in certain online activities or view specific content.

The family's Islamic values emphasize modesty in self-presentation, which conflicts with social media cultures that encourage sharing personal photos and details. They also prioritize community and family time, which can conflict with individual gaming or social media activities.

"Amina wanted to join Instagram like her friends, but we were concerned about the focus on appearance and the potential for inappropriate interactions," explains father Omar. "We needed to find ways for her to connect with peers while maintaining our values about modesty and appropriate social interaction."

The family developed technology guidelines based on Islamic principles while allowing participation in digital culture. They focused on platforms and activities that aligned with their values while teaching the children to articulate their family's choices to peers. They also connected with other Muslim families to share strategies and create community support for raising children with religious values in a digital world.

Socioeconomic Factors in Digital Access and Parenting

Economic circumstances significantly affect families' ability to provide devices, internet access, and digital literacy support that children need for academic and social success. These differences create digital divides that affect children's opportunities and development in ways that extend far beyond simple technology access.

Resource Availability and Quality

Higher-income families can provide individual devices, unlimited internet access, and frequent technology updates that ensure children have optimal experiences with digital tools. They can also afford educational technology, learning apps, and enrichment opportunities that support academic development.

Lower-income families often must make difficult choices about technology spending, may share devices among multiple family members, and may have unreliable internet access that affects children's ability to complete homework or participate in online learning.

These resource differences affect not only children's academic performance but also their social connections, as peer relationships increasingly rely on digital communication and shared online experiences.

Digital Literacy Support Systems

Families with higher education levels and professional experience with technology often provide informal digital literacy education that supplements what children learn in school. Parents can help children evaluate online information, understand privacy settings, and navigate complex digital environments.

Families without these backgrounds may struggle to provide guidance about digital citizenship, online safety, and healthy technology use. Children may need to rely on school-based digital literacy education or learn through trial and error, which can leave them vulnerable to online risks.

Long-Term Opportunity Impacts

Digital divides during childhood can affect long-term educational and career opportunities as technology skills become increasingly important for academic and professional success. Children who lack access to quality technology experiences during their formative years may struggle to catch up later.

However, economic constraints can also foster creativity and resourcefulness as families find innovative ways to access technology and maximize limited resources. Some children develop strong problem-solving skills and appreciation for technology that serves them well in their future endeavors.

Language Considerations for Immigrant Families

Families navigating multiple languages face unique challenges in digital parenting as they balance heritage language maintenance with English-dominant digital environments. These decisions affect children's cultural identity development and family communication patterns.

Heritage Language Maintenance Through Technology

Technology can support heritage language development through access to content in native languages, communication with extended family in home countries, and participation in global communities that share cultural backgrounds.

However, children often prefer English-language content that aligns with peer interests and educational requirements. Families must find ways to encourage heritage language engagement without making it feel like a burden or restriction.

Digital Communication Across Generations

Technology can bridge communication gaps between generations when grandparents and other family members in home countries can maintain relationships through video calls, messaging, and photo sharing. These connections help children understand their cultural heritage and maintain family bonds.

However, technology can also highlight language barriers when children become more comfortable communicating in English while older family members prefer heritage languages. Families need strategies for ensuring that technology supports rather than undermines family communication.

Cultural Content Navigation

Parents must help children navigate between heritage culture content and mainstream American digital culture. This includes finding appropriate content in heritage languages while helping children understand cultural differences in online communication styles and social norms.

Children need support in developing cultural code-switching skills that allow them to communicate appropriately in different cultural contexts both online and offline.

Religious and Cultural Values in Technology Use

Faith communities and cultural groups often have specific values and guidelines about technology use that differ from mainstream American approaches. Families must find ways to honor these values while ensuring children can participate successfully in American educational and social environments.

Modesty and Self-Presentation

Many religious and cultural traditions emphasize modesty in self-presentation, which can conflict with social media cultures that encourage sharing personal photos and information. Families need strategies for teaching children to represent themselves online in ways that align with family values.

This might include guidelines about appropriate photo sharing, privacy settings that limit audience reach, and alternative ways to participate in peer social activities that don't require compromising family values.

Community and Individual Balance

Religious and cultural traditions often emphasize community connection and family loyalty over individual expression. Families may need to find technology approaches that support community values while allowing children to develop individual interests and capabilities.

Spiritual and Ethical Development

Faith-based families often prioritize spiritual development and ethical decision-making in ways that affect technology choices. They may seek educational content that aligns with their values and avoid entertainment that conflicts with their beliefs.

Children need support in understanding how their family's values apply to digital environments and in making technology choices that reflect their spiritual and ethical commitments.

Diversity Framework for Culturally Responsive Interventions

Professionals working with culturally diverse families need frameworks for providing digital parenting support that respects different cultural values while protecting children's wellbeing and development.

Cultural Assessment and Understanding

Effective interventions begin with understanding each family's specific cultural background, values, and goals rather than making assumptions based on ethnicity or religion. This includes learning about cultural attitudes toward authority, individual versus collective decision-making, and traditional approaches to child-rearing.

Professionals should also understand how families' immigration history, economic circumstances, and previous experiences with technology affect their current approaches and concerns.

Collaborative Goal Setting

Rather than imposing mainstream American approaches to digital parenting, effective interventions involve collaborating with families to identify goals that honor their cultural values while addressing safety and development concerns.

This might include finding technology approaches that support cultural identity maintenance, developing strategies that respect family authority structures, and identifying ways to participate in American digital culture without compromising core values.

Resource Development and Community Support

Culturally responsive interventions often require developing resources that don't exist in mainstream programs. This might include finding content in heritage languages, connecting families with others who share similar values, and adapting standard recommendations to fit different cultural frameworks.

Professional may also need to advocate for systemic changes that make programs and services more accessible to diverse families, including translation services, culturally appropriate examples, and staff who understand different cultural perspectives.

Building Inclusive Digital Communities

Creating digital environments that welcome and support culturally diverse families requires intentional effort from schools, community organizations, and technology companies to design programs and policies that work for all families rather than just the mainstream majority.

Educational Institution Adaptations

Schools need policies and programs that acknowledge diverse family approaches to technology while maintaining educational effectiveness. This might include providing multiple options for family communication, offering content in multiple languages, and training staff to understand different cultural perspectives on technology use.

Community Organization Support

Libraries, community centers, and faith-based organizations can provide crucial support for families navigating cultural and digital integration. These organizations often serve as bridges between traditional cultural values and contemporary American society.

Technology Industry Responsibility

Technology companies have opportunities to create products and services that serve diverse communities through inclusive design, multilingual content, and respect for different privacy and communication preferences.

Moving Forward with Cultural Wisdom

Digital parenting in culturally diverse families requires balancing respect for tradition with adaptation to contemporary realities. Families who succeed in this balance often find that technology can actually support cultural identity maintenance and community connection when used thoughtfully.

The goal isn't to eliminate cultural differences in favor of mainstream approaches but to help all families find ways to use technology that support their values while ensuring children's healthy development and social participation.

Success requires ongoing dialogue within families, support from communities that share similar values, and understanding from institutions that serve diverse populations. The children who benefit most are those whose families help them develop cultural confidence alongside digital literacy.

Building Bridges Through Understanding

Cultural diversity in digital parenting reflects the richness of American society and the complexity of raising children who must navigate multiple cultural worlds. Rather than viewing cultural differences as obstacles to overcome, we can see them as resources that enrich our understanding of healthy human development in technological contexts.

The families who thrive are those who view their cultural heritage as a source of strength and wisdom that informs their approach to technology rather than a burden that prevents them from participating in digital culture. This perspective benefits not only individual families but the broader community by demonstrating that there are many effective ways to raise healthy, capable children in our connected world.

Cultural Integration Principles

- Individualistic and collectivistic cultural orientations require different approaches to digital parenting that respect family values while ensuring children's development
- Economic factors significantly affect technology access and digital literacy support, creating divides that impact educational and social opportunities
- Language considerations for immigrant families include heritage language maintenance and cross-generational communication through technology
- Religious and cultural values around modesty, community, and spiritual development require specific strategies for navigating mainstream digital culture

- Professional interventions must include cultural assessment, collaborative goal-setting, and resource development that respects diverse family values
- Inclusive digital communities require intentional adaptation from schools, organizations, and technology companies to serve all families effectively

Chapter 23: Emerging Technologies and Tomorrow's Challenges

Eleven-year-old Maya puts on her virtual reality headset and instantly finds herself standing in ancient Rome, watching gladiators fight in the Colosseum while her teacher explains the historical context. Down the hall, her younger brother Alex speaks to an AI tutor that adapts its teaching style to his learning differences in real-time. Their parents watch this scene with a mixture of amazement and apprehension—technology that seemed like science fiction just a few years ago has become routine parts of their children's education.

Maya and Alex represent the first generation to grow up with truly immersive and intelligent technologies that blur the lines between digital and physical reality. These children will face challenges and opportunities that previous generations never encountered, requiring new forms of wisdom, protection, and preparation that we're only beginning to understand.

The pace of technological change continues accelerating, with quantum computing, brain-computer interfaces, advanced artificial intelligence, and immersive virtual environments moving from research laboratories into consumer applications faster than society can adapt. Generation Alpha children will live their entire adult lives surrounded by technologies that don't yet exist, making preparation more complex than simply learning current tools.

Quantum Computing and Child Data Security

Quantum computing represents both tremendous opportunity and unprecedented threat to the privacy and security of Generation Alpha children. These powerful systems can solve certain types of problems exponentially faster than traditional computers, including breaking many of the encryption methods currently used to protect personal information online.

Current encryption technologies that keep children's personal information secure—from school records to social media accounts—may become vulnerable to quantum computing attacks within the next 10-15 years. This timeline means that information collected about today's children could potentially be accessed and misused when they reach adulthood.

The implications prove particularly concerning for children whose entire lives are being documented digitally from birth. Photos, videos, location data, behavioral patterns, and even biometric information collected during childhood could become accessible to bad actors with quantum computing capabilities.

Quantum-Resistant Security Development

Researchers are developing "quantum-resistant" encryption methods that should remain secure even against quantum computing attacks. However, implementing these new security standards across all systems that store children's data represents a massive undertaking that may take years to complete.

Parents and educators need to understand that information shared about children today may not remain private indefinitely. This reality requires more thoughtful approaches to data sharing and documentation of children's lives than previous generations needed to consider.

Technology companies collecting data about children bear particular responsibility for implementing quantum-resistant security measures and being transparent about the long-term security implications of their data collection practices.

Brain-Computer Interfaces in Education

Brain-computer interfaces (BCIs) that can read neural signals and translate them into digital commands are moving from medical applications into educational and consumer markets. These technologies promise revolutionary approaches to learning and accessibility but also raise profound questions about mental privacy and cognitive development.

Educational BCIs could potentially read students' attention levels, emotional states, and comprehension in real-time, allowing for unprecedented personalization of learning experiences. Students with disabilities could control computers through thought alone, accessing educational opportunities that were previously impossible.

However, brain-computer interfaces also represent the ultimate invasion of mental privacy. If schools or companies can monitor children's thoughts and emotions directly, the potential for manipulation and control becomes enormously concerning.

Educational Applications and Implications

Early educational BCIs focus on detecting attention and engagement levels to help teachers understand when students are struggling or disengaged. These systems could help identify learning differences, attention problems, or emotional distress that might otherwise go unnoticed.

For children with severe disabilities, BCIs could provide communication and learning opportunities that dramatically improve their educational experiences and life outcomes. Students who cannot speak or use traditional input devices could potentially control computers through thought alone.

However, the technology also raises questions about cognitive autonomy and the right to mental privacy. Should schools be able to monitor students' brain states? What happens to neural data collected from children? How do we protect developing minds from technological manipulation?

Case Study 1: The VR Learning Revolution

Jefferson Elementary School implemented a comprehensive virtual reality curriculum that allows students to experience historical events, explore scientific concepts, and practice skills in simulated environments. Ten-year-old Sofia's class takes virtual field trips to ancient civilizations, manipulates molecular structures in chemistry, and practices public speaking in front of virtual audiences.

Sofia initially loved the immersive experiences and found learning more engaging than traditional textbook methods. However, her parents became concerned when she began preferring virtual experiences to real-world activities and seemed to have difficulty distinguishing between simulated and actual experiences.

"Sofia would talk about ancient Rome as if she had actually been there," recalls her mother, Dr. Elena Rodriguez. "She preferred virtual field trips to actual ones and seemed more comfortable in simulated social situations than real face-to-face interactions. We worried that the technology was affecting her connection to reality."

The school worked with families to balance VR learning with traditional experiences and help children understand the differences between virtual and physical reality. They implemented discussions about simulation versus reality and ensured that virtual experiences supplemented rather than replaced real-world learning.

Sofia's experience highlights both the potential and risks of immersive educational technology. While VR provided engaging learning experiences, it also required careful implementation to avoid disconnection from physical reality and real-world social skills.

Case Study 2: The AI Tutor Relationship

Twelve-year-old Marcus struggled with mathematics until his school introduced an AI tutoring system that adapted to his learning style and provided patient, individualized instruction. The AI tutor never became frustrated, provided immediate feedback, and celebrated his progress in ways that built his confidence.

Marcus developed a strong attachment to his AI tutor and began preferring its instruction to human teachers. He would spend hours working with the AI and seemed to form an emotional bond that his parents found concerning.

"Marcus talked about the AI tutor like it was a real person," explains his father, David Kim. "He would say things like 'Mr. AI believes in me' and seemed to prefer the computer's feedback to praise from human teachers or family members. We worried about him forming inappropriate emotional attachments to artificial intelligence."

The school implemented guidelines for healthy AI interaction that included regular reminders about the artificial nature of the tutoring system, balance between AI and human instruction, and discussions about the differences between human and artificial relationships.

Marcus's academic performance improved significantly through AI tutoring, but the experience taught his family about the need for boundaries around emotional attachments to artificial intelligence systems.

Case Study 3: The Quantum Privacy Awakening

The Chen family discovered that their children's school district had been collecting detailed behavioral data about students including location tracking, attention monitoring, and even emotional state analysis through various educational technologies. They learned that this information could potentially be vulnerable to quantum computing attacks in the future.

Eight-year-old Lily and ten-year-old James had been using educational apps, smart whiteboards, and monitoring systems that collected data about their learning patterns, social interactions, and even physiological responses during different activities.

"We realized that the school knew more about our children's daily habits and responses than we did," recalls mother Dr. Sarah Chen. "They had years of data about attention patterns, emotional reactions, and behavioral tendencies that could potentially be accessed by anyone with quantum computing capabilities in the future."

The family advocated for stronger data protection policies and transparency about what information was being collected about students. They also began making more thoughtful choices about which technologies to allow their children to use based on privacy and security considerations.

The experience taught them to consider long-term implications of data collection rather than just immediate benefits of educational technology.

The Metaverse Classroom: Opportunities and Risks

The metaverse—persistent virtual worlds where people can work, learn, and socialize through avatars—represents the next frontier in educational technology. Early metaverse classrooms allow students to collaborate on projects in virtual spaces, attend lectures in simulated environments, and practice skills through immersive experiences.

The educational potential includes global collaboration opportunities where students can work with peers from around the world, experiential learning that would be impossible in physical classrooms, and accessibility features that can accommodate diverse learning needs and physical capabilities.

However, metaverse education also presents significant risks including reality confusion as virtual experiences become more convincing, social development concerns as children spend increasing time in artificial social environments, and privacy violations as virtual worlds collect unprecedented amounts of behavioral data.

Safety and Development Considerations

Metaverse environments require new approaches to supervision and safety as traditional monitoring methods don't translate to virtual spaces. Children need guidance about appropriate behavior in virtual environments and protection from inappropriate content or interactions.

Identity development becomes complex when children can present themselves through avatars that may differ significantly from their physical appearance or personality. This freedom can be liberating but can also create confusion about authentic self-expression.

Social skills development requires careful attention as virtual interactions lack many of the nonverbal cues and emotional nuances that characterize real-world relationships. Children need opportunities to practice both virtual and physical social skills.

Preparing for Technologies Not Yet Invented

University of San Diego research suggests that 65% of today's elementary school students will work in jobs that don't currently exist, using technologies that haven't been invented yet. This reality requires preparing children with adaptable skills rather than specific technical knowledge.

Future-Ready Skill Development

Critical thinking and problem-solving abilities remain valuable regardless of technological changes. Children who can analyze information, evaluate sources, and solve complex problems will adapt successfully to new technologies.

Creativity and innovation become increasingly important as artificial intelligence handles routine tasks. Children need opportunities to develop original thinking, artistic expression, and creative problem-solving that machines cannot replicate.

Emotional intelligence and human connection skills become more valuable as technology handles more cognitive tasks. Children who can understand emotions, build relationships, and communicate effectively will have advantages in an automated world.

Ethical reasoning and moral development help children make good choices about emerging technologies and their applications.

Understanding right and wrong in technological contexts requires strong foundational values and decision-making skills.

Adaptability and Learning Skills

Meta-learning—learning how to learn—becomes essential when knowledge becomes obsolete quickly. Children need strategies for acquiring new skills, adapting to changes, and staying current with technological developments throughout their lives.

Comfort with uncertainty helps children navigate rapid change without becoming overwhelmed or resistant. They need confidence in their ability to figure out new challenges and adapt to unexpected circumstances.

Technology evaluation skills help children assess new tools and determine which ones support their goals versus those that might be manipulative or harmful. Critical evaluation of technology becomes a crucial life skill.

Innovation Watch: Tracking Emerging Digital Trends

Staying informed about emerging technologies helps families and professionals prepare for future challenges rather than simply reacting to them as they arise. However, this requires reliable sources and frameworks for evaluating the implications of new developments.

Reliable Information Sources

Academic research institutions often provide objective analysis of emerging technologies and their potential implications. University research centers, peer-reviewed journals, and academic conferences offer evidence-based perspectives.

Technology industry publications provide information about developments in commercial technology, though these sources may have promotional biases that need to be considered when evaluating claims about benefits and risks.

Child advocacy organizations often analyze emerging technologies from child welfare perspectives, providing valuable assessments of potential impacts on development, safety, and wellbeing.

Trend Evaluation Frameworks

Impact assessment considers how new technologies might affect children's development, learning, relationships, and wellbeing both positively and negatively.

Timeline analysis helps families understand when emerging technologies might become widely available and how quickly they need to prepare for new challenges.

Risk-benefit evaluation provides frameworks for weighing potential advantages against possible dangers, helping families make informed decisions about early adoption versus cautious waiting.

Building Technological Wisdom

The children who will thrive with future technologies are those who develop wisdom about when and how to use powerful tools rather than simply becoming proficient with current devices. This wisdom includes understanding human needs that technology should serve rather than replace.

Core Principles for Future Navigation

Human relationships remain central to wellbeing regardless of technological advances. Children need to understand that technology should enhance rather than replace meaningful human connections.

Physical reality provides experiences and grounding that virtual environments cannot replicate. Children need appreciation for nature, physical activity, and embodied experiences that keep them connected to the non-digital world.

Ethical decision-making becomes more important as technology becomes more powerful. Children need strong moral foundations and decision-making skills to navigate ethical dilemmas that emerge with new technologies.

Critical thinking and skepticism help children evaluate claims about new technologies and resist manipulation or exploitation through technological means.

Preparing for the Unimaginable

The most significant technological developments often surprise experts and emerge from unexpected directions. Rather than trying to predict specific future technologies, families can focus on building foundational capabilities that support adaptation to any technological environment.

Children who develop strong learning skills, ethical foundations, creative capabilities, and human relationship abilities will be prepared for technological futures we cannot currently imagine. These timeless human capabilities provide stability and direction in a rapidly changing technological world.

Technological Horizons

The emerging technologies that Generation Alpha will encounter throughout their lives promise both tremendous opportunities and significant challenges. Success requires building wisdom and adaptability rather than simply learning current tools.

The families and communities that best prepare children for this technological future are those who maintain focus on fundamental human development while thoughtfully integrating beneficial technologies. This balance requires ongoing attention, adaptation, and commitment to placing human flourishing at the center of technological choices.

Future-Ready Development Essentials

- Quantum computing threatens current encryption methods protecting children's data, requiring quantum-resistant security measures and more thoughtful data sharing approaches
- Brain-computer interfaces offer revolutionary educational possibilities but raise concerns about mental privacy and cognitive autonomy
- Metaverse classrooms provide immersive learning opportunities while creating risks around reality confusion and social development
- Preparing for unknown future technologies requires developing adaptable skills like critical thinking, creativity, and emotional intelligence
- Innovation tracking helps families anticipate and prepare for emerging challenges rather than simply reacting to technological changes
- Technological wisdom emphasizes human needs, ethical decision-making, and maintaining connections to physical reality alongside digital capabilities

Chapter 24: Policy, Advocacy, and Systemic Change

Dr. Patricia Martinez sits in the crowded school board meeting, watching parents argue about whether their district should ban social media access on school networks or implement comprehensive digital citizenship education. As a pediatrician and mother of three Generation Alpha children, she understands both sides of the debate—parents' fears about technology's risks and educators' recognition that children need guidance rather than prohibition.

Dr. Martinez represents thousands of professionals and parents who recognize that protecting Generation Alpha children requires more than individual family efforts. The challenges facing these children—from cyberbullying and online predation to addiction-designed algorithms and privacy violations—demand systemic responses that involve policy changes, advocacy efforts, and community-wide initiatives.

The current legislative and regulatory environment struggles to keep pace with technological developments that affect children. Laws written for previous technologies often prove inadequate for addressing artificial intelligence, social media manipulation, and emerging platforms that shape children's daily experiences. Effective protection requires coordinated advocacy that influences technology design, educational policies, and legal frameworks.

Current Legislative Landscape and Future Needs

The legal framework governing children's digital experiences consists of a patchwork of federal and state laws, industry self-regulation, and international agreements that often overlap, conflict, or leave significant gaps in protection. Understanding this complex environment helps advocates identify where efforts can be most effective.

270

Federal Legal Framework

The Children's Online Privacy Protection Act (COPPA) remains the primary federal law protecting children's online privacy, but its 1998 framework struggles to address contemporary technologies. The law applies only to children under 13 and focuses primarily on data collection rather than broader digital wellbeing concerns.

Recent updates to COPPA have expanded definitions of personal information and strengthened parental consent requirements, but many advocates argue that more fundamental reforms are needed to address artificial intelligence, algorithmic manipulation, and the complex ways that modern platforms affect children's development.

Section 230 of the Communications Decency Act provides broad immunity to internet platforms for content posted by users, making it difficult to hold companies accountable for harmful content that affects children. Reform efforts focus on creating exceptions for content that specifically targets or harms children.

The Family Educational Rights and Privacy Act (FERPA) governs how schools collect and share student information, but its framework predates the extensive data collection now common in educational technology. Many advocates call for updates that address learning analytics, behavioral monitoring, and artificial intelligence in educational settings.

State-Level Innovation and Variation

Individual states have begun implementing Age Appropriate Design Codes that require technology companies to consider children's developmental needs when designing products and services. California's code serves as a model that other states are adapting to their specific circumstances.

State privacy laws like the California Consumer Privacy Act include specific protections for minors that go beyond federal requirements. These laws create a complex compliance environment for technology companies but provide stronger protections for children in participating states.

Some states have implemented digital citizenship requirements in education standards, while others focus on cyberbullying prevention or screen time guidelines for schools. This variation creates inconsistency but also allows for experimentation with different approaches.

Advocating for Child-Centered Technology Design

Technology companies make design decisions that profoundly affect children's experiences, but current economic incentives often prioritize engagement and profit over child wellbeing. Advocacy efforts focus on changing these incentives through regulation, consumer pressure, and industry collaboration.

Design Ethics and Children's Rights

Child-centered design principles emphasize safety by default, age-appropriate interfaces, transparency about how systems work, and respect for children's developmental needs rather than simply compliance with minimum legal requirements.

Advocates push for technology companies to conduct child impact assessments before launching products, similar to environmental impact studies for construction projects. These assessments would evaluate how new technologies might affect children's physical, emotional, and social development.

The concept of "childhood by design" suggests that technology companies should build protections for children into their systems rather than adding them as afterthoughts. This includes default privacy settings, content filtering, and time management tools that work automatically rather than requiring parental configuration.

Economic Incentive Alignment

Current business models often reward technology companies for maximizing children's engagement time and data collection rather than supporting healthy development. Advocacy efforts focus on changing these incentives through regulation, taxation, or alternative business models.

Some proposals include restrictions on advertising to children, limits on data collection from minors, and requirements for companies to demonstrate that their products support rather than undermine child development. These changes would require companies to consider long-term child welfare alongside short-term profit.

Consumer advocacy helps parents understand how to use their purchasing power to support companies that prioritize child welfare and avoid those that exploit children for profit. Coordinated consumer action can influence company behavior more effectively than individual choices alone.

Case Study 1: The School District Privacy Victory

The Jefferson County School District faced mounting parent concerns about student privacy when they discovered that educational technology vendors were collecting detailed information about children's learning patterns, behavior, and even emotional responses without clear parental consent or data protection measures.

Parent advocate Maria Santos led a campaign to investigate the district's technology contracts and demand stronger privacy protections for students. The effort revealed that multiple vendors were collecting personal information about children that could be shared with third parties for marketing purposes.

"We found that companies knew more about our children's daily habits and learning struggles than we did as parents," recalls Santos. "They were tracking everything from how long children spent on different problems to their emotional reactions during tests, and we had no idea this information was being collected or how it might be used."

The parent campaign resulted in the district implementing comprehensive privacy audits of all educational technology, requiring vendors to meet strict data protection standards, and providing parents with detailed information about what data was being collected about their children.

The success in Jefferson County inspired similar efforts in other districts and contributed to state-level legislation requiring transparency about educational data collection and stronger parental consent requirements.

Case Study 2: The Social Media Age Verification Campaign

A coalition of parents, child development experts, and privacy advocates launched a campaign to require social media companies to implement effective age verification systems that prevent children under 13 from creating accounts on platforms not designed for their developmental stage.

The campaign, led by child psychologist Dr. Jennifer Walsh, documented how current age verification systems rely on self-reporting that children can easily circumvent. They presented evidence that many platforms were knowingly serving children under 13 despite legal prohibitions.

"We found children as young as 8 years old with active social media accounts on platforms designed for teenagers and adults," explains Dr. Walsh. "The companies' age verification consisted of asking users to click a box claiming they were over 13, which any child could do. Real age verification would require more robust systems."

The advocacy effort resulted in congressional hearings about social media age verification, federal investigations into companies' compliance with COPPA requirements, and proposed legislation requiring technology companies to implement effective age verification systems.

The campaign also influenced some companies to voluntarily improve their age verification processes and develop child-specific versions of their platforms with appropriate safety features.

Case Study 3: The Digital Wellness Education Mandate

Concerned about rising rates of anxiety, depression, and social media-related problems among students, parent advocate David Torres led an effort to require digital wellness education in his state's curriculum standards.

Torres organized parents, educators, and mental health professionals to demonstrate the need for systematic digital citizenship education that went beyond basic technology skills to address online safety, healthy technology use, and digital ethics.

"Our children were getting devices and social media accounts without any education about how to use them safely or healthily," explains Torres. "We were teaching them to drive cars safely but sending them into the digital world without any guidance about navigation or protection."

The advocacy campaign resulted in legislation requiring digital citizenship education at all grade levels, training for teachers to implement these programs effectively, and funding for districts to develop or purchase evidence-based digital wellness curricula.

The success led to similar legislation in other states and influenced national education organizations to develop standards and resources for digital wellness education.

School Board Engagement and Policy Influence

Local school boards make decisions about educational technology, social media policies, and digital citizenship education that directly affect children's daily experiences. Engaging effectively with school boards requires understanding their priorities, constraints, and decision-making processes.

Understanding School Board Dynamics

School boards balance multiple priorities including academic achievement, budget constraints, safety concerns, and community expectations. Effective advocacy frames digital wellness concerns in terms of these existing priorities rather than asking boards to add new responsibilities.

Budget realities affect school board decisions about technology purchases, staff training, and program implementation. Advocates who understand funding sources and budget cycles can time their proposals for maximum effectiveness and offer realistic implementation strategies.

Community politics influence school board decisions as board members respond to vocal parent groups, community organizations, and political pressures. Advocates need broad community support and must address concerns from different perspectives to build consensus around digital wellness initiatives.

Effective Advocacy Strategies

Research-based proposals carry more weight with school boards than emotional appeals alone. Advocates should present evidence about problems, proven solutions, and expected outcomes to support their recommendations.

Coalition building brings together parents, educators, students, and community members around shared goals. Broad coalitions demonstrate community support and provide diverse perspectives that strengthen proposals.

Practical implementation plans help school boards understand how proposed changes would actually work within existing systems and budgets. Advocates should offer specific steps, timelines, and resources rather than general recommendations.

Building Community Coalitions for Digital Wellness

Protecting Generation Alpha children requires coordination among families, schools, healthcare providers, community organizations, and local governments. Effective coalitions bring together diverse stakeholders around shared goals while respecting different perspectives and priorities.

Stakeholder Identification and Engagement

Parents provide personal experiences and emotional motivation for addressing digital wellness concerns. They often serve as effective advocates because school boards and elected officials recognize their legitimate stake in children's wellbeing.

Educators bring professional expertise about child development and practical experience with technology in learning environments. They can provide crucial insights about what works in real classrooms and what barriers exist to implementing new approaches.

Healthcare providers offer medical perspectives on digital wellness and can document the health consequences of problematic technology use. Their professional credibility adds weight to advocacy efforts.

Community organizations including libraries, youth programs, and faith-based groups often have existing relationships with families and can provide platforms for education and advocacy efforts.

Local businesses may support digital wellness initiatives as part of community responsibility efforts or because they need future employees with healthy technology skills.

Coalition Development and Maintenance

Shared goal identification helps diverse stakeholders find common ground despite different perspectives on specific solutions. Successful coalitions focus on broad outcomes like child safety and wellbeing rather than specific technology policies.

Role clarification ensures that different coalition members contribute their unique strengths rather than duplicating efforts or creating conflicts. Parents might focus on community organizing while professionals provide expertise and credibility.

Communication systems keep coalition members informed about ongoing efforts and coordinate advocacy activities. Regular meetings, shared communication platforms, and clear leadership structures support effective collaboration.

Advocacy Toolkit for Making Your Voice Heard

Effective advocacy requires strategic thinking, persistence, and skill in communicating with different audiences. Successful advocates develop expertise in research, communication, and political processes that influence policy decisions.

Research and Preparation

Issue research involves understanding current laws, policies, and practices that affect children's digital experiences. Advocates need to identify specific problems, potential solutions, and examples of successful approaches in other communities.

Stakeholder analysis helps advocates understand who makes relevant decisions, what motivates these decision-makers, and how to frame messages for maximum impact with different audiences.

Evidence gathering includes collecting data about local problems, examples of successful solutions, and expert opinions that support proposed changes. Personal stories and professional research both contribute to compelling advocacy cases.

Communication Strategies

Message development requires crafting clear, compelling explanations of problems and solutions that resonate with specific audiences. Messages for parents emphasize child safety and wellbeing, while messages for policymakers focus on legal compliance and risk management.

Public speaking skills help advocates present their cases effectively in school board meetings, legislative hearings, and community forums. Practice and preparation improve advocates' ability to communicate persuasively under pressure.

Media engagement can amplify advocacy messages through news coverage, opinion pieces, and social media campaigns. Effective media strategies require understanding how different outlets work and what types of stories they find compelling.

Political and Policy Processes

Legislative process understanding helps advocates identify opportunities to influence policy development, amendment processes, and implementation decisions. Different types of policy changes require different advocacy strategies and timelines.

Relationship building with elected officials, school board members, and agency staff creates ongoing opportunities for influence beyond specific campaigns. Long-term relationships often prove more effective than one-time advocacy efforts.

Coalition coordination involves working with other advocacy groups to maximize impact and avoid duplicating efforts. Successful advocates build networks that can mobilize quickly around emerging opportunities or threats.

Technology Industry Accountability

Holding technology companies accountable for their impacts on children requires coordinated pressure from multiple sources including government regulation, consumer action, and industry self-regulation initiatives.

Regulatory Pressure and Compliance

Government agencies including the Federal Trade Commission, Department of Education, and state attorneys general have authority to investigate and penalize companies that violate children's privacy or safety laws. Advocacy efforts can prompt enforcement actions and policy updates.

International coordination becomes increasingly important as technology companies operate globally and children's experiences cross national boundaries. Advocacy efforts that align with international child rights frameworks can influence company behavior more effectively than purely domestic initiatives.

Consumer and Market Pressure

Organized consumer action through boycotts, petition campaigns, and coordinated purchasing decisions can influence company behavior when backed by significant numbers of concerned families.

Investor engagement involves encouraging institutional investors like pension funds and university endowments to consider children's welfare when making investment decisions about technology companies.

Industry Collaboration and Standards

Professional organizations for technology workers can promote ethical standards and practices that prioritize child welfare in product development and business decision-making.

Industry collaborative initiatives bring together companies, advocacy groups, and experts to develop voluntary standards and best practices that go beyond minimum legal requirements.

Long-Term Vision for Systemic Change

Creating a technology environment that truly supports Generation Alpha children's healthy development requires sustained effort over many years. Effective advocacy maintains focus on long-term goals while achieving incremental progress through specific campaigns and initiatives.

Infrastructure Development

Policy infrastructure includes laws, regulations, and enforcement mechanisms that protect children's digital rights and promote their wellbeing. Building this infrastructure requires ongoing advocacy, legislative monitoring, and enforcement oversight.

Educational infrastructure encompasses teacher training, curriculum development, and resource creation that supports digital wellness education in schools. This infrastructure requires sustained investment and continuous updating as technology changes.

Community infrastructure includes organizations, networks, and resources that support families in raising children safely in digital environments. Strong community infrastructure provides ongoing support beyond specific advocacy campaigns.

Cultural Change

Shifting social norms around children and technology requires broad cultural change that influences how families, schools, and communities approach digital wellness. This change happens through education, advocacy, and modeling of positive practices.

Professional development for those working with children ensures that educators, healthcare providers, and youth workers have the knowledge and skills needed to address digital-age challenges effectively.

Public awareness campaigns help communities understand both the risks and opportunities associated with children's technology use, promoting informed decision-making rather than fear-based reactions.

Policy Impact and Community Change

The advocacy efforts that protect Generation Alpha children most effectively are those that combine immediate practical wins with long-term systemic change. Success requires persistence, collaboration, and strategic thinking that addresses both current problems and emerging challenges.

The children who benefit most from advocacy efforts are those whose communities maintain ongoing attention to digital wellness issues rather than responding only to crises. Building sustainable advocacy capacity ensures that children's interests remain represented as technology continues to change and new challenges emerge.

Effective advocacy recognizes that protecting children in digital environments requires changing systems, not just individual behaviors. The goal is creating a world where healthy technology use is the easy choice rather than an ongoing struggle for families and children.

Strategic Action Elements

- Current legislative frameworks like COPPA and Section 230 require updates to address artificial intelligence, algorithmic manipulation, and modern platform effects on children
- Advocacy for child-centered technology design focuses on changing economic incentives and requiring companies to consider child welfare in product development
- School board engagement requires understanding budget realities, community politics, and framing digital wellness concerns within existing educational priorities
- Community coalitions bring together parents, educators, healthcare providers, and organizations around shared goals for child digital wellness
- Effective advocacy toolkits include research skills, communication strategies, and understanding of political processes that influence policy decisions
- Long-term systemic change requires building policy, educational, and community infrastructure alongside cultural shifts toward prioritizing child welfare in technology decisions

Chapter 25: Creating Digitally Healthy Communities

The town of Maplewood looked like any other suburban community until you noticed the details—children playing in parks without devices in sight, families gathered at the community center for digital wellness workshops, and teenagers volunteering as tech mentors for younger kids. This transformation didn't happen overnight, but through the dedicated efforts of parents, educators, healthcare providers, and community leaders who decided that protecting Generation Alpha children required more than individual family efforts.

Three years ago, Maplewood faced the same digital challenges as communities everywhere—rising rates of anxiety and depression among young people, family conflicts about screen time, and concerns about children's social and academic development. Today, it serves as a model for how communities can work together to create environments that support rather than undermine children's healthy relationships with technology.

Maplewood's success demonstrates that creating digitally healthy communities requires coordinated efforts across multiple sectors and sustained commitment to putting children's wellbeing at the center of technology decisions. The most effective approaches combine immediate practical interventions with long-term cultural change that influences how entire communities think about children and technology.

Whole-Community Approaches to Digital Wellness

The foundation of Maplewood's transformation was recognizing that children's digital experiences are shaped by their entire community environment, not just their individual families. Schools, healthcare providers, community organizations, local businesses, and faith communities all influence how children learn to use technology and what messages they receive about healthy digital habits.

Systems Thinking and Coordination

Whole-community approaches begin with mapping all the institutions and influences that affect children's digital experiences. This includes obvious players like schools and families, but also libraries, pediatric offices, youth sports leagues, retail environments, and public spaces where children encounter technology.

Effective coordination requires establishing communication systems that allow different community sectors to share information, align their efforts, and avoid conflicting messages about digital wellness. Regular inter-agency meetings, shared communication platforms, and collaborative planning processes help ensure that community efforts support rather than compete with each other.

Environmental Design and Policy Alignment

Community-wide digital wellness requires examining how physical and social environments either support or undermine healthy technology use. This might include creating device-free zones in public spaces, establishing community standards for youth programs, and ensuring that public institutions model healthy technology practices.

Policy alignment across community institutions prevents children from receiving contradictory messages about appropriate technology use. When schools, healthcare providers, and community organizations share consistent approaches to digital wellness, children experience coherent support for healthy habits rather than conflicting expectations.

Peer Support Networks for Families

One of Maplewood's most successful innovations was creating structured peer support networks that help families navigate digital parenting challenges together. These networks recognize that parents often feel isolated and overwhelmed when dealing with technology conflicts, and that shared problem-solving can be more effective than individual struggle.

Family Circle Development

Family circles bring together 6-8 families with children of similar ages to meet monthly and discuss digital parenting challenges, share strategies that work, and provide mutual support during difficult periods. The circles are facilitated by trained volunteers who help guide discussions and provide resources, but the focus remains on peer support rather than expert instruction.

Successful family circles create safe spaces where parents can admit their struggles without judgment, share both successes and failures honestly, and learn from others facing similar challenges. The long-term relationships that develop through these circles provide ongoing support that extends beyond formal meeting times.

Resource Sharing and Collaborative Problem-Solving

Peer networks excel at sharing practical resources like recommended apps, family media plan templates, and strategies for specific challenges like bedtime battles or homework conflicts. Families can try approaches that have worked for others rather than starting from scratch with trial-and-error methods.

Collaborative problem-solving brings multiple perspectives to bear on complex challenges that individual families struggle to address alone. When one family faces a cyberbullying incident or gaming addiction crisis, the entire network can provide emotional support, practical assistance, and shared wisdom from their collective experiences.

Case Study 1: The Maplewood Transformation

The transformation of Maplewood began when pediatrician Dr. Sarah Martinez noticed increasing numbers of families reporting technology-related problems during routine visits. Instead of addressing these issues individually, she proposed a community-wide response that brought together all the institutions serving children.

The initial coalition included representatives from the school district, public library, community health center, youth sports leagues, and several parent organizations. They began by conducting a community assessment that revealed widespread concerns about children's screen time, social media use, and family technology conflicts.

"We realized that every institution was trying to address digital wellness in isolation," recalls Dr. Martinez. "Schools had one approach, healthcare providers had another, and families were getting inconsistent messages. We decided to align our efforts around shared goals for children's healthy development."

The coalition developed community standards for digital wellness that all participating organizations agreed to implement. These included consistent messages about appropriate technology use, coordinated education programs, and shared resources for families facing challenges.

Within two years, community surveys showed significant improvements in family satisfaction with technology use, reduced reports of technology-related problems in schools and healthcare settings, and increased confidence among parents in managing digital parenting challenges.

Case Study 2: The Teen Mentor Program

Recognizing that teenagers often have more influence on each other than adults do, Maplewood developed a peer mentoring program where high school students receive training in digital citizenship and then serve as mentors for younger children in community programs.

Sixteen-year-old Alex Chen became one of the program's first mentors after struggling with his own social media anxiety and gaming habits. Through the training program, he learned about healthy technology use, digital citizenship principles, and peer counseling skills.

"Working with younger kids helped me understand my own technology habits better," explains Alex. "When I had to explain why certain apps might be problematic or how to handle cyberbullying, I realized I needed to follow my own advice. Teaching others helped me become more intentional about my own digital choices."

The teen mentors work in after-school programs, summer camps, and community events, providing relatable guidance about technology challenges that younger children face. They help with everything from setting up privacy settings to resolving online conflicts to choosing appropriate content.

The program benefits both the younger children who receive peer guidance and the teenage mentors who develop leadership skills while reinforcing their own healthy technology habits.

Case Study 3: The Business Community Partnership

Maplewood's local business community became active partners in digital wellness efforts after recognizing that their future workforce would need employees with healthy technology relationships and strong digital citizenship skills.

Local businesses supported community digital wellness initiatives through funding, employee volunteer programs, and workplace practices that modeled healthy technology use. Several businesses implemented device-free zones and times that demonstrated to the community that successful organizations could function without constant connectivity.

The chamber of commerce organized workshops for business owners about supporting employee digital wellness and creating workplace cultures that prioritized human wellbeing alongside productivity. These efforts helped align business practices with community values about healthy technology use.

"Our businesses realized that investing in community digital wellness would benefit them long-term by developing a workforce that could use technology effectively without being controlled by it," explains chamber president Maria Santos.

The business partnership also provided career exploration opportunities that helped young people understand how to use technology skills productively in workplace environments, connecting their digital literacy to future economic opportunities.

Intergenerational Digital Literacy Programs

One of Maplewood's most innovative approaches involved creating programs where different generations learn from each other about technology rather than assuming that younger people always teach older ones. These programs recognize that both technological skills and wisdom about healthy technology use can flow in multiple directions.

Reverse Mentoring and Mutual Learning

Intergenerational programs pair children and teenagers with older adults for mutual technology learning. Young people help older adults learn to use devices and navigate online environments, while older adults share wisdom about balance, patience, and making thoughtful choices about technology use.

These relationships help bridge generational gaps and provide children with adult perspectives that differ from their parents' views. Older adults often have life experience that helps young people understand the long-term consequences of choices and the importance of maintaining relationships and activities outside of technology.

Cultural and Historical Perspective

Intergenerational programs help children understand that human societies functioned successfully for thousands of years without digital technology, providing perspective about what's essential versus what's convenient. Older adults can share stories about communication, entertainment, and problem-solving before smartphones and internet access.

This historical perspective helps children develop more balanced relationships with technology by understanding that digital tools are means to ends rather than ends in themselves. They learn to appreciate both technological capabilities and the human activities that technology should support.

Measuring Community Digital Health

Creating digitally healthy communities requires systematic approaches to measuring progress and identifying areas that need continued attention. Maplewood developed assessment tools that track both individual and community-level indicators of digital wellness.

Individual and Family Indicators

Family satisfaction surveys assess how comfortable families feel about their technology use, how well technology supports their goals and values, and how successfully they manage technology conflicts when they arise.

Child wellbeing measures include academic performance, social relationship quality, physical health indicators, and emotional wellbeing markers that can be affected by technology use patterns.

Digital citizenship behaviors among children and teenagers provide indicators of whether community education efforts are successfully developing responsible technology use skills.

Community-Level Indicators

Institutional alignment measures assess how consistently different community organizations approach digital wellness and whether their efforts reinforce rather than conflict with each other.

Public space usage patterns indicate whether community environments support healthy technology use through balanced access to both digital and non-digital activities.

Problem incident rates tracked across schools, healthcare providers, and law enforcement help identify whether community efforts are reducing technology-related problems like cyberbullying, online predation, and technology addiction.

Community Organizer's Guide for Building Local Initiatives

Communities interested in developing their own digital wellness initiatives can adapt Maplewood's approach to their specific circumstances and needs. Successful community organizing requires understanding local contexts, building broad coalitions, and maintaining momentum through both successes and setbacks.

Assessment and Planning Phase

Community assessment begins with gathering data about current challenges, existing resources, and stakeholder perspectives. This might include surveys of families, interviews with service providers, and analysis of technology-related problems in schools and healthcare settings.

Stakeholder mapping identifies all the individuals and organizations that affect children's digital experiences and determines their current approaches, concerns, and willingness to participate in coordinated efforts.

Goal setting requires balancing ambitious vision with realistic expectations about what can be achieved within available resources and timeframes. Successful initiatives focus on specific, measurable outcomes while maintaining broader vision for long-term change.

Coalition Building and Engagement

Leadership development identifies individuals from different sectors who can champion digital wellness efforts within their organizations and serve as liaisons to broader community initiatives.

Communication strategies ensure that different stakeholder groups understand how digital wellness connects to their existing priorities and missions rather than asking them to take on entirely new responsibilities.

Resource mobilization combines funding, volunteer time, expertise, and in-kind contributions from multiple sources to support initiative activities without overwhelming any single organization's capacity.

Implementation and Sustainability

Pilot programs allow communities to test approaches on a small scale before implementing broader changes. Successful pilots can demonstrate effectiveness and build momentum for larger initiatives.

Continuous improvement processes help communities learn from their experiences and adapt their approaches based on what works in their specific contexts. Regular evaluation and adjustment keep initiatives responsive to changing needs and circumstances.

Succession planning ensures that initiatives can continue when founding leaders move on or change roles. Building institutional capacity rather than depending on individual champions supports long-term sustainability.

Building Sustainable Digital Wellness Cultures

The most successful community digital wellness initiatives create lasting cultural changes that persist even when specific programs or leaders change. This requires embedding digital wellness values and practices into the normal operations of community institutions rather than treating them as special projects.

Institutional Integration

Policy development within schools, healthcare organizations, and community groups helps ensure that digital wellness principles become part of standard operating procedures rather than

depending on individual initiative or memory. Written policies provide consistency and continuity when staff changes occur.

Training and professional development for people working with children across all community sectors helps build shared understanding and consistent approaches to digital wellness challenges. This includes teachers, healthcare providers, youth program staff, coaches, and other adults who influence children's experiences.

Cultural norm development occurs through consistent messaging, visible modeling of healthy technology use by community leaders, and celebration of positive examples of digital citizenship. Communities that successfully change norms make healthy technology use socially expected rather than exceptional.

Economic and Social Equity Considerations

Creating digitally healthy communities requires addressing the reality that families have different economic resources and cultural backgrounds that affect their ability to participate in digital wellness initiatives. Successful communities develop inclusive approaches that work for all families rather than just those with advantages.

Resource Access and Support

Technology access programs ensure that all families have sufficient device and internet access to participate in educational and community activities without creating financial hardship. This might include device lending programs, subsidized internet access, and community technology centers.

Digital literacy support helps families develop skills for managing technology effectively regardless of their previous experience or education levels. Programs should accommodate different learning styles, languages, and cultural backgrounds rather than assuming universal starting points.

Financial support for families facing technology-related challenges helps ensure that economic constraints don't prevent access to professional help when needed. This might include sliding-scale counseling services, free educational programs, and assistance with technology-related costs.

Cultural Responsiveness and Inclusion

Multilingual resources and communication ensure that non-English speaking families can participate fully in community digital wellness initiatives. This includes translated materials, interpreters for meetings, and staff who understand different cultural perspectives.

Cultural adaptation of programs recognizes that different families may have varying values and approaches to technology use based on their cultural backgrounds. Successful programs respect this diversity while maintaining focus on child safety and wellbeing.

Leadership development within different cultural communities helps ensure that digital wellness initiatives reflect the needs and perspectives of all community members rather than just the most vocal or privileged groups.

Technology Industry Engagement

Digitally healthy communities often find ways to engage constructively with technology companies and industry representatives to advocate for child-friendly design and policies. This engagement can influence corporate practices while building community awareness of technology industry dynamics.

Consumer Advocacy and Education

Community education about technology business models helps families understand how their data and attention are being monetized and makes more informed choices about which companies and products to support.

Coordinated consumer action through boycotts, petition campaigns, and strategic purchasing decisions can influence company behavior when organized at sufficient scale and backed by clear demands for change.

Corporate Partnership and Accountability

Some communities develop relationships with local technology companies or company representatives that allow for dialogue about child-friendly practices and community concerns about specific products or policies.

Corporate social responsibility engagement encourages technology companies to contribute to community digital wellness initiatives through funding, expertise, or policy changes that benefit children.

Industry accountability efforts include supporting regulatory initiatives, participating in public comment processes, and advocating for stronger laws protecting children's digital rights and wellbeing.

Regional and National Network Development

Individual communities achieve greater impact when they connect with similar efforts in other locations to share resources, coordinate advocacy, and influence broader policy changes. Maplewood has become part of a growing network of communities working on digital wellness initiatives.

Knowledge Sharing and Collaboration

Best practice documentation helps communities learn from each other's successes and failures rather than starting from scratch with each new initiative. Shared resources reduce duplication of effort and accelerate progress.

Collaborative research projects allow communities to contribute to the evidence base about effective digital wellness interventions while benefiting from research findings from other locations.

Joint advocacy efforts on state and federal policy issues give communities more influence than they would have working individually to promote child-friendly technology regulations and funding.

Movement Building and Scale

Regional conferences and networking events help community organizers build relationships, share strategies, and coordinate efforts across broader geographic areas.

National organization development creates infrastructure for supporting local communities while advocating for systemic changes that no single community can achieve alone.

Media and communication strategies help raise awareness about community digital wellness approaches and inspire other communities to develop their own initiatives.

Long-Term Vision and Sustainability

Creating digitally healthy communities requires sustained effort over many years and adaptation to changing technological and social circumstances. The most successful initiatives build foundations that can support ongoing work even as specific challenges and opportunities change.

Adaptive Capacity Building

Skill development within community organizations helps build capacity for addressing new digital wellness challenges as they emerge rather than only responding to current problems.

Monitoring and evaluation systems help communities track their progress, identify emerging issues, and adapt their approaches based on changing circumstances and new research findings.

Youth leadership development ensures that young people who grow up in digitally healthy communities become advocates and leaders who can continue the work as they mature.

Legacy and Impact

Institutional change within schools, healthcare systems, and community organizations helps ensure that digital wellness remains a priority even when founding leaders move on or community attention shifts to other issues.

Cultural transformation creates lasting change in how communities think about children and technology, making healthy digital citizenship a normal expectation rather than a special project.

Model development allows successful communities to share their approaches with others and contribute to broader social change around children's digital wellbeing.

Community Wisdom in Action

Maplewood's transformation from a community struggling with digital challenges to a model of healthy technology integration demonstrates that coordinated community effort can create environments where children thrive in digital contexts. The key lies not in rejecting technology but in ensuring that its use supports rather than undermines the fundamental human needs for connection, growth, and wellbeing.

The children growing up in digitally healthy communities like Maplewood develop skills and perspectives that will serve them throughout their lives as technology continues to change. They learn to use powerful tools wisely, maintain strong human relationships alongside digital connections, and contribute to communities that prioritize human flourishing.

The success of community-wide digital wellness initiatives depends on recognizing that protecting Generation Alpha children requires collective action that goes beyond individual family efforts. When entire communities commit to supporting children's healthy development in digital environments, they create cultures where good choices become easier and where children can access the benefits of technology while avoiding its potential harms.

Building Together

The future of Generation Alpha depends not only on the choices individual families make about technology but on the environments that communities create to support healthy digital development. Communities that invest in coordinated digital wellness initiatives are investing in their children's long-term success and wellbeing.

The work of creating digitally healthy communities is challenging and ongoing, but it represents one of the most important investments communities can make in their future. The children who benefit from these efforts will become adults better prepared to navigate an increasingly complex technological world while maintaining their humanity and connection to others.

Community Development Principles

- Whole-community approaches coordinate efforts across schools, healthcare, organizations, and businesses to create consistent support for children's digital wellness
- Peer support networks help families navigate digital parenting challenges through shared problem-solving and mutual encouragement
- Intergenerational programs create mutual learning opportunities where different age groups share both technological skills and wisdom about healthy technology use
- Community digital health measurement tracks both individual wellbeing and institutional alignment to assess progress and identify areas needing attention
- Economic and cultural equity considerations ensure that digital wellness initiatives serve all families regardless of resources or backgrounds

- Sustainable community change requires embedding digital wellness into institutional policies and cultural norms rather than depending on special programs or individual leaders

References

Council on Communications and Media. (2016). Media use in school-aged children and adolescents. *Pediatrics, 138*(5), e20162592. https://doi.org/10.1542/peds.2016-2592

Council on Communications and Media. (2016). Media and young minds. *Pediatrics, 138*(5), e20162591. https://doi.org/10.1542/peds.2016-2591

Carter, B., Rees, P., Hale, L., Bhattacharjee, D., & Paradkar, M. S. (2016). Association between portable screen-based media device access or use and sleep outcomes: A systematic review and meta-analysis. *JAMA Pediatrics, 170*(12), 1202–1208. https://doi.org/10.1001/jamapediatrics.2016.2341

LeBourgeois, M. K., Hale, L., Chang, A. M., Akacem, L. D., Montgomery-Downs, H. E., & Buxton, O. M. (2017). Digital media and sleep in childhood and adolescence. *Pediatrics, 140*(Supplement_2), S92–S96. https://doi.org/10.1542/peds.2016-1758J

Woods, H. C., & Scott, H. (2016). #Sleepyteens: Social media use in adolescence is associated with poor sleep quality, anxiety, depression and low self-esteem. *Journal of Adolescence, 51*, 41–49. https://doi.org/10.1016/j.adolescence.2016.05.008

Orben, A., & Przybylski, A. K. (2019). The association between adolescent well-being and digital technology use. *Nature Human Behaviour, 3*(2), 173–182. https://doi.org/10.1038/s41562-018-0506-1

Przybylski, A. K., & Weinstein, N. (2017). A large-scale test of the Goldilocks hypothesis: Quantifying the relations between digital-screen use and the mental well-being of adolescents. *Psychological Science, 28*(2), 204–215. https://doi.org/10.1177/0956797616678438

Odgers, C. L., & Jensen, M. R. (2020). Annual research review: Adolescent mental health in the digital age: facts, fears, and future directions. *Journal of Child Psychology and Psychiatry, 61*(3), 336–348. https://doi.org/10.1111/jcpp.13190

Kelly, Y., Zilanawala, A., Booker, C., & Sacker, A. (2018). Social media use and adolescent mental health: Findings from the UK Millennium Cohort Study. *EClinicalMedicine, 6,* 59–68. https://doi.org/10.1016/j.eclinm.2018.12.005

Ra, C. K., Cho, J., Stone, M. D., De La Cerda, J., Goldenson, N. I., Moroney, E., Tung, I., Lee, S. S., & Leventhal, A. M. (2018). Association of digital media use with subsequent symptoms of attention-deficit/hyperactivity disorder among adolescents. *JAMA, 320*(3), 255–263. https://doi.org/10.1001/jama.2018.8931

Livingstone, S., & Helsper, E. J. (2008). Parental mediation of children's Internet use. *Journal of Broadcasting & Electronic Media, 52*(4), 581–599. https://doi.org/10.1080/08838150802437396

Valkenburg, P. M., Piotrowski, J. T., Hermanns, J., & de Leeuw, R. (2013). Developing and validating the perceived parental media mediation scale: A self-determination perspective. *Human Communication Research, 39*(4), 445–469. https://doi.org/10.1111/hcre.12010

Moreno, M. A., D'Angelo, J., Kacvinsky, L., Kerr, B., & Zhang, C. (2021). Effect of a family media use plan on media rule engagement in adolescents: A randomized clinical trial. *JAMA Network Open, 4*(3), e213783. https://doi.org/10.1001/jamanetworkopen.2021.3783

Hamm, M. P., Newton, A. S., Chisholm, A., Shulhan, J., Milne, A., Sundar, P., Ennis, H., Scott, S. D., & Hartling, L. (2015). Prevalence and effect of cyberbullying on children and young people: A scoping review of social media studies. *JAMA Pediatrics, 169*(8), 770–777. https://doi.org/10.1001/jamapediatrics.2015.0944

Kowalski, R. M., Giumetti, G. W., Schroeder, A. N., & Lattanner, M. R. (2014). Bullying in the digital age: A critical review and meta-analysis of cyberbullying research among youth. *Psychological Bulletin, 140*(4), 1073–1137. https://doi.org/10.1037/a0035618

Vaccari, C., & Chadwick, A. (2020). Deepfakes and disinformation: Exploring the impact of synthetic political video on deception. *Social Media + Society, 6*(1), 1–13. https://doi.org/10.1177/2056305120903408

Jones-Jang, S. M., Mortensen, T., & Liu, J. (2021). Does media literacy help identification of fake news? Information literacy helps, but other literacies don't. *American Behavioral Scientist, 65*(2), 371–388. https://doi.org/10.1177/0002764219869406

Hutton, J. S., Dudley, J., Horowitz-Kraus, T., DeWitt, T., & Holland, S. K. (2019). Association between screen media activity and integrity of white matter tracts in preschool-aged children. *JAMA Pediatrics, 173*(3), 244–250. https://doi.org/10.1001/jamapediatrics.2018.5056

Lanca, C., & Saw, S.-M. (2020). The association between digital screen time and myopia: A systematic review. *Ophthalmic & Physiological Optics, 40*(2), 216–229. https://doi.org/10.1111/opo.12657

He, M., Xiang, F., Zeng, Y., Mai, J., Chen, Q., Zhang, J., Smith, M. J., Rose, K. A., & Morgan, I. G. (2015). Effect of time spent outdoors at school on the development of myopia among children in China: A randomized clinical trial. *JAMA, 314*(11), 1142–1148. https://doi.org/10.1001/jama.2015.10803

www.ingramcontent.com/pod-product-compliance
Lightning Source LLC
Chambersburg PA
CBHW072113270326
41931CB00010B/1540